Britain
on the Brink

For Jonathan and Christopher

Britain on the Brink

The Cold War's Most Dangerous Weekend,
27–28 October 1962

Jim Wilson

Pen & Sword
MILITARY

Published in Great Britain in 2012 by
Pen & Sword Military
an imprint of
Pen & Sword Books Ltd
47 Church Street
Barnsley
South Yorkshire
S70 2AS

ISBN 978-1-84884-814-6

A CIP catalogue record for this book is available from the British Library.

Typeset in 10.5/12.5pt Palatino
by Concept, Huddersfield.

Printed and bound in England by
CPI Group (UK) Ltd, Croydon, CRO 4YY.

Pen & Sword Books Ltd incorporates the Imprints of Pen & Sword Aviation, Pen & Sword Family History, Pen & Sword Maritime, Pen & Sword Military, Pen & Sword Discovery, Wharncliffe Local History, Wharncliffe True Crime, Wharncliffe Transport, Pen & Sword Select, Pen & Sword Military Classics, Leo Cooper, The Praetorian Press, Remember When, Seaforth Publishing and Frontline Publishing.

For a complete list of Pen & Sword titles please contact

PEN & SWORD BOOKS LIMITED
47 Church Street, Barnsley, South Yorkshire, S70 2AS, England
e-mail: enquiries@pen-and-sword.co.uk
Website: www.pen-and-sword.co.uk

Contents

Foreword

Most of us who lived through the Cold War became used to the threat of nuclear conflict hanging over us. The policy of 'Mutually Assured Destruction' was of little comfort, as the arguments raged for and against the policies of governments both sides of the Iron Curtain. We got on with our lives. But the possibility of war was never too far away.

For several days in October 1962, and one dangerous weekend, that possibility was closer than at any other time during all the Cold War years. Most people in the United Kingdom did not realise how close. The Macmillan Government was desperate not to panic the public, and desperate not to inflame an already terrifying situation.

The Cuban Crisis put the UK squarely into the front-line had the confrontation, centred on Washington and Moscow, led to nuclear conflict. And it so easily might have done, either as a result of a misjudgement or a mistake.

The British public was largely unaware of the appalling dangers they faced. The fact that British nuclear forces went to the highest level of operational alert at any time during the Cold War years, was not even laid clearly before the British Parliament, nor amazingly was it debated by the British Cabinet.

Britain on the Brink attempts to put the British dimension of the Cuban Crisis into context, and records the memories of some of those in Britain's V-Force and missile squadrons who bear personal witness to how close the generation of the 1960s came to facing the awful prospect of nuclear warfare.

I am particularly indebted to former RAF personnel who set down their memories of that grim weekend when the V-Force went to a few minutes readiness, in some cases with crews waiting in their cockpits for the order to take off, and RAF launch crews on ballistic missile bases down the east coast of England waiting for the orders to launch.

My thanks to all at Pen & Sword who have overseen this book to publication. Grateful thanks too to my wife Judith for her patient support and understanding.

Jim Wilson OBE
Carleton Rode, Norfolk

RAF V-Force bases and Thor launch sites in the early 1960s.

Introduction

If the Third World War is fought with nuclear weapons, the fourth will be fought with bows and arrows.

Lord Louis Mountbatten,
Chief of the Defence Staff 1959–65

Fifty years ago the most dangerous days of the entire Cold War took the world to the brink of nuclear conflict.

The Cuban Missile Crisis has been exhaustively written about, documented, and analysed from an American perspective. But potentially, the most dangerous place to have been during those days of mounting tension was Great Britain. The UK was host to American bases that constituted the United States' first-line of nuclear defence. Britain was extremely vulnerable; directly in the sights of the USSR's stockpile of nuclear weapons. Yet the Macmillan Government chose to stand on the margins, and take a risky one-way bet that the crisis would be resolved without war. Ministers decided not to put into practice any of the steps, meticulously planned by civil servants in Whitehall, which were designed to secure some degree of national survival should nuclear conflict break out.

The British public were intentionally kept in the dark about the threat hanging over them. The government seems to have been afraid that to be too open would have caused widespread panic. Its public line during the crisis was one of military non-involvement. American nuclear bases on UK sovereign territory were ordered by their headquarters across the Atlantic to an unprecedented operational alert, only just short of war, without prior consultation with British authorities. There was dialogue on the trans-Atlantic hot-line between President and Prime Minister, but the intention from the American side was more to inform than to consult. Macmillan himself was desperate nothing should be done which could exacerbate an already dangerous situation, even if it meant leaving the nation more vulnerable and exposed should war occur.

By keeping management of the crisis almost exclusively in the hands of himself and his Foreign Secretary, Sir Alec Douglas-Home, the Prime Minister ran a grave risk. It was a risk that, fortunately for him and us, ultimately paid off. But had Khrushchev and Kennedy not reached a deal – and had the cards of international diplomacy fallen differently – the UK could have ended up a virtual waste-land under bombardment from Soviet nuclear missiles. The consequences do not bear thinking about.

Questions still remain over many aspects of the approach the Macmillan Government took in the face of the greatest test of the Cold War. Was the decision to leave the British population so ill-informed justified? Why was the British Parliament not told the full story, even weeks after the crisis was over? Why were carefully planned 'transition to war' precautions, never activated? Were there 'disconnects' between government ministers and British military commanders who were responsible for the UK's nuclear deterrent? The Commander in Chief of Bomber Command certainly thought there were. How closely were the American Strategic Air Command bases in the UK and the RAF's V-bomber and missile forces in touch, and their military strategies aligned?

The experiences of former RAF personnel tell part of the story of Britain on the brink. They show without any doubt that when the ultimate test appeared a reality, the highly trained crews and support personnel, whose role it was to launch Britain's ultimate deterrent, were prepared to discharge their duty whatever the cost.

Cabinet minutes and other documents now de-classified shed a little light; although it is astonishing to find that in October 1962 there were no discussions about UK military alert states or even any reference to specifically military matters during either of the two meetings of the British Cabinet in the crucial days of the crisis. Indeed, the defence secretary made no remarks or submissions at either session of the cabinet. It is even more incredible that at the only meeting of the government's defence committee during the period of mounting tension, there was no mention of Cuba, the world crisis, Britain's nuclear deterrent forces, or their state of readiness, should the dangerous face-off over Cuba have led to an attack on the UK.

The disturbing question remains. Did Macmillan's policy leave the UK fatally exposed if the crisis had resulted in a Third World War? Or was the Prime Minister correct to believe the far greater risk to his country and its people lay in putting in place precautions that might themselves have provoked war? The documentary evidence, such as it is, fails to answer the question. The Cuban crisis was the point at which the temperature fell to its lowest point in the Cold War. It was also the turning point. Although east and west faced each other across the Iron Curtain for many years more, a situation never again developed that looked so menacingly as if it would lead to a Third World War. The conundrum we are left with is why – when as seemed highly likely in 1962 – the UK could have been pitched into the front-line of a global nuclear conflict, the British Government acted as if the country was on the side-lines of this global dispute. The RAF, who then had sole responsibility for Britain's nuclear deterrent, demonstrated by its high state of operational readiness that they were alert to the dangers. But were government ministers as aware as they should have been? And how smoothly did the vital connection between government and military operate during those dangerous days?

Chapter 1

The Unthinkable

We had been on the brink – almost over it.
Prime Minister, Harold Macmillan writing in his memoirs,
At The End of the Day

Throughout the Cold War years the world was never far from the brink of nuclear annihilation. It was an appalling prospect that influenced the lives of everyone who lived through those years. The shadow of a possible nuclear conflict was a factor of daily life. You were aware of it, but closed your mind to it. People learnt to push the unthinkable out of their thoughts, and tried to ignore the frightening reality. To dwell on the horror would have made normal life impossible. You had to trust in the terrible, but so very appropriately-named philosophy of MAD: Mutually Assured Destruction. You had to hope that the leaders of east and west were saner than the policy of the feverish nuclear arms race they espoused; that they, like everyone else on the planet, had a dread of ever pushing the nuclear button. Churchill summed it up in the early years of the nuclear age. He called it 'the equality of annihilation'. In essence it amounted to an insurance policy based on a shared dread of what might happen.

A younger generation probably finds it hard to believe that nuclear annihilation was a real possibility for at least twenty of the Cold War years. It was plausible that America and the Soviet Union would come to nuclear blows. With fleets of bombers and batteries of missiles capable of destroying civilisation many times over, America and the Soviet Union confronted each other at instant readiness. The British were in the unenviable position of being an exposed and very vulnerable 'piggy in the middle' as the United States based elements of their nuclear bombers and missiles on 'the unsinkable aircraft carrier' that was Great Britain. British authorities were, at times, as nervous of American bellicosity as of Soviet imperialism. A 1951 report by Britain's Director of Naval Intelligence, Vice Admiral Eric Longley-Cook, interpreted the American mood as: 'We have the bomb; let us use it while the balance is in our favour. Since war with the Russians is inevitable, let's get it over with now.'[1]

The American theory that war was eventually inevitable and it made sense to start a 'preventive' war while the balance of power was in America's favour, led in 1954 to Winston Churchill urgently seeking a summit between east and west. He too feared American willingness for war.[2]

That was the year the British chiefs of staff produced a doom-laden paper for the cabinet which led to the production of the first British hydrogen bombs. 'We have come to the conclusion that if war came in the next few years, the United States would insist on the immediate use of the full armoury of nuclear weapons with the object of dealing the Russians a quick knock-out blow. We must therefore plan on the assumption, that if war becomes global, nuclear bombardment will become general.'[3]

The chiefs then set out their expectation of the parameters of the Cold War as they and their intelligence experts saw it:

1. Russia is most unlikely to provoke war deliberately during the next few years when the United States will be comparatively immune from Russian attack.
2. The danger the United States might succumb to the temptation of precipitating a 'forestalling' war cannot be disregarded. In view of the vulnerability of the United Kingdom we must use all our influence to prevent this.
3. Careful judgement and restraint on the part of the Allies on a united basis will be needed to avoid the outbreak of a global war through accident or miscalculation resulting from an incident which precipitated or extended a local war.
4. Even when the Russians are able to attack North America effectively, the ability of the United States to deliver a crippling attack on Russia will remain a powerful deterrent to the Soviet Government.
5. It is most probable that the present state of 'cold war' will continue for a long time with periods of greater or lesser tension.[4]

The chiefs of staff were astute in their predictions. The horror of the cold logic of their conclusions was successful in moving the UK into the thermonuclear era. The cabinet papers indicate the way the argument, led by Churchill, went: 'No country could claim to be a leading military power unless it possessed the most up-to-date weapons; and the fact must be faced that, unless we possessed thermonuclear weapons, we should lose our influence and standing in world affairs. Strength in thermonuclear weapons would henceforth provide the most powerful deterrent to a potential aggressor; and it was our duty to make our contribution towards the building up of this deterrent influence.'[5]

So the scenario of the frenetic nuclear arms race became the background to Cold War as the fifties gave way to the sixties. The ever present threat of a Third World War hung like a shadow across life on both sides of the Iron Curtain, until 1962 and the Cuban crisis. Suddenly a global nuclear war looked a terrifying possibility.

For one agonising weekend the spectre of a Third World War moved agonisingly closer and became more frighteningly real. Anyone over the age of fifty today can count themselves a fortunate survivor of a weekend when the world literally stood on the edge of Armageddon. The trigger was America's discovery that the Soviet Union had deployed a nuclear arsenal pointing directly at US cities, virtually in America's own backyard – never mind that the Americans had done exactly the same to the USSR, deploying nuclear missiles in Turkey, Italy and the UK targeted on Soviet cities.

27 and 28 October 1962 were the most dangerous days of the Cuban Missile Crisis. And the missile crisis itself was the most dangerous period in the stalemate of the entire Cold War. Had the policy pursued by the leaders of the east and west turned out differently, or had moves on either side of the east-west divide been misinterpreted – and that could so easily have happened – it is arguable the population of the UK who would have been first to suffer, if not total nuclear annihilation, then massive destruction. Yet at the time, the UK public was largely unaware of the menacing threat it was under, or of the palpable fears and tensions being felt by government ministers in Whitehall. Nor were people in Britain aware that American nuclear forces on bases in the UK had been ordered to a state of readiness just one step below all-out war. American aircraft stood at the end of British runways armed with nuclear pay-loads. Some were actually in the air awaiting the order to head for targets inside the USSR.

As the drama was being played out that crucial weekend, Marshal of the Royal Air Force, Sir Michael Beetham, was Group Captain (Operations) serving in the control bunker at Bomber Command Headquarters near High Wycombe. He recalls the unreal climate outside the operations room as the crisis developed, in sharp contrast to the trauma being felt within Bomber Command Headquarters, as Britain's nuclear forces, and those of the United States stationed in the UK, went to the highest levels of alert in the whole of the Cold

War. Sir Michael clearly remembers the unreal atmosphere as the rest of the nation appeared quite unaware a crisis was brewing that might directly affect them and their very existence. 'When we came out of the bunker for a meal, or took a break outside, the sun was shining and the media were obsessed with some football match. It all seemed quite unreal to us.'[6]

The most striking thing about the Cuban crisis from a British standpoint, is that neither the British people nor the British Parliament were ever told the facts of how close the country went to nuclear war.

Harold Macmillan, Prime Minister at the time of the Cuban crisis, had a reputation of unflappability. However, his grandson, Lord Stockton, has said that as an old man Macmillan only had nightmares about two things from his long life: the traumas he suffered in the trenches of the First World War, and what would have happened had the Cuban missile crisis gone badly wrong.[7] In his own account of his premiership, Macmillan referred to the Cuban 'episode' as 'terrifying'. 'We had been on the brink, almost over it' he wrote. 'Yet the world had been providentially saved at the last moment from the final plunge.'[8] It was the worst weekend of Macmillan's life, and the defining moment of the post-war period in nuclear terms.

The missile crisis, and in particular the events of Black Saturday, 27 October 1962, took the British Government closer to putting into effect its top secret plans for a Third World War, than at any time before or since. During the years of the Cold War extensive and detailed plans, contained in what was called Britain's *War Book*, were assiduously worked on in the most secret corridors of power. Planning for war dominated the lives of groups of civil servants and ministers, who worked to ensure that some form of civil control would be able to continue in Britain in circumstances of nuclear conflict that are almost impossible to conceive, and incalculable in their consequences. The most important of these bodies, where the horrific study of Armageddon was routinely debated and discussed, was the Joint Inter-Services Group for the Study of All-Out War, or in the jargon of Whitehall JIGSAW. Its members consisted of representatives of the three armed services, scientists and civil servants. Between 1958 and 1964 they pondered the answers to questions almost too terrifying to quantify. Lord Louis Mountbatten, Chief of the Defence Staff (1959–65), had called for JIGSAW to be set up, to consider not the 'if' of the Third World War, but the 'when'. The group's findings were reported to ministers, to Lord Louis, and to the Chief Scientific Adviser to the Ministry of Defence, Sir Solly

Zuckerman. No-one knew, if the unthinkable happened, whether the pieces put together by JIGSAW would provide the answer to the nation's survival, if indeed survival was possible. Trying to visualise some kind of future following nuclear warfare, and forecasting how the nation might cope in the direst conditions that they labelled 'Breakdown', was their awesome responsibility. Their nightmare scenario 'Breakdown', was defined in an official ministerial paper dated 1960 as, 'when the government of a country is no longer able to ensure its orders are carried out, either as a result of the collapse of the "machinery of control", or because of a total loss of morale; meaning the majority of those spared became wholly pre-occupied with their personal survival rather than the survival of the state.'[9]

As Sir Kevin Tebbit, a Permanent Secretary at the Ministry of Defence, and a former Deputy Chairman of the Joint Intelligence Committee, recalled: 'Hardly anyone died in the Cold War, but we lived on a daily basis with the risk that everyone might!'[10]

The Cuban crisis began on 14 October 1962 when an American U2 reconnaissance plane flying over Cuba, brought back photographs taken from 65,000 feet that showed beyond any doubt that the Soviet Union was building launch sites for nuclear-armed ballistic missiles capable of striking the United States. The Americans were able to produce photographs with sufficient resolution to show objects as small as two and a half square feet, and the pictures the U2 pilot brought back to his base left the analysts at the CIA's National Photographic Interpretation Center in Washington in no doubt what the USSR was constructing ninety miles off the US mainland.

Just over a week later, on 22 October, as President Kennedy was about to reveal to the world, in a fifteen-minute televised speech, the evidence the Russians were deploying missiles to Cuba, America's armed forces, including those based in the UK, were placed on high alert and ordered from DEFCON (Defence Condition) five all the way up to DEFCON three, just two stages below actual war. The only other occasion, DEFCON three was imposed, was in September 2001 following the terrorist attack on the twin towers in New York.

On 24 October 1962, with surveillance indicating further rapid progress in constructing the missile launch sites, the United States Strategic Air Command's readiness was lifted one notch higher to DEFCON two, the highest state that the military could order short of actual war. The following day Radio Moscow announced the Kremlin had cancelled all military leave and discharges and put all its forces on combat readiness.[11]

In Britain *The Times* reported that the cabinet would meet to consider the implications for the UK of President Kennedy's statement. No mention was made of putting Britain's deterrent forces on a higher state of readiness or of the American strike forces poised to launch a nuclear attack from UK soil.

The consequence of racking up the DEFCON levels meant that for the first time in history all America's long-range bombers and missiles were on full alert. An eighth of the Strategic Air Command's bombers based in the States were at any one time airborne with nuclear weapons on board, refuelled by aerial tankers waiting over Greenland and northern Canada, for instructions to proceed beyond their 'hold' lines to pre-determined targets in the USSR. US nuclear forces in their 'front-line' bases in the UK, America's first line of defence, since flying time to vital targets within the Soviet Union was so much shorter, were placed on a similar level of DEFCON two readiness. Indeed during the crisis the United States despatched an additional thirty B-47s to British and Spanish bases to increase their front-line 'punch'.[12] American aircraft here in the UK were armed with nuclear weapons, and in some instances ordered into the air to await the official code to proceed to their targets. Other US crews on British airfields were put at cockpit readiness, and all of this without the knowledge of the British population or the need for formal authority from the British Government. The nuclear punch which could have been delivered by the United States from UK soil in October 1962 was massive. America ensured the Soviet Union was held at arms length by their policy of forward defence. Her listening posts, early warning systems, and front-line fighter bases in the UK, marked out Britain's role as the prime target for Soviet missiles. When the bombs and missiles started to rain down, the first salvoes would be targeted on British soil. There were plenty of potential targets in Britain for the Soviets to knock out. There were huge bases like Sculthorpe in Norfolk, at that time the biggest nuclear bomber base in Europe with some 10,000 personnel. As well as their UK bomber bases, US Tactical Fighter Wings at Lakenheath, Bentwaters and Wethersfield in East Anglia, equipped with F100 Super Sabres, each capable of carrying 1.1 megaton nuclear weapons, were also poised to strike.

Meanwhile, the British public watched their flickering black and white TV screens, anxious to find out what was happening thousands of miles away in the Caribbean and waited, oblivious of the exceptional nuclear alert called on American bases at their back-doors.

Nor was the British public aware of what was going on at Royal Air Force stations, home to the UK's own nuclear deterrent – the V-Force made up of around 112 V-bombers, and the sixty Thor nuclear tipped ballistic missiles, standing on launch pads at isolated sites down the eastern side of England.

By remarkable coincidence Bomber Command had been involved in a no-notice readiness and dispersal exercise, codenamed 'Micky Finn' on 20 and 21 September, which involved increased readiness on both the V-Force and Thor missile bases. The exercise involved a simulated escalation through the various levels up to Alert two status. The ground had been laid, and the necessary alert postures thoroughly practised, when Air Marshal, Sir Kenneth Cross, Commander in Chief of Bomber Command covertly ordered a real Alert three at 1.00pm on 27 October, placing Britain's nuclear strike force, like the American Strategic Air Command, and beyond the Iron Curtain, Soviet forces, on the closest to a full war footing the military both east and west went to during the whole Cold War.

The British public appeared not to be aware, because the British Government was too afraid of public panic, but the world was edging towards Armageddon. According to his colleagues, Khrushchev was distraught when he heard the American administration had discovered his plan to deploy missiles to Cuba before he could complete the covert deployment. 'The storm is about to break,' he declared. 'It's too late to change anything now.' Significantly, when the crises had passed, the British Ambassador in Cuba, wrote a sobering comment to his boss Sir Alec Douglas Home, the Foreign Secretary. 'If it was a nuclear war we were headed for,' he said, 'Cuba was perhaps a better place to be than Britain!'[13] Those in authority knew what the British public probably did not fully appreciate, that if nuclear exchanges were to happen, Britain was a certain target.

Notes

1. Paper by Vice-Admiral Longley-Cook: *Where Are We Going*, 6/7/1951. (PRO 11/159).
2. Draft cabinet paper, August 1954. (PRO PREM 11/669).
3. PRO, CAB 129/69 'United Kingdom Defence Policy', 23/7/1954.
4. Ibid.
5. PRO, CAB 128/27, 7/7/1954.
6. Author's telephone discussion with Sir Michael Beetham 2008.
7. Peter Hennessy, *The Prime Minister: The Office and its Holders since 1945*. Allen Lane, The Penguin Press, 2000, p. 103.
8. Harold Macmilan, *At the End of the Day*, Macmillan, London, 1973, pp. 214–2.

9. Dr Edgar Anstey of JIGSAW, *Note on the Concept and Definitions of Breakdown*, 10 June 1960. (PRO, DEFE 10/402.)
10. Sir Kevin Tebbit, Permanent Secretary, Ministry of Defence. (Lecture at Gresham College, 2001).
11. Sergei N Khrushchev: *Nikita S, Khrushchev: krizisy i rakety.* Moscow: Novosti, 1991, pp. 273–4.
12. Scott Sagan, *Limits of Safety: Organisations, Accidents & Nuclear War*, Princeton University Press, 1993, p. 63.
13. Document AK1261/667 from British Embassy Havana to Foreign Office London, 10 November 1962.

Chapter 2

America's Front-line

We must not forget that by creating the American base in East Anglia, we have made ourselves the target, and perhaps the bulls-eye of a Soviet attack.

Winston Churchill, 15 February 1951

When the Cuban crisis flared up, the UK was a formidable nuclear power in its own right. It was also in every practical sense the first and the forward line of defence for America. US nuclear strike forces were positioned in Britain specifically to hit strategic targets behind the Iron Curtain, designated by the US Strategic Air Command. This inevitably made the UK a prime target, whether or not Britain had a direct involvement in the origins of a particular conflict. If Cuba had been the trigger for war, as appeared extremely likely in 1962, the United Kingdom was in the front-line. Annihilation without consultation had been the kernel of a long running argument in Britain that had its roots in the immediate post-war period.

In the late fifties, when the US and UK governments were discussing deployment of American intermediate range ballistic missiles in the UK, the Macmillan government thought these first ever operational nuclear rockets to be based in the west would make a powerful contribution to Britain's nuclear deterrent. But there was another view. Some in senior military positions on this side of the Atlantic were sceptical. They considered placing missiles on prominent, easily identified launch pads in a pattern all the the way down the east of England, far from constituting a defensive screen for Great Britain, would serve only as a forward defence for the United States.[1] Instead of a shield protecting the British public, the Thor missiles, they argued, would present a danger to the safety of the UK and its citizens. Self-preservation would dictate the Soviets eliminate the UK missile bases as a prerequisite to winning any nuclear exchange between the Soviet Union and America. The Thor bases were extremely vulnerable; they couldn't be hidden or concealed; and their locations were perfectly well known to the Russians. The British Chief of the Air Staff, Air Chief Marshal, Sir Dermot Boyle, in a note to his fellow service chiefs on 27 January 1958 expressed his serious concerns. The combined chiefs of staff agreed with him, and they passed on their views in a memorandum to ministers. They were opposed they said to being rushed into the Thor missile commitment, which in their view was 'designed to serve American ends more than British.' The missiles were 'highly vulnerable' and since the nuclear warheads would be under American control, Thor could in no way be described as a British independent deterrent.[2] It was a remarkably outspoken comment for Britain's most senior military men to make to their political masters, but it had no effect on the government's policy, and the missile deployment went ahead. The first launch pads became operational in September 1958. In the United States one commentator made a similar deduction about how exposed they were. 'American bases in the UK,' he said, 'would be immensely vulnerable to a Soviet first strike, they were sitting ducks like the American fleet tied up in Pearl Harbor.'

It was a view which also applied to America's Strategic Air Command's bomber bases on UK sovereign territory. But there were powerful counter arguments for supporting a permanent American nuclear presence in Britain. So the vulnerability of the UK's population, and the ever-present threat of a first-strike on the UK, became constant factors in the complex equation of east-west nuclear strategy.

Logic suggested it might suit the United States to fight a nuclear war limited to Europe. If so, as a relatively small country geographically, with a large population, chiefly concentrated in densely populated urban centres, the UK would suffer severely if not terminally, in an all-out nuclear exchange, whether or not the Soviets managed to strike at the United States itself with their limited arsenal of long range inter-continental missiles.

This was the dangerously exposed position the UK found itself in as the Cuban crisis broke on the world scene. The crisis saw US forces across the world placed on an alarmingly high state of readiness.

Three US tactical alert squadrons based in East Anglia and equipped with F-100 Super Sabres capable of carrying 1.1 megaton nuclear weapons, were covertly placed on a high state of alert several hours before President Kennedy announced to the world the crisis in the Caribbean. And their alert readiness was raised without any consultation with the British Government. Bases like Greenham Common, Upper Heyford, Fairford, and Brize Norton went onto a highly secure status, closing down to the outside world. Inside heavily guarded security fences, B-47s were made ready, loaded with nuclear bombs, and awaited orders from SAC headquarters

13

in Omaha, Nebraska. Nuclear armed B-52s flew airborne patrols from UK air-space, their crews primed to receive coded orders from Washington to head for Soviet targets. US Navy ballistic missile submarines at the American naval base at Holy Loch in Scotland went to full alert. Three, equipped with Polaris nuclear missiles, slipped quietly out to sea followed by their tender ship, the USS *Proteus*. As far as the American military were concerned the UK was on close to a war footing, even though the epicentre of the crisis was thousands of miles away in the Caribbean.

The cry of some in the UK, who recognised the dangers to this country as the Cuba crisis escalated was 'no annihilation without representation'. Yet the British Government was playing down the notion that Cuba presented an imminent threat to Britain.

The idea that a threat against the United States inevitably meant a threat against the UK was not new. The dark spectre of possible nuclear war had hung over Britain and East Anglia in particular, where a high proportion of both US and British nuclear forces were based, since July 1950 when the first American nuclear bombs were deployed to the UK. Although the British public was not generally aware of what was happening, at the beginning of the 1950s, Norfolk and Suffolk became host to some ninety sets of the non-nuclear components of America's latest nuclear bombs. They were stored at USAF Strategic Air Command bases at Marham and Sculthorpe in Norfolk, and Lakenheath in Suffolk. The intention was to fly the nuclear cores in from the States if an emergency was declared or if the international situation indicated a movement towards war. It soon became clear, however, this was a totally unrealistic strategy. Events could escalate too quickly to enable the nuclear cores to be delivered in time. The two governments agreed, without any public announcement, that the nuclear bombs, together with their nuclear cores, should be stored on British bases housing American aircraft.

Meanwhile, Britain was manufacturing her own nuclear bomb. The first British built operational nuclear weapons, code-named Blue Danube, were delivered to RAF Wittering near Peterborough in November 1953. Wittering's operational records book hailed the arrival with the comment: 'These bombs will raise the striking power of Bomber Command to an order completely transcending its power hitherto.' But another four months passed before the public was let in on the secret via a statement in parliament about the formation of Britain's nuclear deterrent force – the V-Force – which was to be placed on peak alert at the time of the Cuban crisis.

Protocols governing the US Air Force using British bases to launch nuclear war, date back to the summer of 1946. Shortly after the formation of America's Strategic Air Command in the wake of the Second World War, the Commander of the US Air Force, General Carl Spaatz, visited England to obtain permission in an emergency to use British bases for atomic bomb missions. He obtained the agreement of the Chief of Staff of the Royal Air Force, Air Chief Marshal, Lord Tedder, for five UK air bases to be available for B-29 bombers. It was a deal struck by military officials with no public discussion and no political debate of the potentially serious implications for British sovereignty and political control. This secret administrative agreement, taken rather casually and without a written protocol, was the first step in establishing US rights to base a nuclear strike force in the UK.[3] The following month assembly buildings and loading pits to enable the first generation of cumbersome American atomic bombs to be maintained and handled were installed at five UK bases. In June 1947 the first 'tours' to Europe by Strategic Air Command bombers began as an element of the command's mobility plan to enable America's nuclear strike force to operate from forward European bases. In June 1948, as Berlin became the focus of international attention with a Soviet blockade of land routes into the city, the US Ambassador in London asked the British Government if three groups of heavy bombers could be allowed to come to Britain as a temporary show of strength. A small cabinet committee agreed to the request. The British Cabinet might well have felt that a temporary presence at a time of tension was a reasonable move. However, privately the United States appears to have had long-term intentions from the start. Access to British bases was of critical importance to the US Strategic Air Command's fast developing plans for possible nuclear warfare. As the US Secretary of Defence, James Forrestal, wrote at the time: 'We have the opportunity of sending these planes, and once sent, they would become somewhat of an accepted fixture.'[4] Three bomb groups arrived at Marham, Waddington and Scampton for 'operational training'. They were due to stay for thirty days, but this period was extended to sixty days and when the first tranche of aeroplanes left they were replaced by other groups. A process of regular 'rotation' followed and became routine. So Britain, within convenient flying range of the Soviet Union became the ideal forward base for America. As the US secretary of defence had predicted, the arrangement became permanent and accepted. But the legacy of no unambiguous written agreement, as to the status and the political control of American bases on British soil, remained.

Prime Minister, Clement Attlee's, Foreign Secretary, Ernest Bevin, was so concerned at the lack of a firm agreement which spelled out the terms on which the Americans were allowed to base nuclear forces in the UK, he insisted Britain must have the right to terminate arrangements if the British Government thought it was against Britain's national interests. He was also, not surprisingly, appalled at what the position would be if the US unilaterally chose to use British bases in circumstances where Britain itself was not at war, or if there was a disagreement between the two governments on policy. The UK was sovereign territory. The British Government could not allow US offensive operations to be launched from its territory without UK government consent. There have been suggestions that the US ambassador had given Bevin the assurance he sought, that Britain would be consulted about any plans for the use of British bases in an operational capacity. But these assurances were not put in writing.

In 1950, four further airfields were earmarked for use by Strategic Air Command, those at Greenham Common, Upper Heyford, Fairford and Brize Norton. This took place under an agreement which became known as 'The Ambassador's Agreement' because it was signed between the American ambassador to Britain and the British under-secretary for air. But the actual terms of the agreement remained secret.[5] The Soviet Union had, the previous year, announced it too was a nuclear power and the consequences of that were beginning to 'hit home' in the UK. There was now no doubt that Britain, as America's forward nuclear base would be first to be targeted in any exchange of nuclear weapons. There was no other way the Soviet Union could strike back against the US. It lacked both aircraft carriers and bombers of sufficient range to make a direct attack on North America. But Soviet nuclear bombers were perfectly capable of reaching Britain.

The situation was also crystal clear to the American Government. The safety of the US depended on American nuclear capacity based in the UK. The US Air Force Secretary, Thomas K Finletter, sent a revealing top secret memorandum to the US secretary for defence on 7 July 1950. He wrote: 'We are dependent at this moment almost entirely on the availability of UK bases for the launching of our strategic countermeasures. I haven't any real doubt that the British will come along if we do get engaged in war. But the question is when. I do not like at all the fact that we are almost entirely dependent on the UK ... I know the British well enough to know, that sometimes they can be very slow; and this strategic countermeasure is

16

something which cannot afford to be held up while the British Cabinet is debating about things.'[6]

The other side of the coin was expressed the same year by the British chief of air staff: 'The present situation,' he wrote 'whereby the United States could launch atomic bomb attacks on Russia making use of United Kingdom bases and facilities (without consultation) is intolerable.'[7]

Backbench MPs in Britain were beginning to voice fears that Britain might suffer annihilation without even prior consultation from the American Government, particularly following an overt threat from President Harry Truman to possibly use atomic weapons in the war that had broken out in Korea. In December 1950, Prime Minister Attlee went to Washington for urgent talks over nuclear threats. All he was able to achieve was a none-too-precise personal understanding between him and President Truman. Attlee had been keen to get a written agreement which would set out the exact terms under which bases on sovereign British soil could be used to launch a nuclear attack. He wanted very clearly defined the principle that the United States would not consider using these bases to launch nuclear-armed aircraft without first consulting the British Government.

Before the Attlee-Truman talks no formal arrangements between the two governments had existed. Instead, as has been shown, there were only 'understandings' which were certainly not well defined and were capable of ambiguous interpretation.

Attlee found the Americans adamant that there would be no written agreement. President Harry Truman told the British Prime Minister: 'It will not be in writing, since if a man's word isn't any good, it isn't made any better by writing it down.' The only paragraph in the communique following the talks between the two men that touched upon the key issue read: 'The President stated that it was his hope that world conditions would never call for the use of the atomic bomb. The President told the Prime Minister that it was also his desire to keep the Prime Minister at all times informed of all developments which might bring about a change in the situation.'[8] This was, of course, a long way from the certainty, spelt out in text, that Attlee wanted, which would have set down unequivocally that neither the US nor the UK would use nuclear weapons without prior consultation with each other; in other words an agreement which gave the UK a meaningful veto.

Attlee, in a statement to parliament on 14 December 1950, gave the impression that his talks with the President had been perfectly satisfactory and he made no mention of the fact that the Americans had disputed the British understanding of the outcome, particularly over the vital question of promising 'consultation'.

An American assessment in the early 1950s suggested that the UK would be crippled by an attack in which forty atomic bombs were dropped. 120 would irrevocably destroy the country, and in a general war the American Strategic Air Command could not expect more than a few weeks use of its UK forward bases. Despite the UK's vulnerability as host to America's forward nuclear attack force, the security of the UK, the American planners added, must necessarily be a British primary responsibility.

When Churchill regained the premiership in 1951, while he appreciated the deterrent value of US air bases on British soil, he feared, as had Attlee, America might be provoked into a preventive or retaliatory attack from the UK, which would plunge Britain into a conflict not of her making or necessarily of essential concern to her national interests. It would be easy for the United States to fight a nuclear war far away from its homeland, at the price of the devastation of the UK.

Churchill met Truman for talks in January 1952 in an effort to get assurances. The outcome of these discussions was a memorandum that stated: 'We reaffirm the understanding that the use of these bases in an emergency would be a matter for joint decision by His Majesty's Government and the United States Government in the light of the circumstances prevailing at the time.'[9]

The legal basis for the US military presence in Britain, and the consequences of America's use of British bases from which to launch a nuclear assault, remained a source of controversy for British governments for the rest of the Cold War years. The 1952 Churchill-Truman communiqué was the first and only time a framework for the use of the bases in the UK by American forces was ever set down in black and white. Politicians and commentators have frequently criticised its vagueness and its lack of precision. Some on the British side thought the phrase 'a matter for joint decision' gave the UK a veto. Most Americans felt it did no such thing, and that it was never intended to. Even its status is questioned. It did not have the authority of a legal treaty or contract. Nevertheless it was the basis for the deployment of America's formidable nuclear bomber squadrons and the first operational intermediate ballistic missiles – sixty Thor nuclear tipped rockets – on launch pads in the UK in 1958/59. Fundamental questions were left open. In many people's minds the status of the bases and terms for their use remained opaque and unaccountable.

Early in 1960, the Americans made further approaches to the British Government for forward nuclear weapons facilities, this time for a nuclear submarine base in Britain. That year the cabinet secretly gave their approval for an operational base on the Clyde, with the ironic name, Holy Loch. The deal, in exchange for the right to buy US Skybolt missiles to be launched by Britain's V-bombers, once again, increased the UK's vulnerability. In the event Skybolt was cancelled by the Americans, but in the negotiations leading to Holy Loch, Macmillan attempted to improve the terms of British control over US nuclear bases in the UK. He instructed his then Defence Minister, Harold Watkinson, to strike a hard bargain, but it seems nothing was achieved that built upon the previous loose arrangements. He recorded in his memoirs that he wanted to: 'Look carefully again at the precise terms of the agreement for the American bases, in order to ensure they were watertight,' but while the intention was there he found that the Americans were not prepared to re-open the matter.[10]

The Prime Minister made another attempt to get agreement on more stringent terms in July 1960. An RB-47 bomber from the USAF base at Brize Norton, was shot down by the Soviets over the Barents Sea on 1 July. Russia accused the Americans of violating Soviet air-space and aware that the offending plane had originated from an air base in the UK, the Soviet Government sent a protest note to the British over the use of British bases for spy-flights over Soviet territory. Did Britain know about these flights, the Soviet Government asked. Had there been joint decisions between the British and American authorities? The question put the British in something of a dilemma. Following the Soviet protest the Ministry of Defence issued a statement asserting the flight was perfectly legal and had been undertaken for 'scientific purposes'. It added that both the object of the mission and its flight plan had been known to the ministry.[11]

Little more than a quarter of an hour later the ministry withdrew its statement. When Macmillan was asked to explain why in the House of Commons, he declined. A persistent MP followed this up by asking him to comment on U-2 spy flights from US bases in East Anglia. Again he refused to give an answer, saying that 'These questions have a bearing on either the scope of intelligence activities, or the way in which they are conducted and controlled.' He added that it had never been the government's practice to discuss such matters in the House and it would be contrary to the public interest to depart from that precedent. So the crucial issue of control and consultation was once again evaded.[12]

Following these incidents a Foreign Office delegation led by a senior civil servant went to Washington to discuss the basis on which the Americans operated from British bases. No clear statement was issued as a result of that delegation's discussions with the American Government, but it is clear that the terms of the Attlee/Truman 'understanding' were not changed. *The Times* reported on 15 July 1960, 'The talks are expected to proceed smoothly towards an understanding which will probably involve no actual change in the 1951 agreement.'[13]

In November 1960 when protests were vociferous in Scotland about the new American Polaris base at Holy Loch, Macmillan acknowledged in the House of Commons that: 'The target (Holy Loch) like every other target in the country will be important, but no more important, and perhaps a little less important, than the bomber bases ... We have to accept the situation that our danger is spread, and that we are all in it.'[14]

These questions were particularly pertinent as tensions racked up over the Cuban missile crisis and units of America's Strategic Air Command stationed on British soil were ordered on 24 October 1962 to a far higher state of war readiness than their Royal Air Force counterparts. Critics of the powerful American nuclear presence in Britain felt it inevitably tied the government of a leading European nation much too closely to the strategic interests of the United States. In America it was maintained, and still is, that a US President could neither politically nor legally curtail his right to direct United States forces in their use of nuclear weapons, wherever they might be based. This fundamental constitutional premise therefore inhibited any American Government from being clearer and more open about any 'understanding' arrived at between Britain and the United States over the use of American power from British soil.

Two years before the Cuban crisis emerged, America mounted a world-wide 'nuclear co-ordination exercise' code-named 'Black Rock'. It lasted throughout the month of May 1960 and was in effect a rehearsal of America's nuclear war plans. On at least two occasions during the exercise United States bases in Britain were ordered to a very high level of war readiness. A Labour MP, William Warbey, wrote to Macmillan protesting that the alerts might have been put in place to influence the US-Soviet summit that took place in May 1960, and in any case placed Britain in a difficult position diplomatically. The Prime Minister took a calm view for public consumption, but privately was deeply concerned. Publicly he said 'the alerts were merely a way of practising communications and readiness,' and that 'there was no question of an error of judgement which might plunge the world into nuclear war.' Privately, however, he instructed the Minister of Defence, Harold Watkinson, to protest to the US authorities that Britain had not received prior notification of a simulated raising of the atomic stakes. The Prime Minister felt America should have given the host country warning of what their forces were doing on British soil. The US secretary of defence in his response, made it clear that until that point there was no arrangement in force to 'warn Britain of alerts at British bases during periods of increased world tension and for exercise purposes.' He promised in future any decision to alert US forces in the UK would be notified to the British Government in advance.[15] It revealed just how informal arrangements between the two governments were over matters that implicitly affected British national interests and the safety of the British public. But that assurance seems quietly to have been forgotten when, as the Cuban crisis emerged, US nuclear armed aircraft were covertly placed on a high state of alert.

Macmillan was well aware, indeed publicly accepted, that American bases in the UK placed Great Britain squarely in the cross-hairs of the Soviet Union. At a press conference in 1957, following the agreement between him and President Eisenhower to deploy American inter-mediate range nuclear ballistic missiles targeted on the Soviet Union to RAF units in England, Macmillan openly acknowledged this step would make Britain the free world's first nuclear attack target. 'We can't help that,' he added.

When the Cuban crisis happened and America placed its Strategic Air Command bases in Britain on an unprecedented DEFCON Two alert, the UK was informed, but only at the operational level of Bomber Command. There seems to have been no formal discussion between the US and UK governments. Indeed it was left to Macmillan to personally persuade the American Supreme Commander of NATO, General Lauris Norstad, not to issue a full mobilisation order across the whole of NATO which might well have provoked a much more aggressive response from the Soviet Union and its Warsaw Pact allies.

Notes

1. Chief of staffs' memo to ministers, January 1958. Humphrey Wynn: *RAF Nuclear Deterrent Forces*, HMSO, London, 1994, p. 288.
2. Deputy chief of air staff memo to air council, January 1958, Wynn, p. 289.
3. Duncan Campbell: *The Unsinkable Aircraft Carrier*, Michael Joseph, London, 1984, p. 31.
4. US Defence Secretary, James Forrestal: Diary note, 17 July 1948. Ibid, p. 29.

5. Ibid, p. 32: Ambassadors Agreement.
6. Ibid, p. 33: American Air Force Secretary, Thomas K Finletter, memo to US Secretary of Defense, 7 July 1950.
7. Marshal of the RAF Sir John Slessor, 1950 (Quoted in Duncan Campbell: *The Unsinkable Aircraft Carrier: American Military Power in Britain*, Michael Joseph, London, 1984, p. 34).
8. Attlee/Truman communiqué, December 1950.
9. Churchill/Truman communiqué, 9 January 1952. Quoted in *The Unsinkable Aircraft Carrier*, p. 44.
10. Harold Macmillan: *Pointing the Way, 1959–61*, Macmillan, 1965.
11. *The Unsinkable Aircraft Carrier*, p. 58.
12. *The Times*, 13 July 1960.
13. *The Times*, 15 July 1960.
14. Hansard, 1 November 1960.
15. Joint chiefs of staff files, Section CCS3180, emergency readiness plans. *Unsinkable Aircraft Carrier*, p. 57.

Chapter 3

Jigsaw Puzzles

*In 1960 and again in 1962 JIGSAW maintained that deaths greatly
underestimated the effects of nuclear attack, and that there is little
point in saving people from immediate death without securing the
means of keeping them and the nation alive during the following
months.*

Dr Edgar Anstey, JIGSAW member, 20 May 1963

Throughout the Cold War there were government officials deep
inside Whitehall's corridors of power whose job it was to 'think the
unthinkable'. They were engaged in the grimmest, most secret task of
the Cold War years. They had to assume a Third World War would
happen, and to prepare the country to face Armageddon; to quantify
the enormity of British deaths, casualties, and destruction; and to
imagine how the British state, or what was left of it, could continue
to function. Others had the responsibility of charting the probable
steps that would lead to nuclear war. Through gathering the correct
intelligence, and observing the significant signs, the government
hoped it would be possible to gain sufficient time in the lead-up to
nuclear conflict, to put into operation detailed contingency plans
contained in what was termed the government *War Book*, and therefore give the UK the best possible chance of surviving in some form
when the mushroom clouds erupted.

In February 1962, seven months before the Cuban crisis, Britain's
Joint Intelligence Committee (JIC) compiled a list of probable pointers
to Soviet preparations for nuclear conflict. It was a comprehensive
catalogue consisting of sixty-four different factors over and above
those obtained from observing any obvious deterioration in the
general political situation. Seventeen of the indicators were on a 'red
list' of primary preparations those which the Soviet Union would
consider essential to make before launching a surprise attack on the
west. A further forty-seven were on an 'amber list', those which fell
into the bracket of the more important of the additional preparations
for war which the Soviet Union might make if achieving strategic
surprise was not considered possible. Together these indicators

ranged from the obvious, like increased states of readiness through-out the Soviet armed forces, to the more obscure, for instance abnormal censorship of Soviet forces' mail. The objective was to notice change and assess its significance.[1] But the strategy assumed British intelligence would be able to detect an identifiable period for the build-up to war over a matter of weeks or months. Despite this, when the Cuban situation broke, it came as almost a complete surprise. Events moved very swiftly towards the brink of a Third World War. There was no time to put into practice the planned practical steps to war, like the evacuation of vulnerable people from areas of most danger, even if the government had wanted to do so. A panicking population was the last thing the Macmillan government wanted. So publicly the alarm bells were muted.

The JIC had the task of analysing and interpreting all the intelligence coming in from British Intelligence's covert sources, from spies on the ground and from electronic eavesdropping. It was distilled and went into a weekly digest for ministers. As early as 1957 the JIC had noted the possibility of war breaking out as a result of the Soviet Union making nuclear weapons available to a third-party power.[2] But that initial forecast got lost in the increasing focus of war resulting from the protracted east-west problems over Berlin. The intelligence experts in 1962 were also very aware of the possibilities of 'war by accident or miscalculation', but in the divided capital of Germany, not in the Caribbean.

Their 1962 paper gloomily entitled 'The Likelihood of War with the Soviet Union up to 1966' ended with the following passage: 'Even when there is no particular political tension, each side now has a proportion of its nuclear strike forces constantly at immediate alert. There must always be a risk, however remote, that by pure mechanical or electrical accident, one of the missiles might be launched; or that through misunderstanding one might be launched through human agency without this being the intention of the government concerned; or that one side might interpret the evidence of its early warning devices to mean that an attack had been launched by the other when in fact this was not so.'[3]

Government advisers visualised war might break out as a result of miscalculation of the consequences of a move the other side considered intolerable. Or it could occur because one side or the other falsely believed there had been a weakening in the determination to use nuclear force. Or war might be precipitated as a result of one side or the other failing to foresee the consequences of policies being pursued by a third party or third state, with which it was associated.

All these eventualities were strands of JIC thinking shortly before the Cuban crisis rapidly raised the stakes of global war. All of them were factors involved in the Cuban situation. Yet, out of the blue, Cuba still caught Britain and the United States unawares.

In 1962, despite that suggestion of war being triggered as a result of the Soviet Union adopting a policy with a 'third party' that could lead to fatal consequences, the intelligence chiefs in the UK had their eyes firmly fixed on the possibilities of war erupting in Europe. The Berlin Wall built menacingly and without warning in August 1961, represented the brutal face of the Iron Curtain. Armed Russian and American battle tanks had recently faced each other at Checkpoint Charlie. The conventional thinking was if any flash point was to pitch the world into conflict, the spark would be ignited in that divided city.

Government advisers, whose grisly task it was to plan, step by step, the UK's transition to war, and determine how to grapple with the appalling horrors that would result, had to ponder the probability of national collapse. In the grim lexicon of nuclear planning the experts coined the word 'breakdown' to describe the ultimate situation where a state is reduced to a position where any form of national revival is problematic. By 'breakdown' they meant the point at which the citizens no longer had the will to respond to orders, where the government had lost contact with the machinery of control, and the mass of people were preoccupied with their own survival and the survival of their families, rather than the survival of the country.[4]

The people pondering the enormity of these terrifying 'what ifs' were known as the Joint Inter-Services Group for the Study of All-Out War, or JIGSAW for short. It was the grimmest forum for the solution of Dr Strangelove puzzles. This group wrestled with the problems and the probabilities of Armageddon, deep inside Britain's secret state, for six years of the most intense period of Cold War.

The JIGSAW group tried to estimate the level of nuclear attack that would reduce the UK to 'breakdown'. They calculated that twenty-five megaton nuclear explosions, strategically targeted across the country, would be sufficient to cause UK breakdown. The United States and the Soviet Union they believed, would probably be capable of absorbing up to 450 megaton strikes before either country slumped into nuclear breakdown. However, by then the results of damaging radiation would spread far beyond their boundaries and begin to poison the population of countries across the world. The really shocking statistic was that both the United States and the Soviet Union had the capacity in the early sixties to deliver this scale of strike even after they had been subject to a pre-emptive attack by their major adversary.[5] Breakdown would happen, the experts concluded, when fifty per cent of the population had been rendered ineffective. On just such arguments, almost too awful to contemplate, the survival of the planet and its peoples rested.

Members of JIGSAW were in Washington in April 1960 and co-incidentally again in October 1962 just as the Cuban crisis was breaking. They were discussing the consequences of nuclear war with their opposite numbers in the United States – the US weapons supply evaluation group. A Ministry of Defence member of JIG-SAW, an eminent psychologist, Edgar Anstey, impressed on his American colleagues the British view that in the event of a nuclear attack there was little point in saving people from immediate death without securing the means of keeping them, and the nation, alive during the following months. The US agencies had not accepted that 'breakdown' could occur in such a vast country as America. For political reasons it was a difficult concept to swallow. The exchange of views with the JIGSAW members resulted in the Americans confronting some of the more appalling and sobering consequences of all-out nuclear war, in which many hundreds of megaton strikes could be made against American targets. Anstey spoke passionately about the dangers of escalation and the need for negotiation and conciliation rather than pre-emptive attack. His stark exposition of the British findings may well have influenced the Americans, and particularly President Kennedy, in the face-down with the Soviet Union that was about to shock the world.

The year before Cuba, in July 1961, a bizarre conversation took place in Moscow. Khrushchev and the British Ambassador, Sir Frank Roberts, were both at a production of the Moscow ballet company. In an exceedingly grim conversation, given the nature of the occasion and the surroundings, Khrushchev claimed in a global nuclear war, the UK, West Germany and France would all perish on day one. The Soviet leader posed the question to Sir Frank: 'How many bombs would be needed to put the UK out of commission?' The British Ambassador, intentionally under-estimating, said he thought maybe six. Khrushchev scoffed. He said he had heard an anecdote about pessimists and optimists. Roberts was a pessimist. The optimists thought it would take at least nine nuclear bombs. But, said Khrushchev, the Soviet general staff had earmarked several scores for use against the UK. The Soviet Union had a higher opinion of the UK's capacity to survive than the UK authorities had![6]

Pre-Cuba the conventional wisdom had it that transition to war would follow three distinct phases. A 'precautionary' stage of perhaps seven days or more of growing international tension. A 'destructive' phase lasting forty-eight hours to a week, when the nuclear bombardment would fall. And a 'survival' phase when what remained of government, devolved to twelve regional centres, or bunkers, staffed by ministers, officials, police and the military, focused on trying to prevent the situation of total national 'breakdown' that so haunted the minds of civil servants and ministers. Central Government, if it survived, would retreat to a secret bunker hoping to oversee nuclear retaliation, and maintain some form of civil control.

By the early 1960s it had been agreed that any kind of shelter policy for the population would entail such a massive programme, it was unaffordable, and in any case probably a sheer waste of money. Nevertheless ministers and officials who would occupy the government bunkers hoped to survive and to work in shelters paid for by those same taxpayers left to fend for themselves. Some home defence spending remained. Around £150 million in 1960–61, concentrated on four main areas. These were the pre-attack evacuation of children, mothers, expectant mothers, the aged and infirm – some eleven million people in all; stockpiling of food, oil, and medical supplies to aid survival in the post-attack period; the securing of public utilities and communications – though the probable devastation would have made this problematic; and finally provision of those bunkers from which it was hoped some element of civil control might be exercised. Civil defence, as it was known during the Second World War, directed at rescue and recovery, was not considered practical to cope with the level of destruction a nuclear war would cause. Evacuation from major cities was of debatable use. Many of the most significant military targets were in rural areas, in the Second World War the very places evacuees were sent for safety. The philosophy of survival gave way to the philosophy of deterrence. Money was better invested, the government thought in deterring war than in spending huge sums to ensure the maximum number should survive a war.

This was the gloomy assessment outlined in Duncan Sandys' Defence White Paper published by the Conservative Government in 1957. When it came to discussing the provisions for national nuclear defence it had this to say: 'It must frankly be recognised that there is at present no means of providing adequate protection for the people of this country against the consequences of an attack by nuclear weapons. Though in the event of war, the fighter aircraft of the RAF would unquestionably take a heavy toll of enemy bombers, a proportion would inevitably get through. Even if it were only a dozen, they could with megaton (hydrogen) bombs inflict widespread devastation.'[7] The white paper's conclusion, which set the policy of 'defence' in a nuclear world where weapons were becoming ever more destructive, was that 'the only existing safeguard against major aggression is the power to threaten retaliation with nuclear weapons.'

The underground nerve centre from which survival was destined to be co-ordinated – if the worst happened and the Soviets had not targeted and destroyed it first – was deep below Box Hill in the Cotswolds near to Corsham. It was referred to in 1962 by the code word 'Burlington'. Prior to that, it had been 'Stockwell'. Subsequently, it was changed to 'Turnstile'. Its location, even the meaning of the code itself, was a closely guarded secret. Ministers and civil servants in the know called it simply 'The Quarry'. The need for secrecy was paramount, hence the variety of covert names. Had the Soviet Union known its location and its use, and there is some evidence to believe its secrecy had been compromised by August 1962, it would have been targeted by one of the first Soviet missiles to strike. No one believed it could survive a direct hit, or even one a mile or more away.

A review in 1964 considered that the geology of Great Britain was such that the only sure way of a nucleus of government surviving a direct hit, would be to encapsulate all the personnel within a pressure vessel at a depth of 3,000 feet underground. Such a vessel might ensure the survival of at least some of its occupants, but rock displacement would almost certainly have blocked its exits and its communications, so the chances were no one would ever emerge from it!

The only time the 'quarry' came near to be used to shelter elements of the British Government was during that ominous Cuban crisis weekend in October 1962. Had a cabinet meeting arranged for the afternoon of Sunday, 28 October taken place as scheduled, the Third World War plans would have been set in motion. It would have triggered the move of some 210 people, key to mounting the UK's nuclear retaliation, plus several thousand other civil servants and technicians out of Whitehall to the rudimentary facilities of life in the 'quarry'. Macmillan and some of his main colleagues would have remained in Whitehall until definite warning of a forthcoming nuclear attack had been received when on the issuing of the code word 'visitation' they would have been transferred by helicopter from horse guards parade to the 'quarry'. The battle for survival of the country and the UK state would have begun.

When he became Prime Minister in 1957, at a time the V-Force was coming on stream forming the British nuclear deterrent, Macmillan was first in the office with the awesome responsibility of having his finger on the thermonuclear button. Britain's first H-bombs were operationally available in 1961. The reasons for retaining an independent nuclear capacity for the UK were set out in a memorandum by the secretary of state for air:

1. To retain our special relation with the United States and, through it, our influence in world affairs, and especially our right to have a voice in the final issue of peace or war.
2. To make a definite, though limited, contribution to the total nuclear strength of the west.
3. To enable us, by threatening to use our independent nuclear power, to secure United States co-operation in a situation in which their interests were less immediately threatened than our own.
4. To make sure that in a nuclear war, sufficient attention is given to certain Soviet targets which are of greater importance to us than to the United States.[8]

The unspoken fear within government was that at some future date the Americans might, for whatever reason, revert to a policy of isolationism, in which case Britain would have to have an independent deterrent of its own. Furthermore, possession of a nuclear deterrent would, in Macmillan's view, ensure a place for Britain at 'the top table' in discussions of international significance. It conferred 'great power' status, at a time when Britain was losing its empire. This was not the American view. Robert McNamara, the US Secretary of Defence, frequently complained that the British deterrent was 'unnecessary'. But the nuclear deterrent had been presented to the British people as essential to international influence and national security.

The Prime Minister was the only person able to authorise a nuclear strike, and his ministerial authorisation was essential before the order to launch was given. It was therefore vital that as far as possible the Prime Minister was always contactable. A problem existed when he was travelling in the Prime Ministerial car. In the fifties and sixties there were no mobile phones to offer quick and reliable communications when the Prime Minister was on the move. In October 1961, exactly a year before the Cuban crisis, Macmillan received a memorandum from the cabinet office suggesting a way of overcoming the obvious problem of authorising nuclear retaliation swiftly if the Prime Minister was temporarily out of contact. The proposal was the appointment of two deputies to take on the awesome responsibility in his place. The following day Macmillan replied giving his nominations with a macabre touch of 'black' humour. He wrote with a Shakespearian allusion: 'I agree the following: First Gravedigger – Mr R A Butler. Second Gravedigger: Mr Selwyn Lloyd'[9]

In the early sixties communications were by no means as developed as they are today. Lord Mountbatten rightly felt that there should be some equivalent in the UK, of the military officer who accompanied the President of the United States at all times, carrying the codes that would unleash nuclear retaliation. The reality was radar might give up to ninety minutes warning of an attack by Soviet nuclear bombers, but with no ballistic missile early warning system in operation until the year after the Cuban crisis, attack by Soviet nuclear rockets would be without any warning – the feared 'bolt from the blue'. The US controlled Ballistic Missile Early Warning System (BMEWS), of which Fylingdales in North Yorkshire was just one of three locations, the others being in Alaska and Greenland, did not become operational until 1963.

The solution, dreamt up in Whitehall, was unearthed by Peter Hennessy in 2009, from papers released to the public records office and described in his book *The Secret State*. A memo dated 30 January 1961, suggested that a radio should be installed in Macmillan's car so that messages could be sent in plain language via the Automobile Association. The system was installed in May 1962, and it was planned that in an emergency a message would be relayed via the AA to the Prime Ministerial limousine, to get the PM as fast as possible to the nearest telephone. Another memo contained in all seriousness a reminder that at all times government drivers should ensure they carried four pennies with them so that a call could be made to launch the V-Force from a GPO call box! There was of course the possibility of a reverse charge call, but that might take a few moments longer, when the safety of the entire population was at stake! Whitehall war planners needed both a sense of humour and a sense of proportion. The entire nuclear deterrent with its vast technology of V-bombers, nuclear bombs, and complex missile systems, rested on the AA getting the Prime Minister to a call box! Had they known, Soviet intelligence would never have believed it![10]

But these 'Dad's Army' arrangements still did not address the question of a nuclear 'bolt from the blue' either killing the PM or making it impossible for him to authorise retaliation. It was agreed in January 1962 that should such an attack occur, or if nuclear bombs had burst in the UK before any authority had been given for a nuclear response, the commander in chief, Bomber Command would be given certain powers to order a nuclear response on his own initiative. That was the position during the Cuban crisis. The commander in chief was told he had the power to order all his bombers airborne under positive control – that is awaiting an order to proceed beyond their stop lines; to seek contact with the Prime Minister or his deputy, and if possible also the United States authority responsible for launching strategic nuclear weapons from the UK; and in the last resort when it was confirmed a nuclear attack had been made on the UK, to order entirely on his own responsibility nuclear retaliation by all the means at his disposal.[11] So in the worst scenario a British response would have been a military, not a government decision. The means at the commander in chief's disposal were considerable. Bomber Command had 112 V-bombers under his command and sixty nuclear tipped Thor missiles, although the missiles were subject to American control of the warhead, and a dual launch procedure which required both an American and a British key to be turned before the missile could be fired.

In 1962 the V-Force alone was committed to target thirty-five nuclear bombs on fifteen Soviet cities with populations in excess of 600,000, and twenty-five bombs on twenty-five cities with populations in excess of 400,000. This would have resulted in deaths and casualties on an unimaginable scale. Armed with megaton bombs, it was estimated at this level the V-Force attack would result in some eight million killed and a further eight million injured.[12]

Notes

1. PRO, CAB 158/45 JIC 'Indications of Sino-Soviet Bloc Preparations for Early War' 26/2/1962.
2. PRO, CAB 158/29 JIC 'The Possibility of Hostilities Short of Global War Up to 1965' 20/9/1957.
3. PRO, CAB 158/44 JIC 'The Likelihood of War with the Soviet Union up to 1966' 9/2/1962.
4. PRO, DEFE 10/402 'Note on the Concept and Definitions of Breakdown' 10/6/1960.
5. Peter Hennessy, *The Secret State: Preparing for the Worst*, Allen Lane, London, 2002, p. 185.
6. PRO, FO 371/160546, 'Soviet Attitudes towards Peace, Treaty and Status of Berlin' 17/8/1961.
7. 'Defence: Outline of Future Policy': Cmd. 124 (HMSO 1957).
8. PRO, Air 8/2400 'Medium Bomber Force: Size and Composition'; Defence Board, 'The V-Bomber Force and the Powered Bomb' 29/10/1958.
9. PRO, CAB 21/6081, *'Machinery of Government in War'*: Ministerial Nominations 6/10/1961.
10. Peter Hennessy *The Secret State: Preparing for the Worst*, pp. 191–3.
11. PRO DEFE 25/49 'Nuclear Retaliation Procedures' 23/1/1962.
12. PRO AIR 8/2400 'Russian Capacity to Absorb Damage'.

Chapter 4

'Tit-for-Tat'

We would be doing nothing more than giving them a little of their own medicine.

Nikita S Khrushchev, April 1962

The Cuban Missile Crisis occurred at a time when America was acutely sensitive to any challenge which could raise the stakes of nuclear war. President John F Kennedy had come to office promising 'Communist domination in this hemisphere can never be negotiated.' He declared at his inauguration in January 1961: 'We pledge to work with our sister republics to free the Americas of all such foreign domination and tyranny.' Kennedy's nightmare was that the communist revolution that had installed Castro in Cuba would lead to revolution spreading throughout Latin America. He could not countenance that. Khrushchev, ideological romanticist that he was, was prepared to take a massive risk to enable it to happen.

Kennedy's inauguration speech captured the doctrine of a new era. 'Let every nation know, whether it wishes us well or ill, that we shall pay any price, bear any burden, meet any hardship, support any friend, oppose any foe, to assure the survival and success of liberty. We will do all this and more.'[1]

The mood of Kennedy's 'New Frontier', inferred that if America's vital interests were threatened, the United States would defend them with utmost vigour. But the young President initially pursued a policy that was both provocative and unsuccessful. The failed Bay of Pigs landings against Fidel Castro's Cuba in April 1961 set the scene for the Cuban crisis the following year. Kennedy was determined to overthrow Castro's revolution, but the attempt to achieve this through the landing of anti-Castro Cuban exiles at the Bay of Pigs was a dismal failure. In Moscow, Khrushchev saw it as a clear indication of the counter-revolutionary resolve in Washington. He reasoned that there would be a repeat, and this time America would strike with far greater force. 'The fate of Cuba and the maintenance of Soviet prestige in that part of the world preoccupied me,' Khrushchev later recalled. 'We had to think up some way of confronting America with more than

words.'[2] The Bay of Pigs adventure humiliated the Kennedy administration and strengthened relations between Havana and Moscow.
Washington's on-going covert effort to subvert Fidel Castro's regime,
conducted under the code name Operation Mongoose, played a
significant role in fomenting the missile crisis.

A factor in the United States failing to detect the build up of
offensive weaponry on Cuba, was what some analysts have called
the 'photo-gap'. For five crucial weeks the Kennedy administration
'shot itself in the foot' by limiting U2 surveillance flights over the
island. Two over-flights were scheduled for August 1962. The first
on 5 August was too early, by a matter of days to capture any telling
evidence about what would soon be an unprecedented military build
up on the island. The second flight took place on 29 August after
some days of delay due to bad weather. This photo-reconnaissance
mission detected a surface to air missile site, a SA-2 the same type
of missile that had been used by the Soviets to shoot down Francis
Gary Powers' U2 in the USSR in 1960. With a mid-term election fast
approaching, Kennedy did not want publicity over the discovery of
ground to air missiles. He also did not want surveillance to be conducted in a 'provocative' manner. The next scheduled mission was
on 5 September when further SAM sites were discovered. Secretary
of State, Dean Rusk, argued that losing a U2 over Cuba would compromise Washington's unquestioned right to fly spy missions in
international waters along Cuba's periphery, and given the island's
narrowness, offshore flights were probably sufficient. Four over-flights
were agreed for September, two in international waters and two which
would nip in and out over small portions of central and eastern Cuba.
This considerably limited the photographic 'take' during a period
when the offensive missiles began to arrive. Recognisable missile
equipment would have arrived on Cuba around 17 or 18 September
yet because Washington had denied itself the opportunity to produce
'hard information' the missiles' presence was not established until a
full month later.[3]

Discovering missiles in Cuba, targeted straight at American cities
and at the vital military assets of the United States, made the US feel
more vulnerable than at any time in her history. It was a challenge
Kennedy could not countenance. Confrontation was inevitable, but it
threw up unparalleled risks. The Cuba situation posed a problem
that challenged the prestige of the leadership on both sides and left
scant space for compromise. Secretary of Defence, Robert McNamara,
recalled later: 'The world came within a hairs breadth of nuclear
war ... we came so close both Khrushchev and Kennedy felt events

were slipping outside their control.'[4] Kennedy's own advisers were telling him that in any conflict, ten million Americans would be killed, even if the Soviets targeted only military bases and facilities. But the President was given precious little assurance such precise targeting was even possible. Most military bases in the United States, as in Europe and the USSR, were located in and around cities, so collateral damage would have been extensive. For the first time America was face to face with a threat Europe had lived with for a decade.

In Britain Prime Minister, Harold Macmillan, recorded his thoughts on dealing with Khrushchev in September 1962, before any one knew the Cuba crisis was brewing: 'I felt instinctively anxious lest the President and I were being deceived or lulled into a false security,' he wrote. What lay behind Khrushchev's manoeuvrings, sometimes threatening, sometimes friendly? Was there some new plot hatching? Were we to wake up one morning faced not merely with verbal disputations but by actions which might prove the terrible prelude to the Third World War?'[5] His musings were spot-on. His dire forebodings, fuelled by concerns over Berlin and the failure of the Vienna summit in June 1961 where Khrushchev had all but humbled Kennedy, were to be dramatically fulfilled.

Khrushchev was so committed to Castro and the Cuban revolution that he was prepared to risk his country and possibly the world itself on Castro's behalf. After the crisis was over Castro admitted as much. 'Nikita loved Cuba very much,' he said. 'He had a weakness for Cuba you might say – emotionally, and so on – because he was a man of political conviction.'[6]

In Khrushchev's own words 'We had to establish a tangible and effective deterrent to American interference in the Caribbean. But what exactly? The logical answer was missiles.'[7]

Khrushchev felt the United States could hardly object. America had placed her own intermediate range missiles in Britain, Italy and Turkey, all aimed at the Soviet Union. How could the Americans possibly oppose the Soviets doing the same? 'The Americans would learn,' Khrushchev swore, 'just what it feels like to have enemy missiles pointing at you. We'd be doing nothing more than giving them a little of their own medicine.'

In Britain, as soon as he had heard that the Soviets were installing missiles in Cuba, Macmillan made much the same point. As he recalled in his memoirs, after he had received a briefing from President Kennedy he considered how to draft his response: 'One could, of course, promise general support,' he wrote. 'But I had to remember that the people of Europe and Britain had lived in close proximity to Soviet missiles for several years.'[8] To the UK it was nothing new.

In the end Macmillan settled for tact. He forbore reminding the US President that the threat his country now faced from Cuba was very similar to that the UK had lived under for years, and no different to the threat the west had posed close to the borders of the Soviet Union by deploying missiles to Britain, Italy and Turkey.

Khrushchev was understandably ultra sensitive to the American missiles levelled at his country, particularly those closest just across the Black Sea. He had a habit of greeting visitors to his dacha on the Black Sea shore by handing them a pair of binoculars and telling them to look towards the south. 'What do you see?' he would ask. When they replied nothing but sea and sky he would take the binoculars back and putting them to his own eyes, would bellow, 'I see American missiles in Turkey targeted at my dacha!' No wonder in his eyes Khrushchev saw his Cuban adventure as nothing more than a 'tit for tat'.

But, as the British JIGSAW planners had observed, in stressful times, war could easily result from a miscalculation. Given that Khrushchev had sent the missiles in total secrecy, while lying to Kennedy that he had no such intention, the Americans saw the move as a dangerous provocation. They interpreted the policy as offensive, a threat to the United States. Not, as Khrushchev belatedly protested, 'defensive' weapons placed to defend Cuba – not to confront America. 'Offensive missiles in Cuba have a very different psychological and political effect in this hemisphere, than missiles in the USSR pointing at us,' Kennedy warned.[9] But he refused to equate the Cuban situation with the threat America had deployed in Europe against the Soviet Union.

Notes

1. Annual Message to the Congress and the State of the Union, 30/1/1961.
2. Nikita S Khrushchev: *Khrushchev Remembers*, translated and edited by Strobe Talbott: New York, Bantam, 1971, p. 546.
3. Max Holland: *The Photo Gap that Delayed Discovery of Missiles in Cuba*, www.cia.gov/csi/studies/vol49 no4.
4. Interview for CNN 'For the Record' 18/6/1998.
5. Harold Macmillan, *At the End of the Day*, Macmillan, London, 1973, p. 179.
6. Blight, Allyn and Welch: *Cuba on the Brink: Castro, the Missile Crisis and the Soviet Collapse*, p. 259, New York, Pantheon, 1993.
7. *Khrushchev Remembers*, p. 546.
8. Harold Macmillan: *At the End of the Day*, p. 187.
9. Kennedy meeting with advisers: 'The Kennedy Tapes: Inside the White House during the Cuban Missile Crisis', 22/10/1962.

Chapter 5

Castro's Concerns

Why should it seem we are doing something secretly, covertly, as if we were doing something wrong to which we have no right?

Fidel Castro, July 1962

The America people were enthusiastic over their young, new President. They admired his charm and his powerful and fluent speeches. They believed him when he promised a new era for the American people.

In Britain a speech by Kennedy on 4 September 1962 should have started alarm bells ringing. The White House was under pressure from some Republican quarters, particularly New York Senator, Kenneth Keating, a member of the senate foreign relations committee, and from elements within the CIA, who were prone to believe the increasing rumours circulating of an arms build-up in Cuba. Kennedy and his advisers believed these rumours were being stirred up for political purposes by his opponents and by disgruntled individuals within the CIA. But the President should have taken them more seriously.

In the middle of August aerial film obtained by the CIA had shown Soviet cargo ships heading for the Caribbean. Some were riding unusually high in the water suggesting the huge crates secured on their decks concealed objects that were in fact relatively light-weight. Stories from Cuban refugees arriving in Miami told of long truck conveys on Cuba's roads before dawn. Each vehicle carried a cylindrical object hidden beneath a tarpaulin. Military intelligence concluded these were SA-2s, surface to air missiles, to protect Cuba from invasion. John McCone, Director of the CIA, was rather more suspicious. He guessed the SA-2s, if that was what they were, were being installed to protect an even more threatening secret – ground to ground missiles capable of hitting American cities. Reports also circulated of large numbers of Russian speaking 'tourists' in Cuba ostentatiously dressed in Hawaiian shirts. The CIA speculated correctly they were in reality Soviet troops in disguise!

Stung by criticism, largely from his political opponents, Kennedy issued a warning to the Soviet Union on 4 September that: 'If evidence were to appear of any organised combat force in Cuba from any Soviet bloc country ... or of the presence of ground to ground missiles; or of other significant offensive capability either in Cuban hands or under Soviet direction and guidance ... the gravest issues would arise.'[1]

Commenting later about that warning, McGeorge Bundy, Kennedy's principal national security adviser, recalled it had been issued because of the demands of domestic politics, not because the administration seriously believed that the Soviets would do anything as crazy from America's standpoint as placing of Soviet nuclear weapons in Cuba.[2]

Had Khrushchev taken the warning he could, had he wished, have halted Operation Anadyr, as the Cuban adventure was referred to in Moscow, the very next day. As of 5 September no ground to ground nuclear tipped missiles or their warheads had arrived in Cuba. But the Soviet leader did the exact opposite, he speeded up delivery of weapons en-route, particularly the nuclear ballistic missiles. He also ordered the despatch of tactical nuclear weapons to the Caribbean. Finally he gave the Americans more wholly untruthful assurances that nothing provocative was going on in Cuba, which in Kennedy's eyes made the Soviet deception far worse when the truth emerged.

The day Kennedy issued his warning, the Soviet Ambassador to Washington, Anatoly Dobrynin, told the President's brother, Attorney General Robert Kennedy, that 'There would be no ground to ground or offensive weapons placed in Cuba.' 'Chairman Khrushchev,' he added, 'liked President Kennedy, and he did not wish to embarrass him.'[3] Six days later the Soviet Government issued a further statement saying the arms being delivered to Cuba were 'solely for defensive purposes.'

Kennedy followed up his first warning to Moscow with another delivered at a White House press conference on 13 September, following further Soviet assurances they had no intention of deploying 'offensive' weapons to Cuba. 'If at any time the communist build-up were to endanger or interfere with our security in any way,' Kennedy declared, 'including our base at Guantanamo, our passage to the Panama Canal, our missile and space activity at Cape Canaveral, or the lives of American citizens in this country, or if Cuba should ever attempt to export its aggressive purposes by force or the threat of force against any nation in this hemisphere, or become an offensive military base of significant capacity for the Soviet Union, then this country will do whatever must be done to protect its own security and that of its allies.'[4] Unmistakeably this was a declaration that

America would use ultimate force, if the USSR mounted a direct threat to its vital interests.

Fidel Castro took a different view from the man in the Kremlin. He welcomed the Soviet weaponry to his island but he deprecated the secrecy with which it was being done. He wanted the whole operation to take place openly. In early July his brother, Raul Castro, had been in Moscow for five weeks drawing up the formal five-year treaty which would regulate the stationing of Soviet troops in Cuba. In August the Soviet ambassador to the island, Aleksandr Alekseyev, delivered the finished treaty to Havana where Castro went through it in detail and suggested some revisions. It was taken back to Moscow in late August by Che Guevara.

During the whole time the details of the treaty were being discussed, the Cubans were urging Moscow that the agreement between two sovereign nations, perfectly legal in international law, should be made public, but without the details of the actual weapons to be based on the island.

Fidel Castro kept putting the same question to the authorities in Moscow. What happens if the operation is discovered while the arms build-up is covertly underway? 'If our conduct is legal, if what's more it is correct, why should we do something that may give rise to a national scandal? Why should it seem we are doing something secretly, covertly, as if we were doing something wrong to which we have no right?'[5]

Khrushchev's dismissal of Cuban doubts is significant. He was reported as telling Guevara: 'You don't have to worry. There will be no big reaction from the US. If there is a problem we will send in the Baltic Fleet.'[6]

But Castro remained concerned. He feared the deal, if carried out secretly, would damage his revolution's image in the rest of Latin America and fuel feelings that were running high between Cuba and the United States. Castro had swallowed Khrushchev's boasting that the USSR possessed hundreds of inter-continental ballistic missiles capable of reaching the United States from Soviet territory, so to some extent he doubted the need for an arsenal of nuclear missiles based on Cuba and targeted on the United States. But if the USSR, which was far more experienced in international affairs than was his government in Cuba, wanted to increase the defensive power of the entire socialist camp, he felt Cuba should not base refusal on 'narrow self interest'.[7]

Subsequently, some of the American officials involved in the crisis admitted it was much less likely the US Government would have sought, or been able to insist on a Soviet withdrawal, had the whole operation been seen in the eyes of the international community to have been agreed openly, under a properly constituted treaty between the USSR and Cuba. That after all, is exactly what America had done when it deployed its intermediate nuclear missiles to Turkey, Italy and the UK.

Notes

1. Michael Bechloss: *The Crisis Years: Kennedy & Khrushchev 1960–63*, Harper Collins, New York, 1991, p. 347.
2. Ibid, p. 420.
3. Robert Kennedy: *Thirteen Days: A Memoir of the Cuban Crisis*, Norton, New York, 1969.
4. Public Papers of the Presidents of the United States: John F Kennedy, 1962, pp. 674–5.
5. James Blight, Bruce Allyn, David Welch: *Cuba on the Brink: Castro, the Missile Crisis, and the Soviet Collapse*, Pantheon, New York, 1993.
6. James Blight, David Welch: *On the Brink: Americans and Soviets Re-Examine the Cuban Missile Crisis*, Hill & Wang, New York, 1989.
7. William Taubman: *Khrushchev: The Man and his Era*, Norton, New York, 2003.

Chapter 6

The View From Moscow

What if we throw a hedgehog down Uncle Sam's pants?
Nikita S Khrushchev, April 1962

Why was Khrushchev prepared to risk provoking a nuclear war in October 1962? Installing strategic nuclear weapons in Cuba, particularly those targeted on the American homeland was a huge gamble. He had other choices. If he wanted to protect Cuba and Fidel Castro's communist rule, which was one of his key aims, he could have sent Soviet troops equipped with conventional weapons. If he wanted to escalate the threat, and pose a more serious challenge to the United States, who had demonstrated by the Bay of Pigs adventure and by other covert hostile acts, their intention to rid Cuba of communist rule, he could have sent troops armed only with tactical nuclear weapons, arms not capable of reaching American soil but powerful enough to make an American invasion of Cuba virtually impossible. The strategy Khrushchev adopted posed hugely disproportionate risks if his only aim was to protect Cuba from possible US invasion. The policy he planned to implement in complete secrecy, authorising his diplomats to lie when challenged about it, raised the stakes to the brink of a Third World War.

Khrushchev summed up his thinking in his own words in his autobiography *Khrushchev Remembers*: 'If we installed the missiles secretly, and then the United States discovered the missiles after they were poised and ready to strike, the Americans would think twice before trying to liquidate our installations by military means. I knew the United States could knock out some installations, but not all of them. If a quarter, or even a tenth of our missiles survived – even if only one or two big ones were left – we could still hit New York, and there wouldn't be much of New York left ... The main thing was that the installation of our missiles in Cuba would, I thought, restrain the United States from precipitous military action against Castro's government.'[1]

In Khrushchev's mind the missiles were deployed to intimidate, to frighten. But he risked everything by shipping in missiles and thousands of troops in secret, banking on getting the launch pads operational before the United States discovered what was happening under their noses, less than 100 miles off the American coast.

Khrushchev had another objective. He had been boasting internationally that the Soviet Union was mass-producing intercontinental missiles capable of reaching the United States and obliterating American cities from launch sites deep within Russia. He claimed in a well-publicised speech that Soviet arms factories were turning missiles out 'like sausages.' In fact, by the end of 1959 the USSR only had six operational missile sites with the ability to launch missiles of sufficient range to reach the American mainland. US reconnaissance and human intelligence had provided enough information for America to call his bluff. Indeed, the Soviet leader admitted as much in his memoirs 'It always sounded good to say in public speeches that we could hit a fly at any distance with our missiles ... I exaggerated a little.' His son Sergei Khrushchev, who was a trained rocket engineer, was more explicit. 'We threatened with missiles we didn't have,' he said.[2]

In February 1962, a month after Kennedy became President, the senate foreign relations committee was told by Defence Secretary, Robert McNamara, that America had established a clear military superiority of ballistic missiles for use in any major nuclear conflict. At the time of the Cuban crisis the US had between eight and seventeen times the number of operational nuclear weapons than the Soviet Union possessed.[3] In March 1962, in a reversal of America's former policy, Kennedy stated publicly that Khrushchev must not rely on the United States never striking first. If her vital interests were threatened she would do so. And he added, 'we have a second strike capability which is at least as extensive as that the Soviets can deliver by striking first. Therefore, we are confident that the Soviets will not provoke a major nuclear conflict.' But that was exactly what Khrushchev was contemplating.

He was on the back foot and knew he had to act. If Cuba was invaded and defeated it was he who would be blamed. Similarly, he risked bearing the blame for the loss of the nuclear advantage he had so boldly claimed.

His military commanders were well aware of the advantages of the American Minuteman intercontinental ballistic missile. They knew full well the superior numbers of inter-continental missiles the United States possessed. Because Minuteman contained solid fuel it could be launched within minutes, hence its name. The equivalent Soviet R-16 ICBM took several hours to prepare for firing because it had to be filled with unstable liquid fuel before it was ready for launch. But while the USSR had a limited number of ICBMs it had considerable stocks of medium and intermediate range missiles. Infiltrating batteries of these into Cuba would more than double the warheads Khrushchev could train on American cities. At a stroke he would redress the nuclear balance and restore his own personal credit.

In his memoirs the Russian leader wrote: 'In addition to protecting Cuba, our missiles would have equalised what the west likes to call "the balance of power". The Americans ... would learn just what it feels like to have enemy missiles pointing at you; we'd be doing nothing more than giving them a little of their own medicine ... We Russians have suffered three wars over the last half century ... America has never had to fight a war on her own soil ... and made a fortune as a result. America has made billions by bleeding the rest of the world.'

Khrushchev's aim was to have his missiles in Cuba trained on the 'soft underbelly' of the United States as speedily as possible. The advantage this would give him was considerable. It would enable him to outflank America's early warning radar screen which was predicated on missiles arriving from a completely different direction. The medium-range missiles could reach and destroy Washington, the Panama Canal, Cape Canaveral, even Mexico City. The intermediate-range ones could hit most of the major cities in North and South America from Lima in Peru to Hudson Bay in Canada. Having installed them secretly, when he was ready, probably at the United Nations general assembly planned for November, he would dramatically reveal to Kennedy and the wider world the threat now posed at America's back-door. However, he appreciated committing the Soviet Union to such a risky venture had to be a collective decision. The outcome might very well be war with the United States, a war that once ignited would rapidly spread to Europe. He needed the acceptance and the support of his colleagues on the Presidium.

In April 1962 he broached his plan with his Defence Minister, Rodion Malinovsky, who had been anxiously discussing with his boss the unequal nuclear balance, particularly following news that America's Jupiter missiles had become operational on bases in neighbouring Turkey. Together with the sixty Thor missiles, which since 1959 had stood launch-ready on bases in the east of England, the fifteen Turkish Jupiters, and a further thirty Jupiter missiles in Italy, posed an ever-present threat the Soviet Union could not ignore. Khrushchev startled Malinovsky with the comment: 'What if we throw a hedgehog down Uncle Sam's pants?'[4] It would take a decade for the Soviet Union to equal America's fast launch long-range ballistic missile arsenal through the slow process of weapons development and production. Cuba was a rapid way of achieving equality.

The following month, at a small group of his senior colleagues, Khrushchev outlined his idea in greater detail. With the missiles operational on Cuban launch pads he said he could speak to the Americans as an equal. He was convinced American leaders would take a pragmatic view. They would realise the Soviets were only copying what America had already done. By deploying missiles in the UK, Italy and Turkey they had not tipped the world into nuclear war. Why should a similar deployment by the USSR be a cause for conflict? It was a view he repeated when Oleg Troyanovsky, his foreign policy aid, voiced his strong reservations. Troyanovsky thought the plan ignored the mood in the United States and took no account of probable US reaction. He also felt it unrealistic to expect such an ambitious plan to be successfully carried out in total secrecy. Success depended on springing a surprise under the noses of American intelligence.[5]

Khrushchev insisted he was doing nothing the Americans hadn't already done by placing nuclear weapons close to the borders of the Soviet Union. The difference, of course, was America had been completely open about its policy, in the international forum, and with its NATO partners. The United States had not infiltrated their missiles to threaten the Soviet Union covertly.

Anastas Mikoyan, Soviet first Deputy Prime Minister, who was regarded as something of an expert on Cuba having travelled there to meet Castro in 1960, also doubted the wisdom of transporting and installing the missiles in secret. He feared Khrushchev's plan would trigger a world crisis and considered the whole scheme dangerous.[6] But Khrushchev would have none of it, and set out to marshal support for his policy. His experienced Foreign Minister, Andrei Gromyko, told him that putting missiles in Cuba would cause a political explosion in the United States.[7] But still Khrushchev stood firm.

In his memoirs he claimed the decision was from the outset worked out in collective leadership. It took two or three searching discussions before his colleagues decided it was 'worth the risk'. He wanted his comrades to accept and support the decision with a clear conscience and a full understanding that the consequence might be war with the United States. 'Every step we had taken had been carefully considered by the collective,' he wrote in his autobiography.[8]

He persuaded the Soviet defence council, the USSR's highest civil-military group, to call for an initial operational plan and on 24 May the combined defence council and the Presidium agreed to deployment pending a report from a delegation that had been despatched to Havana.

By 10 June the delegation was back in Moscow reporting Castro's positive reaction to the plan, and confirming the military feasibility of deploying missiles on the island and the necessary Soviet forces to accompany them. The Presidium rubber-stamped the decision to proceed that they had in effect made some weeks earlier. Khrushchev had gained all the support he needed.

The man put in overall charge of Operation Anadyr, was an elderly general whom Khrushchev liked and trusted as an old comrade, although it was questionable whether he was the best choice to undertake a mission where deception and diplomacy were essential. General Issa Pliyev had fought in the Russian civil war, at Stalingrad, and against the Japanese in Manchuria. Khrushchev chose him against the view of his general staff, who insisted the operation should be commanded by an experienced general of the Soviet Strategic Rocket Force.

The first of an armada of ships left discreetly for the Cuban port of Cabanas in mid-July. In total eighty-five passenger ships and freighters were involved in the operation, sailing from six Soviet ports ranging from Sevastopol in the southern Crimea to Severomorsk near Murmansk. Instead of a small force which might have been able to sneak into Cuba with a minimum of fuss, which is what Khrushchev initially had in mind, the Russian military insisted on transporting over 50,000 men, together with huge amounts of equipment, medical facilities, at least three months supplies of food, and of course the crucial missiles and their nuclear war-heads. The missiles were particularly difficult to camouflage or conceal. It was asking almost the impossible to transport them and the entire accompanying force to Cuba under the eyes of American reconnaissance without it being detected, let alone establish it there with all the operational facilities required. The civil engineering alone was enough to provide a tell-tale giveaway to American photographic reconnaissance planes.

Thirty-six medium range rockets, which could hit targets at a distance of 1,200 nautical miles, together with their launchers, and twenty-four intermediate range missiles, which could hit targets 2,000 nautical miles away, made up the lethal core of the shipment. The nuclear warheads accompanying them were between ten and

44

thirty-five times more potent than the bomb that had flattened Hiroshima at the end of the Second World War. In all, the Soviet force consisted of five missile regiments, each with its own support base of technicians and administrative staff. To defend the missiles and their launch bases were three surface-to-air missile regiments; two cruise missile regiments; thirty-three helicopters; a squadron of eleven Il-28 bombers equipped with conventional bombs, and six more aircraft fitted with nuclear bombs; a transport and communications squadron of eleven planes; four motorised rifle regiments; thirty-four tanks; a naval fleet of submarines, cruisers, and destroyers; and a brigade of missile-launching patrol boats.

In total these units would normally require nearly 51,000 men. But in September the numbers were slimmed to 45,000 – far more than the 10,000 men American intelligence assessed had been landed on Cuba, when the United States eventually detected the build-up.

Secrecy began at the disembarkation ports where loading and movements took place under the cover of darkness. The troops were not told where they were going, but they were ordered to build false structures on deck from wood to hide the nature of the lethal cargo being carried. The servicemen were ordered to dress in civilian clothes, and once they reached the area where US reconnaissance operated they were only allowed on deck at night in small groups. The eighteen to twenty day trip to the tropics with temperatures rising uncomfortably high and living conditions below decks primitive, was far from a pleasure cruise.

On arrival in Cuba conditions got no better. Military equipment had to be unloaded during darkness, hidden from view and taken to operational positions at night. The troops maintained total radio silence to foil US listening devices. To provide solid foundations for the missile launch sites, massive concrete blocks were shipped all the way from the USSR and many were moved into place by sheer manpower because the rocky topsoil made it impossible to use heavy earth-moving plant.

Once located at their launch sites the missiles were even more difficult to conceal. Palm trees gave them little cover and because of the multiple difficulties the Soviet troops faced, deployments were running well behind schedule. By mid-September the medium range missiles had been delivered, but their nuclear warheads which arrived under KGB guard, did not get to Cuba until 4 October. The ship carrying the longer range intermediate missiles was still at sea when the Americans spotted what was going on. Throughout the crisis period they remained on board a Soviet ship alongside a Cuban

45

dock. By 14 October eighty cruise missile warheads, six nuclear bombs for the Il-28 bombers, and twelve Luna warheads had reached their destination, stored in hastily built bunkers near to the missile pads and to the airfields where the Soviet bombers were housed.

While the ballistic missiles able to hit American cities were the greatest provocation to the US administration, the tactical nuclear weapons Khrushchev despatched in September were possibly the most dangerous. They included Luna missiles with two-kiloton warheads, which could be used against any American force attempting to invade the island. Khrushchev's initial instructions allowed Soviet commanders on Cuba to use these without any further direct authorisation from Moscow. Had that happened the Americans would inevitably have responded with nuclear weapons of their own. On 22 September, the day President Kennedy revealed to the world what was happening in Cuba, Khrushchev rescinded his earlier orders and said use of nuclear weapons required authorisation from Moscow. But realistically, as at least one Soviet general has since reflected, in the heat of war with Soviet troops desperately defending their bases on Cuba, little or no possibility of further support arriving to assist them and poor communications back to Moscow, could anyone guarantee these tactical nuclear weapons, or even the more powerful cruise missiles, would not have been used? As William Taubman wrote in his comprehensive biography of Khrushchev, *The Man and his Era* 'If such a rocket had hit US troops or ships, if thousands of Americans had died in the atomic blast, would that have been the last shot of the Cuban crisis or the first of a global nuclear war?'[9]

Notes

1. Nikita S Khrushchev: *Khrushchev Remembers*. Translated by Strobe Talbott. Boston: Little, Brown, 1970.
2. Ibid.
3. John Lewis Gaddis: *The Cold War*, p. 78.
4. Aleksandr Fursenko and Timothy Naftali: *One Hell of a Gamble: Khrushchev, Castro & Kennedy 1958–1964*, New York. Norton, 1997, p. 171.
5. Oleg Troyanovsky: *The Making of Soviet Foreign Policy*, p. 235.
6. Blight and Welch: *On the Brink*, p. 238.
7. William Taubman: *Khrushchev: the Man and his Era*, p. 544.
8. *Khrushchev Remembers*, translated by Strobe Talbott, Boston, Little, Brown, 1970.
9. *Khrushchev: The Man and his Era*, p. 548.

Chapter 7

Sunday, 14 October –
Monday, 22 October

The Russian bear has always been eager to stick his paw in Latin-American waters. Now we've got him in a trap, let's take his leg off right up to his testicles. On second thought, let's take off his testicles too!

General Curtis Le May, Chief of Staff, US Air Force,
October 1962

Washington
On 14 October a U2 spy-plane flying an early morning reconnaissance mission over the western part of Cuba, produced the first clear evidence of the existence of Soviet offensive missile sites on the island. It was not until eight days later, 22 October, that Macmillan was officially informed of this potential threat to world peace.

The U2 pilot, Major Richard Heyser, brought the exposed film back to his base near Orlando in Florida and from there it was flown to the Naval Photographic Centre in Maryland to be developed. Nine hundred and twenty eight separate pictures were printed off for analysis. The next day those prints reached the National Photographic Interpretation Centre and by late in the afternoon the experts there had indisputably identified three medium range ballistic missiles sites near San Cristobel.

Analysts also detected eight large, medium range missile transporters and four erector-launchers already in their firing positions. The assurances the Soviet ambassador to Washington had given just a few days before that there were no Soviet offensive weapons being deployed to Cuba had been proved to be a lie.

In the evening of Monday, 15 October the CIA reported the evidence that their worst fears had been proved correct to McGeorge Bundy, President Kennedy's principal national security adviser. Kennedy himself had been involved in a strenuous round of political campaigning, so Bundy decided to leave breaking the dramatic news that might well have the potential to trigger global conflict until the morning of Tuesday, 16 October. Having been given a detailed assessment, the President immediately called a meeting of his main advisers, the group that came to be known as the executive committee, or ex-com for short. By the time the group had convened it was almost noon, and the news had got worse. Further reconnaissance had detected nearly forty medium range missiles on Cuba – all quite capable, should they be armed with nuclear warheads, of hitting and destroying American cities or military targets. The ex-com group was adamant the missiles must be removed. Khrushchev had deliberately deceived Kennedy, betrayed him, and lured him into a position of false security. Kennedy saw the situation both as a test to him personally and a test of America's national will. If Khrushchev was allowed to get away with stationing offensive nuclear weapons at America's back door he would inevitably try other adventures and Kennedy feared, as did Macmillan when he was made aware of the situation, that Berlin would be the next crisis point.

The President decided to keep knowledge of Soviet intentions on Cuba totally secret until he had determined on a course of action. Not even his closest ally Great Britain, where a considerable portion of America's nuclear force was stationed, would be tipped off that the world was moving towards the possibility of global conflict. On Wednesday, 17 October the executive committee was deliberating the options, wavering between launching immediate air strikes on the Soviet offensive missile sites as a precursor to a massive invasion, or instituting a blockade of the island coupled with a demand the missiles must be removed. If the demand to remove them was not met then air strikes and an invasion would be the inevitable outcome. The military were bullish. The joint chiefs of staff pressed for overwhelming air strikes and an invasion. Others in the ex-com group counselled a more considered line. Kennedy was in the midst of political campaigning and to cancel his programme would have raised inevitable questions when his firm policy was to keep knowledge of what was happening in Cuba securely under wraps until an agreed course of action had been thrashed out. So the President carried on with his planned engagements while still wrestling with the problem of whether to strike hard or be more cautious.

On Thursday, 18 October the Soviet Foreign Minister, Andrei Gromyko, was due to have a meeting with Kennedy. It took place at 5.00pm in the Oval office. In a drawer of the President's desk was a file containing the incriminating reconnaissance photographs which revealed the truth of what was happening on Cuba. Gromyko, unaware the President knew the truth of Soviet intentions for Cuba, condemned American 'intimidation' of Havana. He said Soviet assistance to Castro posed no threat to any other nation. 'Were matters otherwise,' the Soviet foreign minister said, 'the Soviet Government would never have been a party to rendering such aid.' Kennedy reemphasised the warning he had issued on 4 September that if there was evidence of an organised combat force in Cuba from any Soviet bloc country, or of the presence of ground to ground missiles, or any other offensive capability, the gravest issues would arise.

Gromyko was shaken by the confrontation, his notes of the meeting sent back to Moscow described the situation as 'the most dangerous development since the end of the war,' and 'he had no idea where it would end.' The issue of nuclear ballistic missiles on Cuba had not been mentioned because Kennedy was not prepared to reveal what he now knew to be the truth. Had Kennedy spoken openly about the missiles, Gromyko later revealed, he would have responded on the lines that had been agreed in Moscow, to the effect that the Soviet Union had provided Cuba with a small number of missiles of a purely defensive nature and their purpose was not to threaten anyone. As it was, the Soviet authorities maintained their policy of outright bare-faced deception.

On the evening of Gromyko's meeting with Kennedy the executive committee took a straw vote which indicated support for a blockade by eleven votes to six. The following day, Friday, 19 October with the President still on his campaign trip, the view swung back to launching a massive bombing strike against Cuba. The Air Force Chief of Staff, the bullish hard-line General, Curtis LeMay, argued that if the United States failed to use force it would be seen internationally as weak and as bad as the appeasement at Munich in 1938. The President's brother, Attorney General, Robert Kennedy, repeated the argument for a blockade, but there were powerful voices still demanding a showdown, even if that risked nuclear retaliation against the United States. Still the British and other European governments remained unaware of the growing danger to world peace.

Kennedy used the excuse of a slight infection to abandon his campaign trail appointments on Saturday, 20 October and he returned to Washington where the executive committee was still favouring the use of nuclear weapons. He insisted the more diplomatic option of a blockade should be given more thorough consideration. The agonising discussions continued throughout the Saturday and into Sunday, 21 October. At that point military force seemed the most likely choice. But Kennedy over-ruled the hawks. He still favoured a blockade, or in the more diplomatic language he advocated using, a 'quarantine', backed if Khrushchev failed to withdraw, by an invasion involving over-whelming force.

The President did not 'take the lid' off the secret that threatened world peace until Monday, 22 October. He informed the former President, Eisenhower and congressional leaders and announced that he would address the nation on television that evening.

London

In London, Macmillan had got wind of something alarming happening in the Caribbean in a warning from the British Ambassador to Washington, David Ormesby-Gore, who was a personal friend of Kennedy's. In his memoirs, Macmillan notes that the President had spoken in 'guarded terms' to Gore and although the British Ambassador had given no details Macmillan had sensed that the alarm in the White House was probably about missiles in Cuba. 'So the blow,' Macmillan wrote, 'was destined to fall, not in the east, but in the west – not in Germany but in the Caribbean.'

On the night of Sunday, 21 October Macmillan recalls he began to receive 'long and alarming telegrams'. One from Ambassador Ormesby-Gore stated: 'I have just come from seeing the President. He will be sending you an extremely important message on Cuba by teletype to Admiralty House at about 10.00pm. I think it essential that you should be there to receive it immediately.' The ambassador's message continued: 'President Kennedy particularly stressed that not only were the contents of the message confidential in the highest degree, but the fact that you are receiving a message at this time should on no account become known'.

When it finally came through to Admiralty House, which was being used temporarily as a stand-in for No. 10, as the Downing Street home of the Prime Minister was undergoing extensive renovation, Kennedy's message gave Macmillan serious cause for concern. In his private diary the following day, he wrote ominously: 'First day of the world crisis'.[1]

Kennedy's message confirmed Macmillan's worst fears. The President wrote that he wanted to give the Prime Minister as much time as possible to consider 'the dangers we now have to face together'.

'Photographic intelligence has established beyond question, in the last week, that the Soviet Union has engaged in a major build-up of medium range missiles in Cuba. Six sites have so far been identified, and two of them may be in operational readiness. In sum it is clear that a massive secret operation has been proceeding in spite of repeated assurances we have received from the Soviet Union on this point.'

'After careful reflection, this government has decided to prevent any further build-up by sea and to demand the removal of this nuclear threat to our hemisphere.'

Kennedy's message went on to say that the United States Ambassador in London, David Bruce, would see Macmillan the next day, Monday, 22 October. Ambassador Bruce would have with him the substance of the speech Kennedy would give to the American nation on Monday evening.

Kennedy's urgent message continued: 'This extraordinary dangerous and aggressive Soviet step obviously creates a crisis of the most serious sort, in which we shall have to act most closely together. I have found it absolutely essential, in the interest of security and speed, to make my first decision on my own responsibility, but from now on I expect that we can and should be in the closest touch, and I know that together with our other friends we will resolutely meet this challenge.'

The President concluded with a passage in which he gave a strong inference of his determination not to shrink from using force if necessary. 'What is essential at this moment of highest test is that Khrushchev should discover that if he is counting on weakness or irresolution, he has miscalculated.'

As Macmillan observed, having absorbed the content of Kennedy's message: 'These were not surface to air missiles which might perhaps be represented as defensive armoury against air attack; they were ballistic missiles directed on the great cities of the United States and capable of spreading destruction and death on a colossal scale within a few minutes.'[2]

Macmillan in his memoirs said that at the time he received the President's message over the teletypewriter at Admiralty House, he was not aware that Kennedy's decision had come after long and bitter debate among the President's own advisers. The majority of the President's advisers, Macmillan noted, had recommended an immediate military strike followed by an invasion and occupation of the island. Had the President and his team known what became clear much later, Macmillan recalled, that the missiles were largely in position, and that the force deployed represented a great part of the available nuclear strength of the whole Russian economy, Kennedy might not have been able to resist the arguments in favour of immediate and decisive action. That would almost certainly have involved nuclear weapons, since the Soviets in Cuba had certainly got them.

Macmillan was frustrated and impatient that Sunday night, having to wait until the American Ambassador came to see him the following day. 'It was difficult at so dangerous a moment,' he wrote, 'to reconcile myself to inaction.'[3] After long reflection he decided to keep the news to himself and not even to warn his Foreign Secretary, Sir Alec Douglas-Home, that night.

The American Ambassador met Macmillan at 12.30pm on Monday, 22 October. He brought with him a dossier to prove that contrary to specific assurances given by the Soviet Government and its Foreign Minister, a formidable armoury of medium range and intermediate range ballistic missiles had been secretly deployed on Cuba. They were 'a pistol pointing at America, Canada and South America, which could not be tolerated.' The ambassador told Macmillan that the President's proposed action to impose a quarantine or blockade on all ships carrying arms to Cuba and to threaten a more complete blockade if necessary, might not satisfy the strident 'war' party in Washington and could itself have great dangers of precipitating a clash. Macmillan recalled: 'We speculated a little about the likely response by Mr Khrushchev. Would it be words or deeds?'[4]

The ambassador brought a new statement from Kennedy declaring the Soviet action 'constituted a threat to peace which imperils the security, not only of this hemisphere but of the entire free world'. The Soviet action and the deceit of its leader and spokesmen had to be met promptly and fearlessly. Kennedy made it clear he would be sending a personal message to other European leaders, but he wished Macmillan to be informed first so there could be an opportunity to discuss the situation between them.

'This is a solemn moment for our two countries, indeed for the fate of the entire world,' Kennedy wrote. 'It is essential that the already great dangers before us should not be increased through miscalculation or underestimation by the Soviets of what we intend to do, and are prepared to endure, in the face of the course on which they have so recklessly embarked.'[5]

The President informed the Prime Minister that he had asked his ambassador to the United Nations to request an urgent meeting of the Security Council and to present a resolution calling for withdrawal of missile bases and offensive weapons in Cuba. He asked for the British representative at the UN to back this resolution.

Chester Cooper, a senior CIA officer and assistant to the Deputy Director for Intelligence for Policy Support, who accompanied the ambassador to his meeting with the Prime Minister, recalls that Macmillan was alone except for his private secretary. It was evident Macmillan had 'some advance general knowledge of the developing situation in Cuba.' Some members of the British intelligence community had been in Washington for several days and had been briefed confidentially about the concerns over Cuba. It was clear the Prime Minister had been made aware through UK intelligence sources.

'However, Mr Macmillan obviously had no idea of the extent or precise nature of Soviet offensive capabilities in Cuba. His first reaction, which he addressed more to himself than to the ambassador, was to the effect that the British people, who had been living in the shadow of annihilation for the past many years, had somehow been able to live more or less normal lives and he felt that the Americans now confronted with a similar situation would, after the initial shock, make a similar adjustment. "Life goes on somehow".'

Chester Cooper comments that the Prime Minister was clearly aware that this might be misinterpreted, and went to considerable lengths to explain to the ambassador that this was more of a philosophical commentary on human nature than any indication on his part that he was not sympathetic with the US position or shocked at the news.

'After my recitation of the present Soviet offensive strength in Cuba, Mr Macmillan said that, if the President were convinced that a meaningful offensive capability were present, "that was good enough for him". He did not spend more than a few seconds on the photographs. Although the Prime Minister did not develop this theme in my presence in detail, he did indicate that he felt that a blockade would be difficult to enforce and that the US would have problems in getting solid UN support. He also ruminated about whether it would not have been better to have confronted Khrushchev privately with our evidence and given him a private ultimatum.'[6]

At this point Macmillan alone in Great Britain was aware of the storm that was brewing and the terrifying consequences that might follow. There was a need to keep the situation in perspective. He recalled in his memoirs. 'I had to remember that the people of Europe and Britain had lived in close proximity to Soviet missiles for several years.' What the United States now faced was little different to the situation the British people had lived under for a considerable period as the threats of the Cold War deepened.[7]

When the US Ambassador had left Admiralty House, Macmillan summoned the Foreign Secretary, Sir Alec Douglas-Home and his chief advisers. The Prime Minister's deepest concern was where all this might lead in relation to Europe. If Khrushchev suffered a great loss of face and reputation in Cuba and was forced to withdraw, would he be tempted to move aggressively in Berlin? Perhaps the Soviet leader's real motive was to trade Cuba for Berlin. How do you read the mind of a leader bent on such a risky course? Together Macmillan and Home drafted a reply to the President. Was it, they asked themselves, the whole purpose of Khrushchev's dangerous deceit to 'move forward one pawn in order to exchange it for another?'

Macmillan records that in the first draft of his reply to the President he thought of advising Kennedy to move swiftly and seize Cuba. He was alarmed 'lest Kennedy miss the bus'. He may never get rid of the Cuban rockets except by trading them for US missiles in Turkey, Italy or indeed the UK; in which case Khrushchev would have totally won his point. Macmillan also fretted over the legality of a blockade of Cuba. There was a possibility of it causing international trouble with neutral and even with friendly countries.[8]

The reply Macmillan and the foreign secretary settled on offered America the UK's support, but asked what Khrushchev's likely reaction would be. 'He may reply either in words or in kind or both. If he contents himself with the first he may demand the removal of all American bases in Europe. If he decides to act he may do so either in the Caribbean or elsewhere. If he reacts in the Caribbean his obvious method would be to escort his ships and force you into a position of attacking them. The fire-first dilemma has always worried us, and we have always hoped to impale the Russians on this horn.'[9]

Macmillan went on to speculate on the Soviets' next move. Khrushchev might put pressure on the weaker parts of the free world's defences. This could be in South-East Asia, in Iran, possible Turkey, but most likely Berlin. It could be tempting for him to answer one blockade with another. 'Any retaliatory action on Berlin as envisioned in the various contingency plans, will lead us either to an escalation to world war or to holding a conference,' Macmillan wrote. 'You and I should think over and decide in what direction we want to steer things within the alliance and elsewhere.'[10]

Macmillan ended with a note of caution to the President. He emphasised that while it was new for the American people to feel vulnerable with nuclear missiles targeted at them from Soviet bases within direct range of most of America's major cities, that was exactly the threat under which most Europeans had lived for a considerable time. Opinion in the UK and Europe might therefore not be quite so sympathetic to the position the United States now faced. 'Many of us in Europe have lived so long in close proximity to the enemy's nuclear weapons of the most devastating kind, that we have got accustomed to it. So European opinion will need attention,' Macmillan wrote. 'More worrying,' he continued, 'is that if Khrushchev comes to a conference he will of course try to trade his Cuba position against his ambitions in Berlin and elsewhere. This we must avoid at all costs, as it will endanger the unity of the alliance.'[11]

After briefing the Prime Minister, Chester Cooper accompanied the US Ambassador at a meeting to brief Hugh Gaitskell, Labour leader and George Brown, deputy leader. Gaitskell had feared the President was confusing the issue of the Soviet build-up by making it appear that surface-to-air missiles were offensive weapons. Having seen the evidence he acknowledged his former concerns had been ill-founded. Cooper recalls Gaitskell was visibly shaken by the clear evidence of long-range missiles.

'He made much of the analogy between Cuba and Turkey and brushed aside most of the standard arguments about the difference between the two,' Chester recalls. 'However, he seemed much impressed with the fact that the Cuban missiles were outside the BMEWS (missile detection) system. He felt that this did, in fact, represent a change in the status quo and in the "balance of terror" question.'

George Brown was concerned as to whether the United States had deployed more or fewer Jupiter missiles in Turkey than the Soviets were putting into Cuba, and as to the Soviets' capability for early warning of the firing of these missiles. Brown's point was that if the United States did indeed have fewer missiles in Turkey than the Soviets would have in Cuba and if the Soviets did have an early warning capability, the argument about the equivalence of the Turkish and Cuban bases would be weakened.

'Gaitskell said' Cooper recalls, 'that he had been with the Prime Minister just prior to our discussion and that the Prime Minister expressed annoyance about the lack of advance knowledge of US actions. I pointed out to Gaitskell in fairly strong terms that there were two aspects to the question of advanced knowledge: one was the developing situation in Cuba and the other was US intentions with respect to Cuba. In connection with the former, I told Gaitskell that we had occasion to discuss Cuba with several important people in the British intelligence community who happened to be in Washington during the week of 15 October, and that several of them had been given a formal briefing on Friday, 19 October. We could only assume that they notified their government of the developing situation in

Cuba. With respect to US intentions, I noted that we had hoped to get an advance copy of the President's statement to the Prime Minister twelve hours before the broadcast, but that was not possible because the President himself had not decided on the precise language of his statement until fairly late in the day ... this was unfortunate but in the nature of the circumstances was all that could have been done.'[12]

The Prime Minister had another worrying issue on his mind. The entire US military across the world, and in particular the Strategic Air Command with its forward bases in the UK, had been ordered to DEFCON three (defence condition) the highest state of alert since the Second World War. The order had been put out by the military commanders in Washington using clear, open communication, so the USSR would have been left in no doubt of the seriousness of the situation and the stance of US forces. DEFCON three meant the Strategic Air Command immediately increased the numbers of its nuclear armed bombers on ground alert from 652 to 912, and 183 medium-range B-47 bombers were dispersed to civilian airfields. The scale of B-52 airborne alert was stepped up from twelve training missions to sixty sorties a day. These were aircraft carrying nuclear weapons in the air awaiting authorisation to proceed beyond their 'go–no go' lines. America's inter-continental ballistic missiles were placed on alert and all available Polaris submarines equipped with nuclear missiles were deployed on operations. Many US aircraft based in the UK, were airborne awaiting 'attack' orders to proceed to their assigned targets. In contrast, the RAF's nuclear deterrent – its V-Force and the sixty Thor intermediate nuclear ballistic missiles, operated jointly with the Americans – were not on an equivalent high-readiness state. Only a proportion was on QRA (Quick Reaction Alert) the UK's normal Cold War alert status. However, Washington was urging a full NATO alert which in the UK would have entailed a Royal Proclamation and the call-up of Britain's Reserve forces. Macmillan was desperate not to exacerbate the situation and steer it in a global direction. It was his belief that any over-reaction could put the world on an irreversible path to war. In his diary that night the Prime Minister noted that Washington 'in a rather panicky way' was urging a full NATO alert.[13]

Coincidentally, Macmillan had a long-standing dinner date in London that Monday evening with General Lauris Norstad, Supreme Allied Commander in Europe. This gave the Prime Minister the opportunity to talk privately with him and to urge the general not to follow Washington's advice and issue a NATO alert with all the international consequences that would flow from it. In his memoirs

Macmillan says that Washington had been pushing for a NATO 'alert' with all that that would imply. 'I told him that we would not, repeat not, agree at this stage. Norstad agreed with this and said he thought NATO powers would take the same view. I said "mobilisation" had sometimes caused war.'[14]

During that Monday evening Macmillan received a telegram from the British Ambassador in Washington, David Ormesby-Gore, who had discussed the two options of an all-out air strike to take out all the known missile sites on Cuba or an immediate blockade. The former would result inevitably in a large number of Soviet and Cuban deaths. The ambassador said Kennedy had asked for his views as to which of the two courses the Americans should follow. Ormesby-Gore said in his message to the Prime Minister that he thought very few people outside the United States would think the provocation sufficiently serious to merit an American air attack. Such a course would damage America politically. He said he favoured the imposition of a blockade, but the crucial factor was the possible repercussions in Berlin. Over-reaction by America could provide a 'smokescreen' behind which the Russians might move swiftly against Berlin in favourable conditions to achieve their aims.

The ambassador's note added that President Kennedy had told him he could not help having a sneaking admiration for the audacity of the Soviet strategy. 'They offered this deliberate and provocative challenge to the United States in the knowledge that if the Americans reacted violently the Russians would be given an ideal opportunity to move against West Berlin. If, on the other hand, he (Kennedy) did nothing, the Latin Americans and the United States' other allies would feel the Americans had no real will to resist the encroachments of communism and would hedge their bets accordingly.'[15]

Washington

At 7.00pm (Washington time) on Monday, 22 October, the President went on national television to address his 'fellow citizens' and inform them for the first time what the Soviets were doing on Cuba. His speech shocked and alarmed people across the United States, in Canada and countries in Central and South America. In the UK the President's speech was received soberly. The increase in world tension and the threat to peace was worrying, but the majority of people had no real appreciation that this represented a real and immediate threat to Britain as well.

'The purpose of these bases,' Kennedy told the American people, 'can be none other than to provide a nuclear strike capability against the western hemisphere.' The medium range missiles, he said, were capable of striking Washington, the Panama Canal, Cape Canaveral, Mexico City or any other city in the south-eastern part of the United States, in Central America, or in the Caribbean area. Other launch sites, not yet complete, were designed for missiles to travel more than twice as far and thus would be capable of striking most major cities in the western hemisphere, ranging as far north as Hudson Bay, Canada and as far south as Lima in Peru. Jet bombers designed to carry nuclear weapons were being un-crated and assembled. The urgent transformation of Cuba into an important strategic base constituted an explicit threat to the peace and security of all the Americas.[16]

After describing the deception the Soviets had practised, in denying they were planning any offensive build-up of weaponry, and recounting the false statements made to him by the Soviet Foreign Minister when the photographic evidence was already in his hand, Kennedy declared that neither the United States nor the world community of nations could tolerate deliberate deceptions and offensive threats. 'Nuclear weapons are so destructive and ballistic missiles are so swift that any substantially increased possibility of their use or any sudden change in their deployment may well be regarded as a definite threat to peace.' Kennedy went on to say that the Soviet Union and the United States had, up until now, deployed strategic nuclear weapons with great care, 'never upsetting the precarious status quo.' 'Our own strategic missiles have never been transferred to the territory of any other nation under the cloak of secrecy or deception. Nevertheless, American citizens have become adjusted to living daily on the bull's-eye of Soviet missiles located inside the USSR or in submarines ... This sudden, clandestine decision to station strategic weapons for the first time outside of Soviet soil is a deliberately provocative and unjustified change in the status quo which cannot be accepted in this country, if our courage and our commitments are ever to be trusted again.'[17]

That phrase might have rung somewhat hollowly in a Soviet Union threatened, as it was, by American missiles deployed on 'foreign' soil. But it was welcomed by citizens in America who for the first time faced an immediate threat of the kind Europeans had lived under since almost the start of the Cold War.

Kennedy told the world: 'We will not prematurely or unnecessarily risk the costs of worldwide nuclear war in which even the fruits of victory would be ashes in our mouth – but neither will we shrink from that risk.' Announcing imposition of a 'strict quarantine' of

Cuba, he said all ships bound for the island from whatever nation, would be stopped and any found to contain cargoes of offensive weapons would be turned back. America would not, he added, deny Cuba the necessities of life as the Soviets had attempted to do in their blockade of Berlin in 1948, but neither would they countenance a clear offensive threat.

Moscow

As Kennedy prepared to make his television address, in Moscow, Khrushchev had returned to his residence after taking his customary evening stroll. He was called to the phone and returned grim faced telling his son Sergei 'They've probably discovered our rockets. Nothing else would explain it.' His son asked what was likely to happen now. 'I wish I knew' Khrushchev replied. He then requested that all the Presidium members should gather in the Kremlin in an hour. Asked what the meeting was about, he said 'I'll tell them once we are there.' He left, telling his son not to stay up for him. 'I'll be back late.'[18]

At the crucial Kremlin meeting, Khrushchev was described as 'being red-faced and angry.' 'We were not going to unleash war,' he told his colleagues. 'We just wanted to intimidate them, to deter the anti-Cuban forces.' Then he mentioned two difficulties. 'We didn't deploy everything we wanted to,' and in reference to the formal agreement drawn up between the Soviet Union and Cuba – 'We didn't publish the treaty.' It was tragic he reflected. Instead of preventing war, his strategy now risked one. 'They can attack us and we shall respond. This may end up in a big war.'[19]

Notes

1. Peter Catterall: *The Macmillan Diaries Volume 2 1957–1966*, p. 508.
2. Harold Macmillan: *At the End of the Day*, Macmillan, London 1973, p. 183.
3. Ibid, p. 184.
4. Ibid, p. 185.
5. Peter Caterall: *The Macmillan Diaries Vol II – Prime Minister and After 1957–66*, p. 509.
6. Chester Cooper, quoted from 'The Cuban Missile Crisis of 1962: Presenting the Photographic Evidence Abroad'. Studies in Intelligence Spring 1972. www.cia.gov/library/center-for-the-study-of-intelligence/csi.
7. Harold Macmillan: *At the End of the Day 1961–63*, p. 187.
8. Ibid, pp. 187–8.
9. Ibid, p. 188.
10. Ibid, p189
11. Ibid p. 189.

12. 'The Cuban Missile Crisis of 1962: Presenting the Photographic Evidence Abroad'.
13. *The Macmillan Diaries Vol II*, p. 510.
14. Ibid, p. 510. *At the End of the Day*, p. 190.
15. *At the End of the Day*, p. 193.
16. Public Papers of the President, John F Kennedy, Washington DC: US Government Printing Office 1963.
17. Ibid.
18. Sergei Khrushchev: *Khrushchev on Khrushchev: An Inside Account of the Man and his Era*, translated and edited by William Taubman, Boston, Little, Brown 1990, pp. 265–6.
19. Notes were secretly taken of the Kremlin meeting by Vladimir Malin, Head of the Central Committee's General Department and are quoted in *One Hell of a Gamble: Khrushchev, Castro, Kennedy and the Cuban Missile Crisis 1958–1964*, by Alexander Fursenko and Timothy Naftali, New York, Norton, p. 199.

Chapter 8

Tuesday, 23 October–
Wednesday, 24 October

Mankind's very existence is in the balance
U Thant, Acting General Secretary of the United Nations,
23 October 1962

London

As the crisis deepened the hot-line between the President and Britain's
Prime Minister was busy – sometimes being used as frequently as
three times or more a day. Macmillan recalled later that he and his
foreign secretary often sat up most of the night standing-by for calls
from Washington. The President was prone to forget the difference
between Washington time and London time, which meant that a
call at midnight in Washington came through at 5.00am in London.
As the crisis deepened Macmillan and Sir Alec were, in the Prime
Minister's words, attended by relays of secretaries bringing regular
refreshment.[1]

At 10.30am on Tuesday, 23 October, Macmillan called a cabinet
meeting. The Prime Minister informed his ministers of the alarming
implications of the situation. He read out Kennedy's confidential
messages, the British Ambassador's comments from Washington, and
summaries of the conversations the two leaders had had on the trans-
Atlantic link. In his memoirs, Macmillan noted that his ministerial
colleagues had been 'rather shaken' by what he had told them. The
chilling events had come 'like a bolt from the blue.'[2]

The cabinet minutes record that the Prime Minister reported that
President Kennedy had decided to prevent any further build-up by
sea and to demand the removal of the threat to the western hemisphere. He recognised the seriousness of this step and the danger
that action taken to contain the Cuban situation might have grave
repercussions in Berlin. He had, however, felt it essential to demonstrate to the Soviet Government that if they had counted on weakness
or irresolution, they had miscalculated. The President regretted
the lack of consultation, which had been due to firm evidence of the

Soviet military capability only coming to light in the course of the preceding week. Speed of decision, he had judged, was essential.

Macmillan told his colleagues that he had promised full support in the Security Council, but had asked for help in preparing a legal case to support the broad moral position on a blockade. International lawyers would be bound to make the point that a blockade involving searching ships of all countries was difficult to defend in peacetime, and had also been the subject of controversy in wartime. But he had accepted that precedents were little guide to conditions in the nuclear age.

The obvious answer for the Soviet Union to oppose a blockade in Cuba, would be by imposing a blockade elsewhere. Soviet retaliation in Berlin would lead either to an escalation to world war or to holding a conference. Macmillan said he and President Kennedy should align their policy as soon as the Russian reaction was known, and decide in what direction to steer the course of events both within the North Atlantic Alliance and elsewhere.[3]

Macmillan said his letter to the President had ended by mentioning two aspects that would be bound to cause concern. In the first place European countries had lived for so long within range of Russian missiles they had got used to it and might not fully understand the strength of the United States reaction. Secondly, Mr Khrushchev would be likely, at any conference, to try to trade Cuba for Berlin. This had to be avoided at all costs since it would endanger the unity of the alliance. In his reply, the President had admitted action was dangerous, but inaction would be even more dangerous. His decision had not been influenced by feelings against Cuba. Rather it was the first step in a major showdown with Khrushchev, whose action in Cuba had been so much at variance with all predictions, that it was necessary to revise previous estimates of his level of desperation or ambition.

The cabinet accepted that the British people would expect to be informed of the government's reaction to President Kennedy's speech. In any immediate comment they agreed ministers should take the line that the government was deeply concerned at the provocation presented by Soviet weapons in Cuba; that they had been kept fully informed by the United States administration; they would give strong support to the United States in the forthcoming debate in the Security Council; and they had no objection to a blockade. The final point was not entirely accurate, there had been conflicting discussion about the imposition of a blockade and of the principle of allowing British ships in peacetime to be searched on the high seas. The

Lord Chancellor, Lord Dilhorne, had been asked to consider a legal justification. Cabinet was also told to expect serious repercussions in parliament. The leader of the opposition had given no undertaking to refrain from condemning the United States' action, and some Labour MPs would almost inevitably do so.

In his summing up, the Prime Minister emphasised that among the many possible dangers the risk of a division between the United States and Europe, or between the United States, the United Kingdom and the other countries of the North Atlantic Alliance, was potentially the most serious and would give the greatest advantage to the Soviet cause.[4]

Macmillan, however, did have some brighter news on that Tuesday. That afternoon General Norstad called at Admiralty House to say he had persuaded Washington to be 'more reasonable' and not, at least for now, call an alert across the whole of NATO. Still concerned to calm the situation down, Macmillan noted: 'Either the bombs will fall, or one side or the other will recoil.' He added, 'although it was perhaps not quite so simple as that, there was no need to anticipate the horrors of nuclear warfare by observing all the traditional, almost ritual preliminaries to conventional combat.'[5]

On Wednesday, 24 October, the day the blockade was formally put into effect, the Lord Chancellor's memorandum on the American blockade came through. The 'Top Secret' document hardly offered much in the way of reassurance. Lord Dilhorne stated baldly that in his and the attorney-general's view, the imposition of a blockade or 'quarantine' around Cuba could not be justified under international law and was plainly unlawful. The two law officers suggested the most favourable line of argument in support of the United States was that the conduct of Cuba and the Soviet Union, 'constituted a threat to the United States of such imminence as to necessitate the taking of immediate steps to render that threat nugatory.' But, they said, they doubted this argument could be sustained in the UN Security Council, as the United States' action appeared to be designed to prevent the threat becoming imminent.

'We think it important that we should make it clear to the United States Government,' the law officers' advice said, 'exactly what our views are on the legality of the present blockade ... we do not concede that they have any legal right to search or detain British ships on the high seas.' The memorandum went on to suggest the government should make clear to the American administration, it fully endorsed the decision by the General Council of British Shipping, that the legal rights of British ships should be reserved. 'Although Her Majesty's

Government do not, in present circumstances, intend to stand on their legal rights in the matter, they also must reserve the right to extend such diplomatic and legal protection to British shipping as may be permissible in accordance with international law.'[6]

In a telegram to the United Kingdom mission to the United Nations, the official government line said. 'We see considerable difficulty in the argument about secret disturbance of the balance of power. While the presence of Soviet missiles in Cuba no doubt greatly increases Soviet striking power, it could still be argued that total American nuclear strength was still ahead of Soviet nuclear strength. We think that it would be better to emphasise and elaborate on other points in the President's speech.' They suggested the British representatives should concentrate their arguments in the Security Council, on the fact that the Soviets had taken deliberately provocative action at a time when disarmament negotiations were in progress. The secrecy with which the deployment of Soviet missiles had been conducted, and the deliberately misleading statements they had made on the subject, contrasted with the American attitude towards the stationing of their own missiles on other territories, and could only give rise to the inference that they were not for purely defensive purposes, and therefore constituted a threat to the peace; a tricky line to take in view of American missiles which were manifestly 'offensive' based in Turkey, Italy and England. To what extent the British Government conveyed these critical views to the American administration is not entirely clear. British reservations over the legality of what the United States was doing, were not discussed in any of the phone calls between London and Washington.

Macmillan seems to have chosen to disregard most of the detailed planning that had occupied civil servants and ministers for so long, plotting how the state would deal with an emergency which suggested the country was headed on a path to a Third World War. These were the steps detailed in the government's so-called *War Book*. The year before the Cuban crisis the Cabinet Secretary, Sir Norman Brook, had drawn up contingency plans for just such an eventuality where international tensions escalated to the point where there was a sudden and increased threat to the safety of the nation. His plan envisaged this kind of situation developing, not over Cuba but in Berlin. How the crisis started was not important. It was the way government should react, that Brook was setting down. His plan was for the government to move to a stage where vital decisions could be taken in an orderly and speedy way without the normal peacetime panoply of full cabinet government. His recommendation was to create a structure that would bridge the gap between the usual peacetime operation of Whitehall and what he termed a 'war cabinet'. Brooks' suggestion was the formation of a ministerial committee which could take all the necessary decisions quickly. Chaired by the Prime Minister it would consist of the home secretary, chancellor of the exchequer, foreign secretary, commonwealth secretary and minister of defence. Brook saw it being serviced by an operations room linked by scrambler phone and teleprinter to all the points in central government concerned with the emergency.[7]

Macmillan appears to have rejected all of this. Perhaps the fact that Sir Norman Brook happened to be ill and off work at the time of the crisis and therefore not available to advise the Prime Minister, was the reason Macmillan took no steps to establish an operations room, or a crisis cabinet, in the way laid out in the cabinet secretary's detailed plans. Even more surprising, with American forces in the UK on a DEFCON three alert, poised at a state of readiness never ordered before, for the first twenty-four hours or so of the crisis, Macmillan took no steps to urge the chiefs of staff of Britain's armed forces to bring their services to a level any higher than normal Cold War readiness – not even the UK's nuclear deterrent units, the V-Force and the Thor ballistic missile squadrons. He certainly gave no precautionary orders for 'The Quarry', or as it was known in Whitehall code 'Burlington', to be readied. Nor was there any move to consider any form of evacuation of vulnerable sections of the population. The Royal Observer Corps (ROC) was not activated, even though it had a vital task as the national nuclear warning and monitoring organisation. The service which would plot where the bombs or missiles fell, their probable size and impact, explosive strength, and the direction and path of subsequent fall-out, was never warned to prepare for operational readiness. In the early sixties the ROC operated from 873 scattered under-ground bunkers equipped to monitor bomb-burst, fall-out and radiation. Had the crisis developed rapidly towards war this trained force, manned largely by volunteers, which was essential to the survival of the nation, would almost certainly not have been ready.

In Sir Norman's absence, his role was taken by Michael Cary, the Acting Cabinet Secretary. Had Sir Norman been at his side, it is possible the Prime Minister would have been persuaded to take a different course but Macmillan decided to play the cards very close to his chest and, despite the increasing potential threat to the UK and the nation's implicit vulnerability, he determined to keep management of the crisis largely a matter between himself and the foreign secretary. He wrote in his diary on Thursday, 25 October: 'I told the cabinet about Cuba (which they seem quite happy to leave to me and Alec Home).'[8]

The question needs to be asked, was Macmillan taking a grave risk by not following the steps laid out in Britain's *War Book*? Was he wise not to put in motion necessary steps to prepare the country and the British people and, if war was to be the outcome, as seemed highly likely, give the UK its best chance of survival?

In part, the answer lies in Macmillan's own experiences. He had served in both the first and second world wars. His official biographer, Alastair Horne, records that he had been deeply affected by the book 'The Guns of August' by Barbara Tuchman, which made a persuasive case that war could result from miscalculation or from unwise and premature action, which was what had happened in 1914. It is also true Macmillan feared causing panic in the UK, if the government over-reacted. That was why he had moved so quickly to quash American calls for a NATO-wide alert. But was he taking a huge risk in treating the growing crisis so coolly in the UK, given the alarm being shown in the States, and the belligerent views being expressed by some American military leaders? No doubt it weighed heavily on his mind as he waited for news to come in, and debated the risks with Kennedy.

On the evening of Tuesday, 23 October, Macmillan had his weekly audience with the Queen. His memoirs recall that he tried to explain to her the dangers of the situation. The Queen, he noted, was as usual, 'calm and sympathetic'.[9] Meetings between a Prime Minister and his sovereign remain strictly private, but what an insight it would provide, to know exactly what passed between them on that Tuesday evening.

New York

The United Nations Security Council met to consider developments. The Soviet representative, Valerian Zorin, despite all the clear photographic evidence to the contrary, had the gall repeatedly to deny there were any missiles or launch pads in Cuba. Both Macmillan and his Private Secretary, Philip De Zulueta, had warned Washington that it was essential the actual aerial photographs should be made public as widely as possible. In New York the American Ambassador to the UN, Adlai Stevenson, did just that, producing enlarged photographs at the UN session, evidence which proved beyond doubt the Soviets and their representative were lying. U Thant, then UN Acting General-Secretary, was alarmed matters were slipping out of control.

His comment underlined the very grave fears now being expressed around the world. 'Mankind's very existence is in the balance,' he commented.

Washington

British Ambassador David Ormesby-Gore, whose personal friendship with Kennedy was important at such a testing time, had persuaded the Americans that a 'quarantine' line eight hundred miles from Cuba was too far out to allow Khrushchev time to consider his options before the first Soviet ships reached it leading to a potentially violent face-down. At Gore's suggestion the 'stop line' was shortened to 500 miles from the Cuban mainland.

Sir David and Lady Ormesby-Gore had received a pre-crisis invitation to join the Kennedys on the Tuesday evening for a private dinner dance at the White House. The dance had been cancelled, but the dinner still took place. The British Ambassador found the President in no mood for social chatter, and the two went off together for a private talk about the day's events and what might happen the following day. Sir David was concerned about the sceptical reaction of the British press. Even the leader of the opposition, Hugh Gaitskell had talked about the 'so-called missiles' in Cuba. The ambassador felt it was vital the missile-site photographs should be published as widely as possible in the world's press, especially those that would most readily persuade sceptical audiences that the Soviet missiles were indeed installed and operational. The President sent for the photographs and together the two re-examined them. Ormsby-Gore's shrewd advice persuaded the President to release them for extensive media publication the next day when they made a powerful impact on world opinion.

Setting up a blockade on the high seas rapidly was not too difficult for the Americans. Much of the Atlantic fleet was already at sea and one of the manoeuvres the fleet had practised was the possibility of mounting a blockade. Preparatory work had begun in early October, and consideration of a blockade of the island since its government had turned communist, had been debated for some time. An early October poll commissioned by the White House had shown the public favoured such a move by eight to one.

Moscow

The letter from Kennedy to Khrushchev announcing the blockade of Cuba, reached the Kremlin at 1.00am, as Tuesday gave way to Wednesday, 24 October. When it was translated by Troyanovsky, the Soviet leader's foreign relations adviser, Khrushchev's initial reaction was of relief rather than anxiety. He interpreted America's stance as being neither an ultimatum nor a direct threat of an immediate invasion of Cuba. Khrushchev had been apprehensive of what the Americans might do. Now suddenly his mood changed to elation. 'We've saved Cuba,' he declared. He began to draft a letter telling Kennedy his proposed blockade was, 'a serious threat to peace and security' and amounted to 'naked interference with the domestic affairs of Cuba and the USSR.' He demanded the President 'renounce actions which could lead to catastrophic consequences for peace throughout the world.' Later that day Radio Moscow broadcast military orders putting Soviet forces on higher combat readiness, cancelling all military leave, and in particular ordering the USSR's ballistic missile units to enhanced alert.[10] That evening, looking exhausted, he told his son Sergei that he was accelerating the installation of missiles in Cuba and had given orders to speed up the ships carrying the nuclear warheads. He was particularly concerned those ships with the warheads on board might not slip through before the blockade was imposed. In the event these ships did successfully cross the 'quarantine' line before the Americans could stop them. Sergei seemed shocked that his father appeared to have no contingency plan for what was happening now that the Americans had discovered what the Soviet Union had been secretly planning. He asked his father if he thought nuclear war was now a strong possibility, to which Khrushchev answered thoughtfully: 'It's one thing to threaten with nuclear weapons, it's quite another to use them.'

Washington

The CIA had more grim news for the President on Tuesday, 23 October. New surveillance had shown Soviet cargo ships were still steaming steadily towards Cuba. On the island itself missile launch pad construction was advancing quickly. On the Tuesday evening the President's brother Robert Kennedy called at the Soviet embassy in Washington to speak to Ambassador, Anatoly Dobrynin, who had already, in a cable to Moscow, warned the Kremlin how 'nervous' those in the inner circle of the administration were getting. Dobrynin informed his colleagues in the foreign ministry in Moscow, that the Americans were prepared to go all the way in a test of strength with the USSR. When the President's brother and the Soviet Ambassador met, Dobrynin noted Robert Kennedy was 'obviously agitated.' He asked how the captains of Soviet ships would react when they reached the American quarantine line. Dobrynin said there was no chance they would obey US orders to stop and be searched. Such orders on the high seas were, he said, illegal and unlawful. 'I don't know how this will end,' Kennedy replied, 'since we are determined to stop your ships.'

'But that would be an act of war,' the ambassador responded.[11]

London

Very late that Tuesday night, Macmillan received an urgent telegram from President Kennedy. The Prime Minister recalled, 'It warned me that the critical moment would come if and when the Russian ships met the large blockading forces the Americans had rapidly mobilised.' The telegram read: 'I know of no sure escape from the problem of the first shot. Our best basic source is firmness, now.' It was a question of watching and waiting. The following day the crucial test would be exactly what orders the Soviet leaders in Moscow had passed on to their ship's captains in the Caribbean.

In the UK and in the United States, millions woke up on that Wednesday morning ready to tune into radio or TV to hear how rapidly the tipping point into nuclear war was approaching. Robert Kennedy, watching his brother the President, tense and worried, remembered it as, 'the time of greatest worry.' Ambassador Dobrynin recalled that Wednesday as the most 'memorable' day of his near thirty years as Ambassador to the United States.[12]

Washingon

The blockade was fully imposed on Wednesday at 10.00am, Washington time. At exactly the same time the US Strategic Air Command, in the United States and on its bases in the UK, moved from DEFCON three, one step higher to DEFCON two, just one stage below war. Strategic Air Command more than doubled its nuclear capability. Its number of nuclear-armed bombers was increased from 912 to 1,479; inter-continental missiles on immediate stand-by were scaled up from 112 to 182. Together the total of Strategic Air Command nuclear weapons, those carried by the aircraft and the warheads on the missiles, and those carried by America's Polaris nuclear submarines, all of them waiting for the order to launch, reached a terrifying 2,952. Scores of bombers, many operating out of UK bases, loaded with nuclear weapons, remained airborne around the clock, re-fuelled by flying tankers, waiting over their holding areas of northern Canada, Greenland and the Mediterranean, for the signal to fly direct to their assigned targets in the Soviet Union. The Strategic

Air Command Commander, General Thomas Power, decided without Presidential assent, to announce the order openly, in transparent un-coded form, so the Soviet authorities would be left in no doubt of the aggressive stance the United States had now adopted.

Robert Kennedy scribbled an alarming note on his pad: 'Was the world on the brink of a holocaust and had we done something wrong? ... I felt we were on the edge of a precipice and it seemed as if there was no way off.'

London

In the UK the V-Force and the Thor nuclear armed rockets on their launch pads scattered on isolated sites down the east of England, had all been involved in a major 'Micky Finn' readiness and dispersal exercise the previous month, 20/21 September. The whole of Britain's nuclear deterrent forces had, just weeks before the Cuban crisis, rehearsed moving through the war readiness stages to Alert two, at which point the V-Force was armed with nuclear weapons and despatched to some twenty-six dispersal airfields around the country, to reduce the risk of aircraft being destroyed on the ground should the Soviets mount a nuclear attack. The normal peacetime alert condition for the V-Force was Alert five. Alert four was a precautionary state instituted during periods of international tension. Alert three allowed the Commander in Chief of Bomber Command, during a period of political tension, to take measures to ensure, in the words of the official definition: 'The maximum number of aircraft are made combat ready (loaded with nuclear bombs). At main bases these aircraft planned to operate from home bases are to be prepared for operational take-off; the remainder are to be armed (nuclear weapons) and prepared for dispersal.'

So, despite the unprecedented DEFCON two alert condition of American's Strategic Air Command in the UK, on RAF bases, including the V-Force bomber airfields, and the twenty launch pads each housing three Thor ballistic missiles, there was no heightened readiness on that Wednesday, 24 October, beyond the standard Cold War operational state that meant a proportion of V-bombers and Thor missiles were stood-by at fifteen minutes 'Quick Reaction Alert'. Indeed, on the UK missile bases where American nuclear specialists under the command of Strategic Air Command were solely responsible, through a joint agreement between the American and UK governments, for the nuclear warheads and for arming the missiles, the USAF and RAF crews were bizarrely working side-by-side under vastly different alert states. The American Authentication Officers

(AOs) who were responsible for arming the war-heads, were ordered to wear their war/peace keys around their necks. Normally the key was kept locked in a safe. The AOs were also forbidden to leave their post, adjacent to the launch pad, even for routine calls of nature! The British crews they worked alongside were on routine operational shifts. They stood ready to receive orders to bring missiles to a launch phase, but they were not at the same level of war-readiness as their 'Yankee' colleagues. A recipe for dangerous confusion if ever there was one!

On both sides of the Atlantic, concern and fear was rising. Those now in their late sixties and seventies, may recall the tension they and their families felt as they listened to radio news reports, or watched on flickering black and white television sets the pictures beamed in from America, of Soviet ships at sea and American warships waiting to confront them. Undoubtedly in the UK there was rising concern over the global situation. But what was not known or reported in the British media at the time, was how very close to home all this was. Britain was hugely vulnerable. American bases in Great Britain were on their highest ever alert. American nuclear armed aircraft were on immediate stand-by or airborne from British bases crossing the skies of mainland UK. If the crisis turned into a nuclear exchange the target would have been as much the British homeland as Cuba. That could happen within hours. Nobody had warned the British people that a direct threat to them might be imminent. Macmillan records in his memoirs the pressure he felt. 'We knew that twenty-five Soviet ships were approaching Cuba,' he wrote. 'Fourteen were believed to be carrying rockets. The first clash must thus come soon.'[13]

As the hours passed, the Prime Minister noted: 'No further news came to us that day, 24 October, except a rumour that some Russian ships had turned back. Kennedy phoned me at 11.00pm, London time.' Macmillan records part of the conversation:

President Kennedy: 'As you have probably heard, some of these ships, the ones we're particularly interested in, have turned around – others are coming on, so we ought to know in the next twelve hours whether they are going to try to run it, or whether they're going to submit to be searched. We'll be wiser by tomorrow night, but maybe not happier.'

Macmillan: 'You don't really know whether they are going back or whether they are going to try and make it, do you?'

Kennedy: 'Some of the ships that have turned back are the ones that we were most interested in and which we think would have given us some material. Others are continuing, I think they are just tankers. Now, I don't know whether they are going to make us sink these or whether we are going to be permitted to search them. That's still in question.'

As the conversation proceeded the two leaders got onto the issue of how missiles already on Cuba could be removed. Kennedy explained the most recent surveillance evidence showed the Soviets were continuing to build launch facilities. He and his advisers were going to have to make the fatal judgement whether to invade Cuba or whether to hold off and use Cuba as a 'sort of hostage in the matter of Berlin.' He asked the Prime Minister for his judgement, and he posed the question: 'Do we tell them that if we don't get the missiles out we are going to invade Cuba? Khrushchev would then probably say if we invade it would provoke a general nuclear assault from them, and in any case he would "grab Berlin". Or do we just let the nuclear work go on figuring he won't ever dare fire them, and when he tries to grab Berlin, we then go into Cuba.' A tense Macmillan agreed to think over the alternatives.[14]

Writing in his diary, Macmillan said of this crucial talk with Kennedy over the trans-Atlantic telephone: 'Rather unexpectedly the President asked me straight out the $64,000 question "Should he take out Cuba". I said I would like to think about it.' He noted British Intelligence was reporting that a number of Soviet ships in the early stages of their voyages to Cuba seemed to be returning via the Baltic to Polish or Russian ports.[15]

Moscow

As Wednesday's blockade approached Khrushchev was in two minds how to react. On the Tuesday evening he had ordered Soviet ships to proceed, and told submarine commanders in the Caribbean to fire back if fired upon – most were armed with nuclear-tipped torpedoes. At Wednesday morning's Presidium he suggested stopping some ships. A great many nuclear and other sophisticated weapons had already reached Cuba and been off-loaded, although the intermediate range missiles had not. He was undecided whether to let his tankers continue. A prominent American industrialist, William Knox, president of Westinghouse Electric, happened to be in Moscow. Khrushchev summoned him unexpectedly to the Kremlin and told him that if the US Navy tried to stop Soviet cargo vessels he would order Soviet submarines to sink the US warships. He told Knox he was not intent on the destruction of the world 'but if we all wanted to meet in hell it was up to us.' Later Khrushchev despatched another letter to Washington warning the Americans not to intimidate the

Soviet Union. 'In your heart you recognise I am correct. I am convinced that in my place you would act the same way ... Try to put yourself in our situation and think how the USA would react to these conditions.'[16]

Notes

1. *At the End of the Day: 1961–63*, Harold Macmillan, p. 194.
2. *The Macmillan Diaries Vol II: Prime Minister and After 1957–66*, p. 510.
3. Cabinet minutes 23 October 1962 PRO, CAB/128/36.
4. Ibid.
5. *At the End of the Day*, p. 195.
6. Memo to cabinet from Lord Chancellor, 24 October 1962.
7. PRO, PREM 11/3815 'Organisation of government to deal with a crisis in Berlin'. September 1961.
8. *The Macmillan Diaries Vol II*, p. 510.
9. *At the End of the Day*, p. 196.
10. Sergei N Khrushchev: *Nikita S Khrushchev*, Moscow, Novosti 1991, p. 279.
11. *Khrushchev: The Man and his Era*, William Taubman, p. 564.
12. Arthur M Schlesinger Jr: *Robert Kennedy and his Times*, New York, Random House, 1978, p. 514.
13. *At The End of the Day*, p. 197.
14. Ibid, pp. 198–203.
15. *The Macmillan Diaries Vol II*, p. 511.
16. *Khrushchev: The Man and his Era*, p. 566.

Chapter 9

Stretched Nerves

We believe the Russians will regard the UK as such a threat that
they will aim to render it unusable for a long period, and will not
hesitate to destroy great parts of the UK to achieve this aim.

Joint Intelligence Committee report, January 1955

In Britain fears were rising. Hugh Gaitskell, leader of the opposition Labour Party, called for the Prime Minister to visit Washington without delay. Talking to the President on the trans-Atlantic telephone was not sufficient. The situation was 'far too dangerous'. The balance of war and peace in Europe was threatened. Gaitskell recalled that when the Americans talked of using the atomic bomb in Korea in 1950, Attlee, then British Prime Minister, flew to Washington for direct talks with President Truman. The Labour leader said the position over Cuba was far more dangerous than it had been in relation to Korea twelve years ago. Nothing less than a face to face meeting between the two leaders was acceptable.[1]

Outside the political arena nerves were also stretched. Within Whitehall, although no decisions had been made about protection of the public, plans were secretly being devised to safeguard the nation's most important art treasures from nuclear attack. Four days after Kennedy imposed his naval blockade of Cuba, a group of directors from Britain's foremost galleries were involved in talks to plan the removal, under armed guard, of eleven large pantechnicons full of Britain's most irreplaceable paintings, documents and art treasures to Manod quarry in North Wales and Westwood quarry at Corsham, in Wiltshire. If the situation prevented the treasures from being transported that far there were alternative plans for temporary storage in Gloucestershire and Henley-on-Thames. The directors of the National Gallery, the Tate, the Wallace collection, the Victoria and Albert Museum, the British Museum, the Public Record Office, and the Royal Collection, were asked to produce a list of the most important treasures to be taken to safety if the threat increased and there was a real prospect of the UK being hit by nuclear attack. They realised a huge number of paintings and objects of high value would have to be left to take their chance, and their survival would be slim. The plan was for the convoy of masterpieces to leave London under armed guard at dawn to give the convoy of treasures the best chance of getting away undetected and unimpeded by traffic.

Declassified papers now in the Public Records Office, show that before the plan – code-named Operation Methodical – could be put into operation, questions were asked about the advisability and morality of removing the nation's old masters when no plans were being made to protect the population. Sir Thomas Padmore, the second secretary at the treasury put it bluntly: 'Personally I have very little sympathy with all this,' he informed his minister. 'If this country, and other countries are going to be devastated and destroyed to the degree which would be caused by an all-out nuclear attack, I cannot bring myself to care very much about artistic treasures, however great and however irreplaceable.' If the secret plans became known, it might cause public alarm and panic, prompting people to flee from London. It was bizarre, paintings were being put before people. In the event, the plan was quietly dropped. But a year after the Cuban crisis Operation Methodical was quietly revived and included in national contingency plans. A treasury official noted: 'Whether it will have the faintest chance of succeeding ... is another question; but this exercise has from the very start been based on the premise that there should be no removal of major masterpieces until other overt precautionary measures are being put in train.'[2]

Among those in the know was Anthony Blunt, then surveyor of the Queen's pictures. A few years later he was unmasked as the 'fourth man' in the notorious Soviet spy ring that included Burgess, Philby and Maclean. The chances are, Soviet intelligence knew all about Operation Methodical long before the secret plans were declassified and released to the National Archives in 2002.

Elsewhere in the country members of the largely volunteer-manned Civil Defence Corps, who must have been following the news with mounting concern, were wondering why they had not received any official instructions from government to move to a higher state of alert. So far Macmillan had felt it neither necessary nor advisable to alert or increase the readiness of the 400,000 members of the UK home defence forces. At various places in the country, which felt they were particularly vulnerable if a nuclear war was imminent, civil defence officers were getting anxious that they ought to be warning their volunteers to be ready to be called to action. Mr Eric Ally, the civil defence officer in charge in Norwich, a city particularly at risk as it was down-wind of several RAF nuclear deterrent bases recognised as prime targets in any nuclear exchange, recalled that when he approached the Home Office he was told to do nothing. He approached the town clerk of Norwich at city hall who held the role of local civil defence controller. The town clerk advised him to call the Home Office, the department responsible for civil defence. 'We were told to do nothing as they were hoping the problem would go away!' Mr Ally recalled. 'In those days we had a regional organisation headed by a regional director. They were told by the Home Office to keep their heads down as well. We were not allowed to give any information out to the public officially, but we decided to do so. We showed the 'Protect and Survive' film to parish meetings and we produced our own booklet – and then we had our knuckles well and truly wrapped. You can guess the problems we faced from the bureaucratic establishment.'[3]

So although there was a trained volunteer force of some 400,000 civil defence volunteers available, the Home Office took no steps whatever to put them on stand-by, despite the fact that, within hours, without any publicity and covertly, Britain's deterrent forces would be ordered to fifteen minute readiness or less, with nuclear weapons loaded and in some cases crews in their cockpits.

Government policy not to activate the civil defence force was counter to the claims made in a contemporary recruitment leaflet widely distributed to persuade people to give up their time to assist in the nation's defence. 'Civil defence has the nation in its care,' the leaflet proclaimed. 'Civil defence's responsibilities are enormous – probably far greater than anyone realises before they join. They touch upon nearly every facet of life of the nation. Civil defence volunteers would be ready in a period of alert, to advise the public on how to protect themselves, their families and their homes. If war followed, civil defence could not prevent millions of casualties; but it could help men, women and children to survive and reduce their suffering. Immediately after an attack, civil defence would be in the field: fire-fighting; rescuing the trapped; caring for the injured; caring for the homeless; providing food and water; monitoring the fall-out; controlling civil defence operations; advising and keeping up the morale of the public. In the aftermath of attack it would provide the vital information about local conditions which the central organisation would need.'[4]

That was the promise in the government publicity, but at the most critical time of the entire Cold War, nothing was done to set in motion the training, expertise and good intentions of those who had committed themselves to their communities via civil defence. It flew in the face of the fine words in the Home Office pamphlet: 'Some people take no interest in civil defence because they cannot bring themselves to think that a nuclear war could ever occur. But until general disarmament has been achieved, this country could be attacked with H-bombs. There would be damage on a vast scale from a nuclear attack. Yes. There would be millions of casualties. Yes. But there would not be complete destruction; on any reasonable assumption there would be millions of survivors. These millions would live, but they would need help, your help, which could be given efficiently only if you had been trained. Good intentions would not be enough. Only those whose abilities had been properly trained could bring life, healing and hope to the victims of the war in the long and grim struggle to restore civilised life.'[5]

It appears the bottom line was the government was afraid to panic the public.

In other publications the advice given by Government authorities to people, should a nuclear attack happen, seems now pathetically inadequate. One 1962 leaflet, prepared by the Central Office of Information and headlined 'Survival', warns that the immediate danger from a nuclear explosion would be from heat. It suggests seeking protection by 'placing your body in shadow, under cover, or behind a solid object; if nothing else is available, hide beneath clothing like an overcoat or jacket!' The next danger would be from blast. Here suggestions range from sheltering in a building to hiding in a ditch, a fold in the ground, or if no other cover exists, lying flat to the ground. Finally, the danger from radioactive fall-out is flagged-up. The advice is to retreat to a 'refuge room', a room with the least outside walls, or outside walls 'thickened with boxes of earth or some other way,' and stay there until told, presumably by radio 'what to do next.'[6] All very comforting and reassuring, but totally unrealistic.

In the 1960s, although civil defence was costing around £19 million a year, there was a positive switch of focus from planning to saving lives after a catastrophic H-bomb attack, on the lines of civil defence in the Second World War, to a more modest and less costly objective of ensuring basic national survival and governance. A government paper presented to ministers in March 1958, made it clear that: 'The Russians, either using bombers or ballistic missiles when available, could mount a comprehensive attack on this country. It would be aimed in all probability at nuclear bomber bases and offensive missile launching sites (a total of at least forty to fifty targets) as a first priority ... Even if there were no deliberate attacks on centres of population, the smallness of the UK and the possibility of weapons

going astray, it is very likely that centres of population will be hit ...
if, as is possible, ground burst weapons are used ... extensive areas
of the country would be contaminated by fall-out as well.'[7]

This gloomy, but realistic, assessment made it clear that the
problems of home defence would be made vastly more complex by
bomber bases in rural areas becoming prime targets, so plans to
move civilians from cities into the country were no longer viable. For
the planners, contemplating nuclear war, the problems of effectively
protecting the UK public looked bleak. The Strath Report in 1955 had
recommended a programme of shelter building for the population,
but the cost was estimated at £1.25 bn – around £23 bn at today's
prices. The government considered it unaffordable, but in a period
of extreme tension the government still needed to rally public opinion
and maintain public morale. Some in Whitehall questioned the value
of civil defence in such circumstances, but all those whose job it was
to plan for a Third World War knew it was politically impossible to
abandon it entirely. Possibly that is why it remained as a mere token
'fig-leaf' during the Cuban crisis. To activate it would have risked
public panic, but in extremis the public had the comfort of knowing
civil defence existed, however ineffective it might be in guaranteeing
peoples' actual survival.

In a 1960 government paper entitled 'Public Presentation of Home
Defence Policy' civil servants wrote: 'The primary objective of the
services we have suggested is to ensure that the government has
the means to sustain public opinion in a time of crisis ... in the
absence of authoritative guidance there has been an increasing
tendency for local authorities and their chief officers to conclude
that the government has lost faith in there being any substantial
number of survivors from a nuclear attack and for public opinion
to dismiss the possibility of taking useful measures to mitigate the
effects of nuclear attack. This has made it increasingly difficult, quite
apart from questions of finance, to keep the civil defence organisation alive, and the long term effect on the possibility of rallying
public opinion in a period of tension, is likely to be even more serious.
Unless a consistent effort is made to present the thesis that sensible
plans can and are being made to reduce casualties and to preserve the
structure of society in the unlikely event of the failure of the deterrent,
there is much less likelihood that public opinion would stay firm in
an extreme emergency, when it would be essential for the success of
the deterrent policy that the enemy should believe that public opinion
should stand firmly behind the threat to use nuclear weapons if
necessary. The majority opinion of the committee is that unless a

more positive attitude is adopted, as a background to whichever of the alternative financial proposals is adopted, the danger of acceptance by the public of a 'peace at any costs' policy in a period of tension would be much increased.'[8]

National survival, rather than life-saving operations, emerged as the focus of the home defence review that formed part of the 1961 Defence White Paper.

So ministers were being told three things in the years before the Cuba crisis heightened the threat and worries of war. First, national survival depended on an effective control system in wartime with central and regional government dispersed to hardened bunkers. Second, although it had severe limitations in the thermonuclear age, it was politically impossible to abandon home defence entirely. Third, it was vital to maintain public morale and public support firmly behind the deterrent policy, otherwise the British public might adopt a 'peace at any price' attitude. It seemed the government wanted it both ways.

Three years after the Cuban crisis the film director, Peter Watkins, made the 'War Game' a forty-five minute docudrama about the consequences of a limited nuclear strike on Kent. It was dramatic and well researched. Its message was that the government's civil defence preparations were both deceitful and nonsensical and that even those who hid, as instructed, under the dining table surrounded by sandbags stood little chance of survival. One critic wrote: 'It was so frightening, it showed that in such a holocaust the living would truly envy the dead.' So disturbing was the message that successive governments kept it off the air for twenty years lest it engender panic.

The advice fed to the public was ludicrously unrealistic. A civil defence leaflet issued by the Macmillan Government three years before the Cuban crisis, urged farmers to keep their livestock under cover, make their cellars comfortable and stocked with three weeks' supply of water and tinned food, and watch where they built their haystacks. It was patronisingly useless. After Cuba, the government felt obliged to issue more general advice in case the Soviet Union decided to reduce Britain to a crisp. 'If you have to go outside put on gumboots or stout shoes, a hat or a headscarf, coat done up to the neck, and gloves.' Better, however, to cower under the stairs with a wardrobe against the front door. The leaflet was withdrawn within a year to howls of ridicule.[9]

Macmillan appears to have chosen to steady public opinion at the time of Cuba, by refraining to do anything overt that might have alerted the British public to the deep concerns that were being held in Admiralty House and Whitehall.

Lord Allen of Abbeydale, who was Deputy Under Secretary at the Home Office 1960–62, has said that at the time of Cuba the growing tension was 'treated by the Home Office with complete indifference ... I have no recollection of the Home Office taking any action in response to the rising international crisis in October 1962 ... we had faith in Lord Harlech (David Ormsby-Gore, British Ambassador in Washington) at the time.' He was not surprised that local authority officials who had contacted the Home Office had received no directions from the civil defence department and felt that the Macmillan Government's reaction to the crisis was a very British one 'hoping it would go away!'[10]

But there was one organisation that did respond to the crisis. The giant 185-foot dish antenna of the Jodrell Bank telescope near Manchester was temporarily handed over to the RAF to search for and track incoming Soviet missiles. The ballistic missile early-warning station at Fylingdales in Yorkshire, part of the American BMEWS early warning system, did not become operational until 1963. So, at the time of the Cuban crisis, Jodrell Bank was a desperate stop-gap measure to try to gain some form of early warning of a missile attack. The Ministry of Defence declared a 'state of military vigilance' and arranged for the dish of the telescope to be re-aligned to pick up Soviet missiles at a range of a thousand nautical miles. It would have given the RAF a tiny margin in which to get their V-bombers in the air. But it was hardly a guaranteed warning system. Jodrell Bank had been built for scientific research and there were real concerns that the instrument might confuse missiles with atmospheric phenomena. So, it was conceded, it could not be entirely relied upon to identify an attack with any certainty.[11] But it was better than nothing.

Notes

1. *The Times*, 24 October 1962.
2. *The Independent*, 5 March 2002.
3. Quoted in 'UK Nuclear History Working Paper No. 3' by Robin Woolven, Mountbatten Centre for International Studies. Also email exchange with author, April 2007.
4. Home Office Leaflet, H.O. 6214.
5. Ibid.
6. Central Office of Information Leaflet, prepared for the Women's Voluntary Service, OF11.
7. CAB 134/1476, 'Form and Duration of a Future War', 19 March 1958.

8. CAB 134/2039, 'Public Presentation of Home Defence Policy', 1960.
9. *The Times*, 27 June 2004.
10. Lord Allen of Abbeydale quoted in 'UK Nuclear History Working Paper No. 3'.
11. Sir Bernard Lovell: *Astronomer by Chance*, Macmillan, 1990, p. 322.

Chapter 10

Thursday, 25 October–
Friday, 26 October

It seemed we were on the edge of a precipice with no way off.
Robert Kennedy, United States Attorney General,
25 October 1962

London

Macmillan notes in his diary that he was up early as Thursday, 25 October dawned, despite having burnt the midnight oil the previous nights. He was still keeping management of the British end of events tightly in his own hands and those of his Foreign Secretary, Sir Alec Douglas-Home, and Home's closest advisers in the Foreign Office. The Prime Minister had to make a statement to parliament on the world crisis and he was anxious to prepare his draft and to make sure tensions in Britain were kept at as low a point as possible.[1]

The fact Parliament was due to be prorogued on that Thursday would help him to limit discussion on the subject. MPs were not due to meet again until 30 October, when a new session of Parliament would start. That suited the Prime Minister. 'We had, at least the good fortune to escape daily questioning with all the embarrassment involved,' he wrote in his memoirs.[2] It shows how anxious Macmillan was to keep the level of concern in Britain from rising in the face of the growing global threat.

Washington

In contrast, the mood in the USA was getting close to fear. A poll taken in the States over the previous twenty-four hours had shown one in five Americans believed the blockade of Soviet ships would result in a Third World War. Earlier in 1962 the Kennedy administration had issued a guide to the US public on the facts of thermonuclear war, advising on the steps people could take to provide themselves with limited protection. Twenty-five million copies of the government booklet had been printed and the Department of Defence had allocated nearly $700 million for a civil defence programme, which included the construction of fall-out shelters and the stockpiling of emergency food supplies and medical equipment. Evidence of this came to light in 2006 when a long forgotten storage room under New York's Brooklyn Bridge was opened and revealed 350,000 packs of emergency rations, medical kits and water-drums, dated 1962.

In the White House the closeness of war was brought home when envelopes were distributed to key personnel printed with the instructions, 'To be opened in emergency'. These contained the passes and details of where to go in the event of warning of imminent nuclear attack to be whisked by helicopter to deep shelters.[3] The President's brother noted on 25 October, 'We are on the edge of a precipice with no way off ... President Kennedy had initiated the course of events, but he no longer had control over them.'[4] There was a sense of dread in Washington. The President himself put the odds for nuclear war at between one in three and even.

London
In the UK no steps had been taken to warn the public, or put in hand any preparations for nuclear war. Indeed, Macmillan records in his memoirs: 'Parliament, the press and the public remained remarkably calm, at least at this stage.'[5] But would they have remained so calm if the facts of what was happening and the risks had been widely known? The UK press seemed not to have grasped quite how dangerous events in the Caribbean could be for the UK and Europe.

When Macmillan went to the House of Commons at 11.00am that Thursday morning, he found the Conservative benches packed and the opposition benches also full, especially below the gangway.

The Prime Minister told the House that President Kennedy had made clear to him his 'deep concern about the development of Cuba as a formidable base for offensive ballistic weapons'. The United States had known for some time of the location of a number of surface-to-air missile sites in Cuba, but these missiles, even though they carried nuclear war-heads, could be regarded as defensive.

'Very recently,' the Prime Minister continued, 'a number of medium range missiles – or ground-to-ground – missile sites have been definitely identified in Cuba. Reports from all American intelligence sources confirm that at least thirty missiles are already present in Cuba. Such missiles with a range of over 1,000 miles, could reach a large area of the United States, including Washington and nearly the whole of Central America and the Caribbean including the Panama

Canal. In addition, sites for intermediate range ballistic missiles with an operational range of 2,200 miles have been identified. Further sites for both types of missile are being constructed. All these missiles are designed to carry, and must be presumed to carry nuclear bombs. In addition, Russia has supplied Cuba with IL-28 aircraft of which over twenty have been definitely identified. These bombers are of course offensive and not defensive weapons.'[6]

'These facts which are fully established on the basis of the evidence provided, serious though they are in themselves, took on a more sinister character because of the previous history of this affair. The House may recall that on 4 and 14 September, President Kennedy issued solemn warnings about the build-up of offensive weapons in Cuba and that on 11 September the official Soviet news agency Tass said: "The armaments and military equipment sent to Cuba are designed exclusively for defensive purposes" and added: "there is no need for the Soviet Union to shift its weapons ... for a retaliatory blow to any other country, for instance, Cuba." That amounted to an official disclaimer by the Soviet Government. In addition, as recently as 18 October, Mr Gromyko, the Soviet Foreign Minister explicitly speaking on the instructions of his government, assured President Kennedy in person, that Soviet assistance to Cuba was of a purely defensive character. At that very moment circumstantial evidence to the contrary was accumulating.'

'In view of the President's pledge that the United States would take measures to oppose the creation of offensive military power in Cuba, the Russian action, contrary to their categorical assurances, in developing this power can only be regarded as a deliberate adventure designed to test the ability and determination of the United States. The President, no doubt, formed the view, and, in my judgement, rightly, that to have accepted this would throw doubt on America's pledges in all parts of the world and expose the entire free world to a new series of perils.'

Macmillan informed MPs that the President's blockade was designed to meet a situation that was without precedent. The measures he had taken were not extreme, 'indeed they are studiously moderate in that the President has only declared certain limited types of war material, not even all armaments, to be prohibited. The armaments specified are these: surface-to-surface missiles, bomber aircraft, bombs, air-to-surface rockets and guided missiles, together with their war-heads and equipment. None of the categories specified in the President's proclamation could honestly be described as defensive.'

The Labour leader, Hugh Gaitskell, said President Kennedy had made plain his intention to secure the removal of the nuclear bases in Cuba. That could be done by agreement or by attack. He asked the Prime Minister if he was aware that if there was an attack on Cuba it would be very difficult to see how the Russians would not be able to justify an attack on Turkey. 'If the ground for attack is that there are nuclear bases on neighbouring territories, then I am afraid this seems to follow.' Gaitskell also asked pointedly if the British Government had been consulted before the decision by the President to blockade Cuba was taken. 'If they were consulted, what advice was taken? If they were not consulted, is it not a very unsatisfactory state of affairs that one member of an alliance can take unilateral action, even though this may clearly involve the greatest danger to other members of the alliance?'

Macmillan replied that the President had to act, in his view, very rapidly. Those were the facts and he did not wish to comment further.

Mr Gaitskell pressed again. Would the Prime Minister bear in mind, he asked, the need to impress upon the United States Government the desirability of taking Britain and the other allies into the fullest possible consultation before any further steps were taken in what was becoming a critical situation.

Other members rose to question the Prime Minister, but after just a few had had the chance to do so the Gentleman Usher of the Black Rod, Lieutenant General, Sir Brian Horrocks, was heard knocking on the door of the chamber three times to signal the prorogation of parliament and summon members to attend the Queen's Speech. There were cries of 'no' from some of the opposition back-benches who wanted the debate on the crisis to continue. The demands continued when Black Rod was announced by the door-keeper. As he advanced up the chamber further shouts of 'No, no, no' interrupted his summons for the commons to attend the House of Lords.

The Deputy Serjeant at Arms, Lieutenant Colonel P F Thorne, walked to the table and shouldered the mace. At this stage a Labour MP, Mr Fenner Brockway, attempted to rise to make a point of order. There were more noisy protests as the speaker made no reply, and rose from his chair to lead the procession to the lords. Mr Brockway shouted 'an absolute shame.' Another Labour member, Mr Rankin exclaimed 'to hell with the Lords.' But the session was over. Parliamentary ceremony had taken precedence over the opportunity to debate further the dire threat of possible nuclear war. Macmillan had succeeded in his aim of closing down discussion and keeping a low profile on the whole dangerous affair.[7]

Afterwards, according to commentary by *The Times* political correspondent, some MPs sought to determine when there was last a potentially serious threat to UK national security, or to peace in Europe, which had found the British Government no more than a spectator at the ringside; at worst impotent to have any effective voice in fateful decisions.

The view was, *The Times* declared, that Mr Macmillan had been able to do no more than 'turn the sheet music while President Kennedy played the tune'. There had been no consultation between Washington and London, although there had been some advance information on intentions, but it was clear that an explosion in the Caribbean would have repercussions for peace in Europe. *The Times* political commentator wrote: 'The new reality is that circumstances are not only conceivable but nakedly stated in which there should be no retreat from the brink ... MPs will reassemble at Westminster conscious that some of their illusions have been stripped away to reveal a starker reality; but they know also that the way ahead is beset with dangers which put all our politics in a new perspective.'[8]

Despite the protests in the Commons over the premature ending of the debate on the crisis, Macmillan recorded in his diary that his statement was well received. He had taken precautions to arrange for the prorogation of parliament to be delayed by no more than half an hour beyond its usual time of 11.00am, to ensure proceedings could not be prolonged and too many searching questions asked. His memoirs recall that there was 'a mild demonstration' from MPs who wanted more time to debate the crucial international situation, 'but it amounted to very little.'[9]

At 2.45pm Macmillan held a cabinet meeting. The only note referring to it that he makes in his diary is the peremptory remark: 'I told the cabinet about Cuba (which they were happy to leave to me and Alec Home).'[10] Most of that cabinet meeting was concerned with papers from a committee chaired by the Home Secretary covering many aspects of the future of Britain, including industrial location, housing, office building, transport etc. 'A fascinating discussion' Macmillan called it – but it was on a day when, if world events had deteriorated, Britain might not have had a future!

Sir Alec Douglas-Home opened the discussion in cabinet. He told colleagues that a number of Russian ships believed or known to be carrying military supplies, had been diverted or had been ordered to return home. Others were still on course. The United States naval commanders were under orders to intercept them, using minimum force, but so far no interception had taken place. The acting secretary general of the UN had called on President Kennedy, Mr Khrushchev and Dr Castro to accept a truce for two or three weeks so discussions could take place. No replies to this appeal had yet been received.[11]

The Foreign Secretary said three conditions needed to be met. The dismantling of the missile sites in Cuba; the stationing of United Nations observers in Cuba to witness dismantling; and the stationing of UN observers in Havana to scrutinise incoming cargoes. Unless these conditions could be met it would be impossible for President Kennedy in the present atmosphere to withdraw the United States blockade, and so long as the blockade remained in force it was hard to see how progress could be made. It did not seem there was any action that the Prime Minister could usefully take at this juncture; an early visit to Washington, for example, could easily be misinterpreted as a mission of appeasement.

In discussion, ministers pointed out that it was to be expected that the existence of United States missile bases in Europe would feature increasingly in the case which the Soviet Government would present in defence of their action, and it was unfortunate that at this moment United States representatives in Europe were urging on European governments the desirability of increasing the medium-range missile forces at the disposal of the North Atlantic Alliance.

Summing-up the Prime Minister said that the situation remained extremely serious and it was necessary to avoid at all costs the temptation of reaching a settlement by lowering the resistance of the free world to aggression. It was equally necessary to avoid driving those who felt that they had been the victims of aggression to desperation.[12]

Moscow

In the Kremlin the mood was moderating slightly. Khrushchev had received a cold but incisive letter from Kennedy in which the President said he regretted the crisis, but the Soviets had caused the 'challenge' and they were to blame for the deterioration in relations between the east and west. He hoped the Russian leader would act to restore relations before it was too late. Khrushchev's son noted that the letter helped convince his father that compromise might be the best course of action. The fact that America's military forces had been raised to DEFCON two had shaken him. He regarded it as 'bluff', but admitted it could not be ignored.

A Presidium meeting was called for that afternoon. Khrushchev proposed to his colleagues that he should respond to Kennedy on the lines of: 'Give us a pledge not to invade Cuba, and we will remove the missiles.' His son noted that his father realised Kennedy was under massive pressure to attack Cuba. If that invasion happened how should the Soviet Union respond? Should it launch an attack on West Berlin? That would inevitably lead to war in Europe and once the shooting started there would be no way of stopping it.[13]

New York

Deliberations at the United Nations were not particularly helpful to either Kennedy or Macmillan. The UN's Acting Secretary General, U Thant, had sent a message to Kennedy saying a large number of the permanent representatives of member governments had resolved to appeal to the US and to the Soviet Union to refrain from any action that might aggravate the situation and bring with it a risk of war. He urged Kennedy voluntarily to suspend the quarantine measures America had imposed and stop attempts to search Soviet cargo ships for a period of two to three weeks. In a message to Khrushchev the UN leader urged suspension of all arms shipments to Cuba for a similar period. From America's point of view a voluntary suspension would have allowed the USSR to continue work on the missile sites so the threat to US cities would be greater after two or three weeks than it was now. Macmillan in a call to Washington from Admiralty House, advised the President that after Khrushchev's earlier deceit and duplicity over deployment of offensive weapons on Cuba, it was impossible for the United States to rely on a Soviet promise. The Prime Minister also urged Kennedy to demand there should be some form of inspection, either by the UN or by an independent authority, to ensure work ceased on military installations while negotiations took place. He concluded by advising the President that America should continue its military build-up so she was ready if an attack on Cuba proved unavoidable.

London

Throughout Thursday night further calls came through from Washington to London. Again Macmillan was up until the early hours discussing progress with the President. Khrushchev, despite his more moderate mood earlier in the day, was still insisting his ships must not be searched. It was clear that if the Soviet authorities stuck to this line America would have to face the risk of stopping Soviet ships by force and searching them, or in the worst situation firing on and sinking Russian cargo ships. The critical moment would come during the following afternoon, Friday, 26 October.[14]

del Castro and Nikita Khrushchev. Had Khrushchev been open about his treaty to deploy nuclear issiles to Cuba, as Castro wanted him to be, it is possible he would have won international greement for his action.

esident John Kennedy's and Prime Minister Harold Macmillan's agreement at the Bermuda onference in March 1957 to base American Thor nuclear missiles in the UK, together with the merican decision to base Jupiter missiles in Turkey and Italy, led directly to the Cuba Crisis.

Map showing the range of the missiles Khrushchev intended basing in Cuba, and the targets they were capable of reaching.

US Navy low-level photograph of a medium range ballistic missile site under construction at San Cristobel, Cuba.
(*US National Security Archives*)

reconnaissance photograph of ballistic missile site preparations on Cuba.
(*US National Security Archives*)

Nuclear war-head bunker under construction at San Cristobel, Cuba. (*US National Security Archives*)

President John Kennedy delivering his historic broadcast on 22 October 1962 to reveal that the USS[ ] was covertly deploying nuclear missiles to Cuba. (*US National Security Archives*)

Three squadrons of American F100 Super Sabre aircraft at bases in the UK, each armed with 1.1 megaton nuclear bombs, were covertly ordered to operational alert unknown to the British people, [ ] hours before President Kennedy went on television to announce the USSR was installing missiles c[ ] Cuba. (*USAF*)

-47's of the United States Strategic Air Command based in the UK were loaded with nuclear
eapons and prepared for take-off when the SAC was ordered to Defcon Three on 22 October 1962.
SAF)

uclear armed American B-52 bombers flew airborne patrols from UK bases in UK airspace during
e crisis after the Strategic Air Command had been ordered to unprecedented alert levels and their
K bases 'locked-down'. (USAF)

Fifty-nine of the sixty Thor intermediate-range missiles deployed in the UK were brought to fifteen minutes readiness or less, as the crisis developed. (*Author's collection*)

The three elements of Britain's nuclear deterrent, the V-Force: Vulcan (front), Victor (left) and Valiant (right). The V-Force squadrons were covertly brought to their highest alert during the whol Cold War as the crisis developed.

Vulcan's of the RAF's V-Force formed a core part of the UK's nuclear deterrent. (*Author's collection*)

RAF Vulcans guarded and at readiness.

Air Marshal Sir Kenneth Cross, Commander in Chief of Bomber Command at the time of the Cuban Missile Crisis. He was proud of his Command's level of readiness, but critical of his political masters. (*Ron Case/Hulton Archives/Getty Images*)

Prime Minister Harold Macmillan described the critical week-end of the crisis, 27/28 October 1962, as 'the worst two days of my life'.

Sir Alec Douglas-Home, Foreign Secretary 1960–63. During the Cuban Crisis Harold Macmillan and Sir Alec played the British end of the developing crisis very close to their chests concerned too much openness would panic the British people.

Section of the switchboard and communications centre at the underground Central Government Bunker at Corsham, referred to in 1962 by the codeword 'Burlington'. The scale of the communications network was huge. (*Crown Copyright*)

Chairs, many still in their wrappers, piled up at the Central Government Bunker at Corsham awaiting 4,000 civil servants and Government officials who would face 'Armageddon' together. (*Crown Copyright*)

INDICATIONS OF DANGER

BEFORE ATTACK

FIRST STAGE
There would be an official instruction to take precautions.

SECOND STAGE
Our warning system is designed to provide a warning before an attack reaches this country, giving enough time to get under cover.

DURING ATTACK

The light from a nuclear explosion would warn those not under cover to seek instant protection against the other possible dangers – heat, blast, radioactive fall-out.

AFTER ATTACK

Warnings would be given to those places which fall-out was approaching.

IMMEDIATE DANGER from HEAT

TO PREVENT FIRE

BUILDINGS could be protected at the first indication that danger was imminent, when householders would be asked to prevent fire by :
a. whitewashing windows to keep out heat
b. removing or flameproofing all materials that flame easily if exposed to great heat
c. having simple means of fighting fire, in the house

TO AVOID BURNS

PEOPLE could be protected by being in shadow :
a. under cover or behind a solid object
b. covered by own clothing if no other shadow near enough to duck into

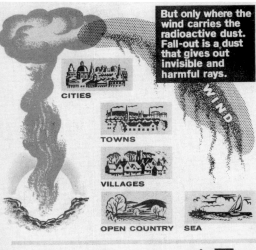

But only where the wind carries the radioactive dust. Fall-out is a dust that gives out invisible and harmful rays.

CITIES

TOWNS

VILLAGES

OPEN COUNTRY   SEA

A REFUGE ROOM would give DISTANCE from the dust DENSITY between us and the dust TIME to allow the radioactivity to decay – all these three safety factors weaken the rays given off by the radioactive dust.

WE WOULD BE WARNED OF ITS ARRIVAL

ACTION: STAY IN REFUGE UNTIL TOLD WHAT TO DO NEXT

SURVIVAL!

We all want to prevent nuclear war.
But, if it ever came, we would all have to know the do's and don'ts that could help many families to survive. This series of five diagrams explains the facts about our protection in the survival areas.

PREPARED FOR THE W.V.S. BY THE CENTRAL OFFICE OF INFORMATION

Government 'Protect and Survive' pamphlets issued to the British public in the early 1960s.
(Author's Collection)

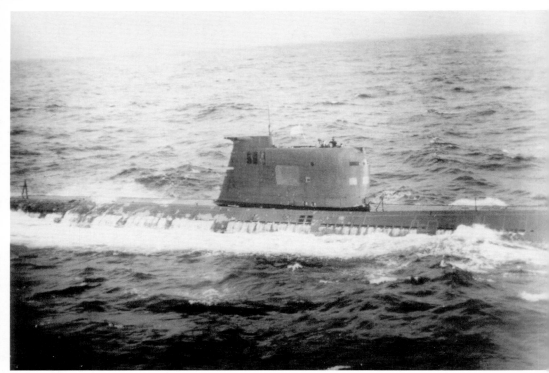

Soviet submarine B59 which came close to triggering World War III when a furious argument broke out after its Captain ordered a nuclear-tipped torpedo to be prepared for firing.
(*US National Security Archives*)

Crates holding Komar guided-missile armed patrol boats on a Soviet freighter headed for Cuba.
(*US National Security Archives*)

Экз. № 2

Тов. ЦК КПСС — т.Серову А.К.

КОПИЯ ИСХОДЯЩЕЙ ШИФРТЕЛЕГРАММЫ № 20076

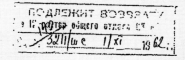

ТРОСТНИК —

товарищу ПАВЛОВУ

На № 8/154

Категорически подтверждается, что применять ядерное
оружие из ракет, ФКР, Луна и с самолетов без санкции из
Москвы запрещается.

Получение подтвердить.

ДИРЕКТОР

№ 76639
27 октября 1962 г.
16.30

отп.1 экз.

Верно: Нач.смены 4 отд.8 Упр. ГШ
ПОЛКОВНИК

/ЛАВРЕНКО/

отп.29.10.62 г. 16.30
Щербакова

Top secret telegram from Moscow to the commander of Soviet forces on Cuba sent at the height of the crisis, 26 October 1962. (*US National Security Archives*)

6.   Partly no doubt because Cuba has thus been so firmly excluded from taking a hand in the shaping of her own destiny, life here, in spite of the acute underlying tension, has been relatively undramatic.   This can also partly be explained by the government's efforts to keep the temperature down and to encourage business as usual in industry and agriculture, both of which have been hard hit by the mobilisation of the militia..   (As the crisis drags on this will become a factor of immense, perhaps decisive importance in an already shaky economy.)   But I think equally important ingredients in what Castro proudly refers to as "discipline and dignified calm" are the stunned confusion and anxiety of the general public, which has shown itself remarkably unenthusiastic about dying for the cause.   Added to which two weeks of windy, wet weather have done nothing to help maintain revolutionary ardour amongst militia on guard duties and in flooded fox holes on the beaches.   The hard core of both the new and the old style communists are probably still just as ready to fight and sacrifice themselves as ever before - but they would, I believe at this moment be on their own.

7.   The same calm has, I am glad to say, prevailed amongst the British colony both white and coloured.   There has so far been no signs of, and indeed no reason for discrimination against ourselves or the nationals of any other country.   An early interest in the possibility of evacuation has subsided as it became evident that if it was a nuclear war we were heading for, Cuba was perhaps a better place to be in than Britain.

/ 8. It

Memorandum from the British Ambassador to Cuba, Herbert Marchant, to the Foreign Secretary, Sir Alec Douglas-Home, in which he says: 'If it was nuclear war we were headed for, Cuba was perhaps a better place to be than in Britain'. (*US National Archives*)

Kennedy told Macmillan that fourteen ships had turned back of their own accord, and these were probably the ones carrying the most sensitive military cargo Khrushchev did not want either to produce or allow to be examined. Those ships still on course for Cuba might be ones that did not have military equipment in their holds but there was no way of being certain. The President insisted, 'We cannot permit him (Khrushchev) to establish the principal that he determines which ships will go and which will not.'

On Friday, 26 October a veritable flood of messages passed back and forth between London and Washington. Macmillan noted in his diary: 'Two long telephone talks with the President. The situation is very obscure and dangerous. It is now a trial of will.' American reconnaissance flights were reporting furious activity in Cuba. Soviet launch emplacements were being finished, and missiles being manoeuvred into place. Il-28 bombers were being assembled and made airworthy. In one call Kennedy referred to photographic evidence of sophisticated special equipment and many self-propelled armoured vehicles. It was during this conversation that Macmillan floated the option he had been considering of temporarily immobilising the Thor missiles in the UK, targeted on the Soviet Union, as a bargaining counter to persuade Khrushchev to back down. Kennedy replied he and his advisers would consider the suggestion, but he was wary of 'too many dismantlings' and Khrushchev might insist on a similar agreement in order to eliminate American missiles from Turkey and Italy. Macmillan's rising concern was that too much pressure on Soviet interests in the Caribbean, could produce new threats and tensions in Berlin and these would escalate the danger for the UK and Europe. In his memoirs, he said his suggestion of using the British-based Thor missiles as an attempt to find an escape for Khrushchev would only have been a temporary measure. He would never have consented to a permanent deal. America's allies in Europe would have felt that to avoid the threat in Cuba the US Government had bargained away their protection and undermined the principles of the NATO treaty.[15]

Macmillan followed up his suggestion of throwing the immobilisation of the UK based Thor ballistic missiles into the argument with a written statement to the President: 'It might be helpful to the Russians' face if we undertook ... to allow the immobilisation of our Thor missiles, of which there are sixty, under UN supervision. This has, of course, the disadvantage that it brings in the concept of bargaining bases in Europe against those in Cuba. Nevertheless if it would turn the scale I would be willing to propose it to U Thant

(UN Acting Secretary General) and it might be less invidious for us to take the lead rather than place the burden on the Turks. You said you would have this idea looked at.'[16]

Macmillan appeared desperate to lower the tension and divert any possible spread of war to Europe where the flashpoint of Berlin deeply troubled him and his foreign secretary. There are no records that show Kennedy displayed any interest in the idea of immobilising the Thor rockets in the UK. It certainly was not discussed at the White House meeting of the ex-com on Saturday morning. Even among Macmillan's own group of closest advisers there were those who felt his suggestion would be construed as looking as if the British were the first to crack. Harold Evans, Macmillan's Press Secretary, recorded in his memoirs that he had voiced his concerns over the 'appeasement flavour which some could see in the Thor proposition.'[17]

Meanwhile the Joint Intelligence Committee in London had been assessing the photographic evidence from the United States using the expertise of British intelligence officers and analysts. A highly secret paper circulated to the cabinet concluded that 'provided nuclear warheads are available, missile units in Cuba could be allocated certain strategic targets on the American Continent, at present allocated to other Soviet forces. If all known sites are completed, we estimate that the overall Soviet initial launch capability against the US will have increased significantly by the end of 1962.' The British experts had carefully assessed the IRBM, MRBM, shore-to-ship missiles, surface-to-air missiles, Komar patrol vessels equipped with anti-ship missiles, air-to-air launch sites, and nuclear warhead storage sites, and given their own highly classified detailed assessment under the restriction that it was for 'UK Eyes Only'.[18]

Washington
Across the Atlantic the greatest ever concentration of American troops and armour was gathering in the south-east of the United States. The British Acting Consul in Miami described the atmosphere in Florida as much like Southern England before D-Day, with troops and armour massing in huge numbers. Kennedy was under intense pressure from his joint chiefs of staff to launch air strikes and an invasion. The military appeared obsessed with finding an opportunity to demonstrate its potential and its power. Some of the generals appeared positively gung-ho in their appetite for war. When asked what the Soviet reaction would be to a surgical raid on their missiles and men, General Curtis Le May snapped, 'There will be no reaction.' Robert

Kennedy recalled acidly that 'many times ... I heard the military take positions which, if wrong, had the advantage that no-one would be around at the end to know.'[19]

Moscow

At his office in the Kremlin, Khrushchev received a file from his intelligence sources informing him that the American plan for the invasion of Cuba was virtually complete and the attack could be launched at any moment. US hospitals were preparing to receive large numbers of casualties and the administration was prepared to go on to a full war footing. The KGB information had a sobering effect in the Kremlin. Khrushchev started drafting yet another communication to Washington. 'We understand perfectly well that if we attack you, you will respond in the same way,' he wrote. 'You too will receive the same that you hurl against us. If war broke out then it would not be in our power to stop it, for such is the logic of war.' If both sides did not pull back they would 'clash like blind moles and then reciprocal extermination will begin'. Khrushchev was prepared to make a proposal, which amounted to the USSR removing its missiles from Cuba in return for an undertaking that America would never invade Cuba and would lift its blockade. That 'deal' wrapped up in a great deal of emotional bluster, arrived in America after 6.00pm Washington time. Khrushchev appealed in so many words to Kennedy to 'save the world from its impending doom.' It seemed the crisis was coming to an end. In fact the worst was still to come.[20]

Notes

1. *The Macmillan Diaries Vol. II*, p. 51.
2. *At the End of the Day*, p. 205.
3. Jim Wilson: *Launch Pad UK: Britain and the Cuban Missile Crisis*, Pen & Sword 2008, p. 132.
4. Robert F Kennedy: *Thirteen Days: A Memoir of the Cuban Missile Crisis*, New York, Norton, 1969, pp. 70–1.
5. *At the End of the Day*, p. 205.
6. Hansard, 25 October vol. 1664 ccl. 1053–64.
7. *The Times*, 26 October 1962.
8. *The Times*, 29 October 1962 'In and Out of Parliament: Backbenchers Shed Some Illusions'.
9. *At the End of the Day*, p. 205.
10. *The Macmillan Diaries Vol II*, p. 512.
11. Cabinet Minutes, 25 October 1962 PRO: CAB/128/36.
12. Ibid.
13. Sergei N Khrushchev: *Nikita S Khrushchev*, Moscow, Novosti, 1991.

14. *At the End of the Day*, pp. 206–8.
15. Ibid, pp. 210–12.
16. PRO: PREM 11/4052 Macmillan to Kennedy teleprinted to Washington, 27 October 1962.
17. *Downing Street Diaries Vol II*, p. 225.
18. Joint Intelligence Committee Report: 'Cuba: Threat posed by Soviet Missiles,' 26 October 1962.
19. Arthur M Schlesinger Jr: *A Thousand Days: John F Kennedy in the White House*, New York: Fawcett Crest, 1967, p. 831.
20. William Taubman: *Khrushchev: The Man and his Era*, p. 569.

Chapter 11

'Black Saturday' 27 October

If the next thirty-six hours were agonising in Washington, they were almost equally so in London.

Prime Minister, Harold Macmillan in his memoirs
At the End of the Day

On Saturday, 27 October 1962, the day that would come to be known as 'Black Saturday', the most dangerous hours of the whole Cold War, were about to start.

Moscow

Because of the time difference Khrushchev awoke in Moscow at around the time Washington was going to bed. The night before he had believed an American invasion of Cuba was imminent. Now he assumed that as the Americans had not attacked in the previous few hours they must be holding back, perhaps afraid of the force they would meet if they attempted to take the island. The day before, Khrushchev's letter to Kennedy had been conciliatory, offering a deal. Now he dictated a new, more hard-line letter, demanding a trade-off with America's missiles targeted on the Soviet Union standing on launch sites across the Black Sea in Turkey. The Soviet Union, he told Kennedy, would give a solemn pledge not to invade Turkey, if the United States would make a similar statement in the security council of the United Nations guaranteeing not to invade Cuba.[1]

'If we can achieve the liquidation of the missile bases in Turkey,' he told colleagues on the Presidium, 'we would win.' Khrushchev knew from Soviet intelligence reports that some public discussions and newspaper reports in the States had mooted the suggestion of a trade-off of some kind, though the Kennedy administration had never formally proposed such a move. Khrushchev thought Kennedy might reject his letter of the previous day as being too vague. It did not occur to him that putting the Turkish element of the deal into the public domain would create problems for the White House, especially among some NATO allies.

Instead of sending his latest message through diplomatic channels, which took an inordinate time to reach Washington, Khrushchev decided to broadcast it openly on Radio Moscow.

Washington

Kennedy and his advisers were shocked. Before they had had time to respond to the proposal sent by Khrushchev on Friday, they were now faced with a completely new proposition. Most of Kennedy's advisers were outraged. The hawks felt by making his new letter public, Khrushchev was acting in bad faith. They were ready to propose immediate military action. But Kennedy still believed a deal could be made. He decided the best tactic was to ignore Khrushchev's new offer and to reply instead to his first letter. In his response he stated: 'If the Soviets would remove all weapons systems from Cuba capable of offensive use, then after adequate UN verification, the United States would remove promptly the quarantine measures and give assurances against an invasion of Cuba.'[2]

Kennedy's response left Washington about 8.00pm Saturday evening and reached the Soviet foreign ministry in Moscow just after 10.30am on Sunday, 28 October. By then Khrushchev's alarm was rising as a result of several disturbing incidents. On the Saturday morning (Washington time) an American U-2 spy plane based at an airfield in Alaska, and airborne on a routine atmospheric 'sampling mission' to detect signs of radiation from nuclear tests, had accidentally strayed into Soviet airspace over the Chukotka Peninsula. The Soviets, alert to the possible implications, had scrambled armed MIG fighters to shoot the spy-plane down. The U-2 pilot broadcast an urgent SOS and a group of American fighter aircraft were despatched to escort the wayward plane back to its base. The American fighters sent to the aid of the U-2, which was then at least 100 miles inside Soviet territory, were armed with nuclear weapons that could be fired on the authority of each individual pilot.[3] The White House was unaware of this alarmingly provocative incident, the sort of event British planners had considered could rapidly lead to the nightmare scenario of war-by-accident.

Around noon on Saturday a far more significant event happened that cast the terrifying shadow of a direct path to war across the already complex crisis. A U-2 gathering fresh photographic evidence of continuing work on the missiles sites on Cuba, was shot down and its pilot, Major Rudolph Anderson killed. Castro had ordered his troops to fire on any aircraft entering Cuban air space. But the limited weaponry the Cubans themselves possessed, meant they failed to hit any of the reconnaissance planes the Americans sent over. The Soviet Air Defence Commander on Cuba, Lieutenant General Stepan Grechko, had asked authority from Moscow to use the Soviet surface to air missiles (SAMs) under his command. Although Moscow had not given its specific authority, the Soviet anti-aircraft units were convinced the attack on Cuba was about to commence. Grechko, or one of his junior officers, gave the fateful order to fire and brought the U-2 down. This undoubtedly constituted an act of war, and it shocked both Washington and Moscow.

In the White House there were immediate demands for retaliation. In Moscow, Khrushchev feared this was the trigger to an unstoppable nuclear conflict. In London, Macmillan agonised over this alarming incoming news. 'It seemed on that Saturday the climax had now been reached,' the Prime Minister recalled in his memoirs. 'The Americans could have no alternative but to launch an attack, at least to destroy the SAM sites.' He wrote, 'The next thirty-six hours were agonising.'[4]

Macmillan was very aware of the vulnerability of the UK if war was imminent. At that stage he had given no orders for the British deterrent forces to move to heightened readiness, beyond the normal fifteen minute quick reaction alert at which a proportion of the V-Force and Thor missiles were always held. The world seemed to be moving inexorably towards the abyss. News coming in from Washington was sobering. Soviet diplomats in the United States capital and in New York, were busy destroying confidential documents.

Robert McNamara, the American Defence Secretary, told his colleagues: 'We must be prepared to attack Cuba, and quickly. If we do and we leave the missiles in Turkey, the Soviet Union will probably attack the Turkish missiles and we cannot allow that without a full military response from NATO.' The conflict that appeared now about to start in the Caribbean would potentially spread rapidly to Europe. By then the whole of NATO and the Warsaw Pact would be involved.[5]

In the south eastern states of America, the military machine was now unstoppable. All the necessary preparations were in train for a full-scale assault on Cuba, if necessary as early as Monday, 29 October, and American military chiefs were contemplating the use of nuclear weapons. A confidential report from the Department of Defence, listed the requirements as almost a quarter of a million men, 2,000 air sorties against key targets in Cuba, and several thousand marines and airborne troops. One estimate of American casualties if an invasion was ordered put losses at well over 25,000.

Caribbean

The US Navy at sea to enforce the blockade were unaware that Soviet Foxtrot submarines, armed with nuclear-tipped torpedoes, were part of the multi-service military force the USSR had despatched to Cuba. Only hours after the shooting down of the U-2, an even more dangerous drama began to unfold. The Soviet submarines had been sent to Cuba to spearhead the development of a major Soviet naval base at Mariel Bay. Under orders from the Pentagon, US ships were carrying out systematic efforts to track any Soviet submarines as part of the naval blockade. The US warships were under orders not to attack the submarines directly, but to try to induce them to surface and identify themselves using practice depth charges to achieve this. Messages outlining the US Navy's intentions were transmitted to Moscow in an effort to avoid any misunderstanding but the information about US Navy intentions was never passed on to the Soviet submarines. The American effort to force the submarines to surface involved considerable risk. Exhausted by weeks spent undersea in difficult circumstances and worried that the US Navy's depth charges were the real thing, senior officers on several of the submarines were sufficiently rattled to consider firing nuclear torpedoes, whose explosive yields approximated to the bomb that had devastated Hiroshima. The Soviet crews having endured weeks submerged, were convinced they were under attack.

It is now clear from records published in Moscow in 2002, that senior officers in several of the Soviet submarines actively discussed firing their nuclear weapons. Aboard one submarine, B-130, which US destroyers had cornered, Captain Nikolai Shumkov, ordered a nuclear torpedo to be prepared for firing. The weapons security officer warned him the torpedo could not be armed without permission from headquarters and reliable communications to get the necessary authorisation were virtually impossible. Tension on board was running so high that the security officer reportedly collapsed under the strain. Shumkov told his crew he had decided he would not fire because to do so would probably mean they would all perish.

Even more dangerous was the situation aboard a sister submarine, B-59. In a remarkable account published forty years later, the communications and intelligence officer, Vadim Orlov, recalled the fraught atmosphere on board as they came under attack from American depth charges. A totally exhausted Captain Valentin Savitsky, unable to establish communications with Moscow and believing that war had already started, ordered the nuclear-tipped torpedo to be prepared for firing. Savitsky shouted 'We're going to blast them now! We will die, but we will sink them all.' Three officers on board – Savitsky, the political officer Ivan Semonovitch Maslennikov, and Commander Vasili Arkhipov – had authority to launch the torpedo if they could not get authorisation from Moscow, providing they all agreed. A furious argument broke out between them, in which only one, Arkhipov, was against making the attack. Eventually he persuaded Savitsky to surface the submarine and await orders from Moscow. At a conference in 2002 which looked back on the crisis, the then former American Defence Secretary, Robert McNamara, acknowledged that Arkhipov, by his persuasive arguments, had almost certainly saved the world from a nuclear war. Had the torpedo been fired, nothing could have stopped escalation to a nuclear conflict. It was that close – but on that Saturday in 1962 there was still the near certainty of an American invasion.[6]

The Soviets sent two further submarines, B-75 and B-88 to the Caribbean and Pacific respectively with specific combat orders. B-75 carried two nuclear torpedoes. It left Russian waters at the end of September and the instructions issued to its commander, Captain Nikolai Natnenkov, were to defend Soviet transport ships en route to Cuba with any weapons, including nuclear, if the ships came under attack. The other submarine had orders to sail to Pearl Harbor and attack the American Naval base there if the crisis over Cuba escalated into a US-Soviet war.

Unknown to the Americans, the Soviet troops on Cuba had among their armaments Luna tactical nuclear weapons. They would almost certainly have been used by the Soviet defenders desperate to stop an American landing, as they knew without a shred of doubt they could not rely on any extra forces arriving to help them defend the island.

Washington

On the American side too there were other potential triggers to war which could have resulted from miscalculation. In order to keep a hugely increased fleet of nuclear-armed B-52s continuously on airborne patrol, it seems some may have flown with weapons whose circuitry had not been fully certified as safe. At Malmstrom Air Force base in Montana, American officers at a Minuteman ICBM site jerry-rigged the launch system so as to give themselves an independent launch capability, by-passing normal safeguards in the scramble to get the maximum of the new silo-based inter-continental missiles ready. In another hugely risky incident, the Air Force tested a long-range Titan ICBM missile at Vandenberg Air Force base in California, just as the crisis was reaching its crescendo. While the missile did not carry a nuclear warhead, the Air Force had mated nuclear warheads to other ICBMs at Vandenberg, and had placed them on alert. Fortunately the Soviets did not detect the launch, or they would certainly have misinterpreted it as part of a nuclear attack. The pressures on the ground on both sides were building to a point where a single mistake, a wrong order, a misjudgement, would have pre-empted the frenetic diplomatic debates that were going on in Washington and Moscow and tipped the crisis into full-scale conflict.

Kennedy's executive committee was in session almost continuously as the grim news flowed in to the White House that Saturday. President Kennedy was beginning to realise that at the climax of the crisis, he did not know, and could not control, all the actions of his own military.[7]

London

Macmillan, with mounting concern, could only watch 'on the side-lines' with very little practical means of influencing the balance between peace and war.

'All through that critical day we waited for news while the President and his advisers struggled to find some alternative to military action,' Macmillan recalled in his memoirs. He vividly remembered his grow-ing concern throughout the hours of agonising in Washington and in London. To add to his concerns devious approaches were being made to the Foreign Office, allegedly from a member of the Russian Mission in London, suggesting the British Government issue an appeal for a summit conference to try to settle the issue. One of these voices urging the UK to broker a conference was a Captain Eugene Ivanov, a London- based officer of Soviet military intelligence. 'This proposal was repeated directly to me through a Conservative MP of high character and standing on Saturday afternoon,' Macmillan wrote. 'Home and I agreed to regard the earlier approaches as attempts to drive a wedge between London and Washington. Even this last appeal seemed to me likely to conceal a trap.'[8]

Indeed it might. The captain Ivanov Macmillan was referring to was ostensibly an assistant naval attache at the Soviet Embassy in London. Actually he was an officer of the GRU, the Soviet military intelligence service. Some security experts believe that one of Ivanov's objectives, when he arrived in London in March 1960, was to find out details of an American plan to arm the West German army with a medium range ballistic missile called 'Sergeant'. The nuclear war-heads would be kept in West Germany under American control until an emergency. At that point German troops would be empowered to use them. The plan and the date the missiles would become operational were highly secret. The Soviet Union had obvious strategic reasons for wanting to learn these details. There was huge sensitivity in Moscow to any move to give West Germany access to nuclear weapons. Khrushchev had taken the decision to build the Berlin Wall, which was erected without warning in August 1961, and he was concerned that NATO's reaction might result in war. Khrushchev had also begun thinking of installing missiles in Cuba. If Moscow could prove that the Americans were about to station nuclear missiles on the West German border, his case for missiles in Cuba would not appear unreasonable.[9]

The scandal that broke with the resignation of John Profumo, Macmillan's Minister of War, in June 1963, and was one of the reasons that led to an end of Macmillan's leadership, appears to have been linked to Ivanov's attempts to get information about the American missiles in Germany. He tried to achieve this via the 'services' of the attractive 19-year-old Christine Keeler, who was having an affair with Ivanov and also allegedly sleeping with Profumo. Keeler was later quoted as saying: 'I was to find out, through pillow talk from Jack Profumo, when nuclear warheads were being moved to Germany.'

At one of the tensest moments of the Cuban missile crisis Ivanov, acting on the instructions of the Soviet ambassador in Britain, seems to have been active in trying to resolve the situation to the USSR's advantage by advocating British intervention. He made the approach through a mutual friend, Stephen Ward, with whom he was a frequent visitor to Lord Astor's Cliveden estate (as were the notorious Christine Keeler and her friend Mandy Rice-Davies). Ivanov used Astor's name to approach Sir Harold Caccia, Permanent Under Secretary at the Foreign Office, and suggest Britain should take the initiative to call a summit conference to resolve the Cuban stand-off. The gist of Ivanov's message to Caccia was 'that the Soviet Government looked to the United Kingdom as their one hope of conciliation.'[10] The Ivanov inspired phone call was made on Wednesday, 24 October. Caccia forwarded it to the British ambassador in Moscow, who was 'sceptical about both the information and the initiative.'[11] The following day, again at Ivanov's suggestion, Ward persuaded the Tory MP Sir Godfrey Nicholson, to meet Ivanov. The Soviet GRU agent urged Nicholson to go to the Foreign Office and press for a conference. On 'Black Saturday', 27 October, Ward, again at Ivanov's behest, also tried to use the Earl of Arran, a Foreign Office official, to reinforce the suggestion of a summit. Arran met Ivanov who said he had been instructed to 'get a message to the British Government by indirect means, asking them to call a summit meeting in London forthwith.'[12] Ivanov assured him Khrushchev would respond favourably to a British invitation to take part in a conference and that Britain would get all the credit for breaking the deadlock. Macmillan noted in his diary that he suspected this was a trap to drive a wedge between the UK and the US at a critical moment. Although nothing came of Ivanov's efforts, the fact that he used Khrushchev's name, presumably with the specific permission of the Kremlin, shows the level at which his moves were being orchestrated.

Ivanov returned to Moscow in March 1963 as soon as the story about Christine Keeler appeared in the newspapers. The journalist Brian Freemantle, a commentator on intelligence matters, wrote at the time: 'In no way did Ivanov return to the Soviet Union under any odium. He may have failed to obtain any military secrets from his shared liaison with Christine Keeler, but his other success in compromising the war minister was enormous – causing huge embarrassment to a British Conservative Government and the downfall of a war minister. His rewards would have been considerable.

Washington

Theodore Sorensen, a member of the National Security Council, recalled the fear within the executive committee as the 'Black Saturday' news grew grimmer and grimmer. 'If the Soviet ships continued coming, if the SAMs continued firing, if the missile crews continued working, and if Khrushchev continued insisting on concessions with a gun at our head then – we all believed – the Soviets must want a war and war would be unavoidable.'[13] Under-secretary of State, George Ball, recalled: 'It was unmistakeably 'Black Saturday', one might reasonably infer from the evidence that the Soviets really intended war and were simply stalling until they were better prepared.'[14] What played on the mind of the President and his advisers was the nightmare that the Soviets might decide that as total war was inevitable, they would launch a pre-emptive nuclear strike against the United States. Black humour brought some relief.[15] 'I hope you realise,' Kennedy said at one point, 'that there's not enough room for everyone in the White House bomb shelter!'

A private meeting that Saturday evening in Robert Kennedy's room at the justice department, between the President's brother and the Soviet Ambassador, Anatoly Dobrynin, was an attempt to impress on the Soviet diplomat in no uncertain terms that time was running out for both sides. Robert Kennedy spelt out that if the USSR refused to remove their offensive weapons then the United States would remove them by force. If the Soviet Union retaliated then 'before this is over, while there might be dead Americans, there would also be dead Russians.' Robert Kennedy made the point emphatically that the military were insisting that reconnaissance flights over Cuba must continue and the next time a U-2 was fired on the Americans would retaliate. The United States was also preparing to bomb the missile sites and this would lead to a terrible chain reaction which would assuredly end in nuclear war. There were 'hot heads' both in the military and in the administration who were 'spoiling for a fight,' he said. A solution was urgent and this was probably the final chance to find one. Kennedy made it clear that if the Soviets removed the missiles under United Nations supervision, the United States would agree not to invade Cuba. The US he inferred were also prepared to remove the Jupiter missiles from Turkey. The US Government he said would not make that promise publicly, because to do so would appear to the Turks and the rest of NATO that America had sold out under pressure from Moscow in order to protect the American public at the expense of the defence of Europe. However, Robert Kennedy made it clear that the ambassador had his word, and the word of his brother, the President, that missiles in Turkey would be dismantled in four to five months. The agreement would have to be kept strictly secret. Only a handful of people in Washington would know about it. That was the carrot. Kennedy's stick was that his brother needed a response from Khrushchev by the next day.[16] In truth it was not too difficult for the Americans to offer up the Jupiter missiles as a bargaining counter. They were becoming old technology and could, in time, be replaced by Polaris submarines patrolling in Turkish waters. Removing the missiles, provided the Soviets carried out their part of the bargain, would be a far better option than bombing Cuba intensively, or mounting an invasion and risking a nuclear war.

Following that meeting, Robert Kennedy wrote a memorandum summing up the strong line he had taken with Ambassador Dobrynin. 'I told him this (the shooting down of an unarmed U-2 reconnaissance plane and the death of its pilot) was an extremely serious turn of events. We would have to make certain decisions within the next twelve or possibly twenty-four hours. There was very little time left. If the Cubans were shooting at our planes, then we were going to shoot back ... He raised the point that ... we were violating Cuban air space. I replied that if we had not been violating Cuban air space then we would still be believing what he and Khrushchev had said – that there were no long-range missiles in Cuba. In any case, I said, this matter was far more serious than the air space over Cuba and involved people all over the world. I said that he had better understand the situation and he had better communicate that understanding to Mr Khrushchev. Mr Khrushchev and he had misled us. The Soviet Union had secretly established missile bases in Cuba while at the same time proclaiming, privately and publicly, that this would never be done. I said those missile bases had to go and they had to go right away.'[17] Robert Kennedy stated in his memorandum that he was not giving the USSR an ultimatum, but a statement of fact. Khrushchev should understand that if he did not remove the offensive weapons, the United States would remove them.

In communicating this to Moscow, Dobrynin conveyed to the Kremlin that the President's brother had appeared extremely agitated 'the first time I have seen him in such a condition.' He had stressed emphatically to him that the Americans believed time was running out. An attack, the consequences of which could not be predicted, was imminent. In his cable to the Soviet foreign ministry, revealed in the 1990s, Dobrynin quotes Kennedy as saying: 'The US Government is determined to get rid of those bases – up to, in the extreme case, of bombing them, since I repeat, they pose a great threat to the security of the USA. But in response to the bombing of these bases, in the course of which Soviet specialists might suffer, the Soviet Government will undoubtedly respond with the same against us, somewhere in Europe. A real war will begin, in which millions of Americans and Russians will die. We want to avoid that in any way we can, I'm sure that the government of the USSR has the same wish. However, taking time to find a way out is very risky (here R Kennedy mentioned as if in passing, that there are many unreasonable heads among the generals, and not only among the generals, who are itching for a fight.) The situation may get out of control with irreversible consequences.'[18]

On the matter of the Turkish-based Jupiter missiles, Dobrynin's memo said: 'And what about Turkey?' I asked R Kennedy. 'If that is the only obstacle to achieving the regulation I mentioned earlier, then the President doesn't see any insurmountable difficulties in resolving this issue,' replied R Kennedy. 'Formally the deployment of missile bases in Turkey was done by a special decision of the NATO council. To announce now a unilateral decision by the President of the USA to withdraw missile bases from Turkey – this would damage the entire structure of NATO and the US position as leader of NATO, where, as the Soviet Government knows very well, there are many arguments ... However, the President is ready to come to agree on that question with N S Khrushchev, too. I think to withdraw these bases from Turkey,' R Kennedy said, 'we need four to five months. This is the minimal amount of time necessary for the US Government to do this, taking into account the procedures that exist within the NATO framework.'[19]

Dobrynin's memo then added: 'R Kennedy then warned that his comments about Turkey are extremely confidential; besides him and his brother only two or three people know about it in Washington.'

Khrushchev himself in his memoirs picked up the startling point in Dobrynin's memo that some military leaders in Washington were itching for a fight. In *Khrushchev Remembers* translated and edited by Strobe Talbott, he recalls Dobrynin reporting that: 'Even though the President himself is very much against starting a war over Cuba, an irreversible chain of events could occur against his will. That is why the President is appealing to Chairman Khrushchev for his help in liquidating this conflict. If the situation continues much longer the President is not sure that the military will not overthrow him and seize power. The American army could get out of control.'[20]

This seems a wild exaggeration, but Dobrynin was an experienced, careful and responsible diplomat, respected on both sides of the Iron Curtain, and according to the original memorandum he certainly noted that Robert Kennedy had made some remark about the impatience of some of the American generals. Dean Rusk, American Secretary of State at the time in his own memoirs, *As I Saw It*, says Khrushchev either genuinely misunderstood or deliberately misused Robert Kennedy's statement. 'Obviously there was never any threat of a military takeover in this country. We wondered about Khrushchev's situation, even whether some Soviet general or member of the Politburo would put a pistol to Khrushchev's head and say "Mr chairman launch those missiles or we'll blow your head off!" '[21]

In Washington tensions that Saturday night were close to breaking point. Some in the administration, particularly those closest to the negotiations, wondered whether they would survive the next few days. Dobrynin and the staff in the Soviet embassy in Washington shared their fears. An American attack was widely expected on Monday, 29 October or Tuesday, 30 October at the latest.

Havana

In Cuba there was both fear and anger. On Friday, 26 October Castro had become convinced an American invasion was imminent, at least within the next twenty-four to seventy-two hours. Ever since the Bay of Pigs attempt Castro had almost a paranoia that the Americans were determined to overthrow his government. At around 2.00am Saturday, 27 October a highly stressed Castro turned up at the Soviet Ambassador, Alekseyev Aleksandr's apartment in Havana. The two consumed a substantial amount of beer and sausages, then Castro started to draft an urgent message to Moscow. He feverishly dictated some ten versions before he was satisfied. The import of Castro's message to Khrushchev was terrifying. Aleksandr realised he was prompting the USSR to launch an immediate pre-emptive strike against the United States.

Castro told the ambassador that he did not want his country to suffer the perfidy of allowing the imperialists to strike first and wipe Cuba off the face of the earth, which would be the certain result if the United States used its massive nuclear force. He wanted the Soviet Union to be the first to 'fire' – to launch a nuclear attack against the United States, even if his country perished, as it almost certainly would in the ensuing conflagration.

He later explained he was convinced an American attack was coming. The Soviets would respond with nuclear weapons causing an American nuclear retaliation in return. But he did not want Khrushchev to let the Americans strike first. 'There should be no hesitation' he told Moscow. 'I dared to write a letter to Nikita aimed at encouraging him. That was my intention. The aim was to strengthen him morally, because I knew that he had to be suffering greatly, intensely. I thought I knew him well.'[22]

The letter crafted by Castro and translated by Aleksandr, read: 'If the imperialists invade Cuba with the goal of occupying it, the danger that aggressive policy poses for humanity is so great, that following that event the Soviet Union must never allow circumstances in which the imperialists could launch the first nuclear strike against it. That would be the moment to eliminate such danger for ever through an act of clear legitimate defence, however harsh and terrible the solution would be, for there is no other.'[23]

Although Castro appeared to be accepting the virtual elimination of his island in an American nuclear attack, it is possible that he had swallowed Khrushchev's boasts about the overwhelming missile supremacy of the USSR and that he believed after a Soviet first strike on the United States, America would have been so weakened, her response would have been minimal.

Castro's alarming message arrived in Moscow early in the morning of Sunday, 28 October. Troyanovsky, who was permanently camped in the central committee building as the crisis unfolded, received the telegram and called Khrushchev at home. Castro's sentiments appalled and scared the Soviet leader. He rightly interpreted it as a call for the Soviet Union to launch an immediate all-out nuclear strike against America. Castro, he concluded, had completely misunderstood Moscow's purpose which was not to attack the United States but to ensure the United States did not attack Cuba.[24]

There seems no doubt Castro's intention was to urge a Soviet nuclear pre-emptive strike on the United States. Years later he claimed to have been willing to die if necessary in a nuclear conflagration.[25]

London

Deep concern was being felt in London where, because of the time difference, Sunday dawned without any news of Soviet concessions. Macmillan had had little sleep throughout the Friday and Saturday nights. He was experiencing some of the most worrying days of his life, knowing that the peace of the world was on a knife edge, and aware of Britain's total vulnerability if the crisis ended in nuclear conflict. He knew it was going to be a day on which he might be forced to take unprecedented decisions with unthinkable consequences for the British public.

Macmillan had other worries on his mind as well. Britain was inevitably a 'player' in the Cuban crisis. Britain had a role as a colonial power in the Caribbean. Jamaica and Trinidad had gained independence in August 1962 with the collapse of the ill-fated West Indian Federation, but Britain still had responsibility for a number of islands in the former federation, together with the British Virgin Islands, the Bahamas, Bermuda, British Honduras, and British Guiana. So America was not just dealing with a dispute in Cuba that affected only the safety of its own people. The British Government had a duty to the citizens of those outposts of the Commonwealth in the Caribbean quite apart from concerns about any conflict quickly enveloping Europe, the UK and the rest of NATO.

Macmillan had made it clear to the Chief of Air Staff, Marshal of the Royal Air Force, Sir Thomas Pike, on Saturday, 27 October that if the situation deteriorated further overnight he intended calling a crucial cabinet meeting on the Sunday afternoon and he would require all the chiefs of staff to be in attendance. It would be a meeting where decisions over war and the very survival of the nation would have to be made. Even though he knew Kennedy was probably only forty-eight hours from launching an invasion and a bombing campaign, on Saturday, Macmillan had briefed Pike that he was 'adamant that he did not consider the time was appropriate for any overt preparatory steps to be taken such as mobilisation.' He did not want Bomber Command to be officially alerted, although he did want the force to be ready to take 'appropriate steps' should they become necessary. Macmillan told his RAF chief of staff that once the American invasion force was ready, President Kennedy would probably authorise action, only informing his allies once the operation was in progress rather than consulting with the UK in advance.[26] In other words, US forces based in Britain might be called into action without prior consultation with the UK Government.

The Prime Minister had also arranged for Peter Thorneycroft, the Minister of Defence, to meet with all the service chiefs at lunch-time on Sunday, 28 October to co-ordinate military advice before the expected full cabinet meeting in the afternoon. That cabinet would have to take some of the most serious and significant decisions any British Cabinet had had to face.

Following the Prime Minister's meeting with the chief of air staff at Admiralty House at 11.00am on 'Black Saturday', Sir Thomas contacted the Commander in Chief of Bomber Command, Air Marshal Sir Kenneth 'Bing' Cross, who immediately within the powers that had been conferred on him, covertly, and on his own responsibility, ordered his command to alert condition three. Technically, alert three was a 'precautionary alert', the precursor to the next level alert two which demanded generation of the maximum number of aircraft to combat serviceability. Cross' order was implemented as unobtrusively as possible. Operational staff who were either on leave or off base were called back by phone or through the police knocking on their doors. Macmillan had told Sir Thomas he wanted Bomber Command to be 'ready' and key personnel available on their stations, but he specifically ruled out making the dramatically raised alert level public knowledge or that any preparatory steps should be taken overtly. Any broadcast on the BBC to notify crucial staff they were required back at their bases was specifically ruled out. Normally an alert three would have been followed by the next stage in war readiness, alert two, the movement of the V-bombers to their dispersal airfields. Each main bomber base had six dispersal stations, widely scattered across the UK, which they could use to minimise the chances of the whole force being wiped out in a first strike attack.

Marshal of the Royal Air Force, Sir Michael Beetham, who was Chief of Air Staff at the time of the Falklands War, was group captain (operations) in 1962, serving in the control room at Bomber Command headquarters. Speaking at an RAF Historical Society seminar in 2001 he recalled: 'We got the message from government, from Macmillan, that no overt action was to be taken. So anything that we did decide to do had to be done quietly. We couldn't for instance use the BBC to recall people from leave, as we would have liked to have done. In fact we were so successful that nothing ever seemed to appear in the press, despite the fact that we had generated the entire V-Force to a very high state of readiness. We even put the crews in their cockpits at one stage, but basically they were held at fifteen minutes' notice. Ideally, once the bombs were on board, what we wanted to do was move on to the next stage in our pre-planned alert procedure, which would have dispersed the V-Force. We were forbidden to do this, however, so aircraft had to stay at their main bases.'[27]

Another Group Captain, Roy Boast, commanding officer of the Helmswell complex of Thor missile bases recalled: 'I was advised by the air officer commanding group on the Saturday morning that we were on stand-by for the 'real thing' but that apart from the early recovery of the missile on routine maintenance, manning procedures would be as for any other day with all the launch sites continuously manned. I did not inform my wing or squadron commanders of the AOC's message, but anyone abreast of the news would have recognised for himself the full implications. The next thirty hours seemed most unreal doing all the normal things with my wife and daughter (my son was away at school and had the best chance of us all of survival). Perhaps the worst thing was to realise that the station and dispersed sites would be hit and destroyed shortly after we had fired our own missiles, or before if the Russians chose to make a pre-emptive strike.'[28]

So for those 'in the know', the seriousness of the UK's position that 'Black Saturday' was very obvious. The majority of the British people were blissfully unaware that if the 'face off' being conducted thousands of miles away in the Caribbean, in Moscow and in Washington, resulted in a wrong move, a misjudgement, or, as seemed very likely, the Soviet leadership added to their aggressive policy by grabbing West Berlin, they too and the rest of Europe would inevitably and swiftly be involved in nuclear war.

The headquarters of Bomber Command was linked by direct line to the headquarters of America's Strategic Air Command in Nebraska. Generally the two control centres were in frequent contact and the commanders of the UK and US nuclear strike forces were normally in regular communication. But it seems as the crisis developed these usually close communications ceased. Air Marshal Sir Kenneth Cross, gave his recollections of that tense period to Group Captain Ian

107

Madelin, former Director of the Ministry of Defence's Air Historical Branch in a recorded conversation in 1993. Cross recalled that as the crisis grew discussion between him and the Air Ministry and between him and his opposite number at headquarters of Strategic Air Command was almost non-existent. This was not for lack of trying. Cross said he frequently tried to contact the Air Ministry for instructions, but with little success and the state of communications with Strategic Air Command was similar. Cross' frustration can be imagined. His responsibilities as commander of the nation's deterrent forces were immense, yet he was clearly being constrained by the lack of direction by the UK's higher political/military leadership. 'Once the Cuban missile crisis started, there was no one at the end of the phone, and there was no one at the end of the phone until it was over' he said.[29] There is some evidence to suggest Cross had been 'badgering' the MOD, Air Ministry and Whitehall for some direction for the previous five days of the crisis. Political considerations stood in the way of him taking all the precautionary measures to increase the readiness of his forces that he felt were necessary. He concluded this was deliberate policy on the part of ministers. But it put him as commander of Britain's nuclear deterrent forces, in an unenviable position. He was de facto in charge of Britain's nuclear response and had the delegated authority to launch an attack on the Soviet Union under certain extreme conditions. He must have been aware of the actions being taken in the United States by General Thomas Power to raise the readiness of American Strategic Air Command. He must have known of the mismatch between the alert levels of the nuclear strike forces each side of the Atlantic, and particularly between RAF and the USAF personnel on bases in the UK.

In a letter to the Vice Chief of Air Staff, Air Marshal Sir Wallace Kyle, when the crisis was all over, Cross wrote: 'Despite having everything ready to bring seventy-five per cent of the aircraft in the command to readiness, we could not give the order for fear of the effect it might have (if it became known) on the very tense negotiations between Washington and Moscow.'[30]

Another senior officer, Air Vice Marshal Stuart Menaul, recalls that in the early hours of 'Black Saturday' Sir Kenneth Cross went into the Bomber Command operations room to hear the latest news from America.[31] Such was the gravity of the situation and the growing tension in his operational headquarters, Cross must have been relieved to have had contact with the chief of the air staff a few hours later. It gave him the opportunity to place the UK's V-Force and the RAF's Thor nuclear tipped missiles on the highest level that they were ordered to in the whole of the Cold War, roughly equating to the state of readiness his American colleagues had been placed on three days earlier. Up until that time, Cross on his own initiative had implemented all the measures which could be done routinely and covertly. There is evidence he wanted to go further and disperse his V-bombers, but he needed ministerial authorisation to do so. Authorisation Macmillan had expressly ruled out. As a result of Cross' new instructions from the chief of the air staff, his alert three order, flashed to V-Force bases, increased the number of fully armed aircraft at quick reaction alert, on fifteen minutes to take-off or less on most operational stations, from three to six. In at least one instance, RAF Waddington, the number was tripled to nine aircraft armed and ready to go. Across the Thor missile bases all except one of the sixty Thor missiles were brought to within fifteen minutes of firing.[32] That was a training missile, and subsequently efforts to place that too on fifteen minutes to launch were also made.

Following Sir Thomas Pike's meeting with the Prime Minister on 'Black Saturday' he called a meeting for 2.30pm where he briefed his fellow chiefs of the armed services, the First Sea Lord, Admiral of the Fleet, Sir Caspar John, and Chief of the Imperial General Staff, General Sir Richard Hull. The Chief of the Defence Staff, Lord Louis Mountbatten was away from London and was not at the crucial meeting. According to the minutes of that meeting,[33] the chiefs were informed that senior officers and civil servants in the Air Ministry, Admiralty and the War Office had been warned to be available at one hour's notice. The chiefs of staff discussed the advice they would offer the full cabinet, if and when it was called the following day. They concluded that while precautionary measures could be taken by Bomber Command, those few V-bombers abroad should not be recalled at this time (though they were the following day). The chiefs agreed it was essential for Bomber Command to be dispersed as soon as the situation warranted, in order that its deterrent effect should be seen to remain credible. Without dispersal to widely scattered air-fields the whole of the V-Force would have been 'sitting ducks' had the USSR decided to launch a peremptory attack. These measures were the most effective that could be implemented to comply with the Prime Minister's instructions that there should be no 'overt' steps and no general military mobilisation. They would give necessary political assurance to the United States. If America mounted an offensive against Cuba, as the President had threatened in the next forty-eight hours, the chiefs agreed the most likely Soviet reaction would be to occupy West Berlin. Military advice was that West Berlin was indefensible against the substantial conventional forces the Russians had available, and existing plans to mount 'probes' along the ground access routes to the city would be 'useless'. The Prime Minister, they agreed, should be advised of this so that he might urge the President to restrain General Norstad, the Supreme Allied Commander in NATO, from ordering any such action. The British military chiefs concluded that as soon as there were positive indications that the United States proposed to strike against the Cuban mainland, Bomber Command should be dispersed. That would have been put into effect immediately the code-word 'Framework' was flashed to all the RAF's operational stations. It would also have immediately put into effect the detailed provisions in Britain's secret *War Book*. A move against West Berlin would have placed the whole of the peace of Europe into jeopardy. The chiefs were informed the US invasion force would not be ready until the 29 October at the earliest. The British Government would be told before any definitive action was taken, but this would take the form of 'information rather than consultation'.

There is no indication in American Government records, that either high-level military or political authorities in the States were aware the British nuclear deterrent forces had been covertly, placed on an alert three level. The only British forces whose alert state the President was notified of, were those RAF resources directly under the command of the supreme allied commander Europe. These were RAF Valiants and Canberras which had been armed with American nuclear weapons. They stood at a high state of readiness on bases in the UK and West Germany. The American general who commanded United States Air Forces in Europe (CINCUSAFE), General Truman Landon, interpreted the orders issued by General Lauris Norstad, the supreme commander of NATO in Europe (SACEUR), in his own way. Norstad had ordered no measures should be taken which could be considered provocative or might disclose operational plans. But Landon went close to ordering a full DEFCON two alert. He independently ordered a discrete increase in the overall capability of his forces to be effected in a gradual and unobtrusive way. Significantly, this included an increase in the number of nuclear-armed aircraft on quick reaction alert loaded with high-yield thermonuclear weapons in place of less destructive, lower-yield nuclear bombs. A number of these aircraft were stationed in the UK, notably at RAF Marham in Norfolk.

On Sunday, 28 October Macmillan noted in his diary: 'I am writing this in a state of exhaustion, after being up all Friday and Saturday nights to about 4.00am. The difference of hours between America and

England is the cause. It is impossible to describe what has been happening in this hour by hour battle – in many ways rather like a battle ... All through Saturday night the strain continued.'[34] In fact, as the fate of the world swung between peace and war that Sunday morning, the defining moment of the Cold War was reached. Air Marshal Cross, Bomber Command's Commander in Chief, stood all the aircraft in his command to full readiness.

Harold Macmillan's official biographer, Alastair Horne, in a foot-note to his chapter on the Cuban missile crisis, says, new information now suggests that Britain did go to the brink of mobilisation: 'As the crisis worsened the commander in chief Bomber Command, a relatively lowly air marshal, decided to prolong and increase the alert even further. At this stage the British nuclear forces became capable of being launched within fifteen minutes, or less, on 230 targets in the Soviet Union and Warsaw Pact countries.'

The distinguished Cold War historian, Peter (now Lord) Hennessey, notes in his book *The Secret State* that it is very likely the cabinet meeting Harold Macmillan planned for the afternoon of Sunday, 28 October 1962 would have officially authorised a move to what was defined in the *War Book* as the precautionary stage in transition to war. This would have led to the formation of a small war cabinet probably consisting of Macmillan, Alec Douglas-Home (Foreign Secretary), Henry Brooke (Home Secretary) and Peter Thorneycroft (Defence Secretary). It is probable Rab Butler, the First Secretary of State and Deputy Prime Minister would also have been included as a member.

If the situation worsened, this group, together with the cabinet secretary, other senior government officials, the chief of defence staff, and probably the chief scientific adviser would have been taken by helicopter to 'The Quarry' (Burlington) to receive a stream of signals detailing the deteriorating world crisis. Had the threat of war actually tipped into Armageddon and the UK was under nuclear attack it would have been from 'The Quarry' that Macmillan would have issued authorisation for nuclear retaliation.[35] Standing by, at alert condition three that Sunday in October, Britain's nuclear deterrent force was poised ready to provide it.

Notes

1. Foreign Relations of the United States: 1961–63 vol. 6, pp. 178–81.
2. Ibid, pp. 181–2.
3. Scott Sagan: *Moving Targets: Nuclear Strategy and National Security*, Princeton, Princeton University Press, 1989, p. 29.
4. *At the End of the Day*, p. 213.

5. Richard Reeves: *President Kennedy: Profile of Power*, New York, Simon & Schuster, 1993, pp. 418–9.
6. National Security Archive: 'US and Soviet Naval Encounters During Cuban Missile Crisis'.
7. Scott Sagan: *The Limits of Safety: Organisations, Accidents & Nuclear Weapons*, Princeton University Press, 1993.
8. *At the End of the Day*, p. 213–4.
9. Chapman Pincher: *Too Secret Too Long*, Sidgwick & Jackson, London, 1984, p. 321.
10. Christopher Andrew: *The Defence of the Realm: Authorised History of MI5*, Allen Lane, London, 2009, p. 497.
11. Ibid.
12. Ibid.
13. Michael O'Brien: *John F Kennedy: A Biography*, New York, Thomas Dunne Books, 2005, p. 669.
14. Ibid, p. 669.
15. Ibid, p. 667.
16. Foreign Relations of the United States 1961–63, Vol XI Cuban Missile Crisis and Aftermath, Doc 96.
17. Ibid.
18. Dobrynin's cable to the Soviet foreign ministry, 27 October 1962: National Security Archive, George Washington University (Cold War International History Project).
19. Ibid.
20. *Khrushchev Remembers* translated and edited by Strobe Talbott, Boston, Little, Brown, 1970, pp. 551–2.
21. Dean Rusk as told to Richard Rusk: *As I Saw It*, New York, Norton & Co, 1990, pp. 238–40.
22. James Blight & David Welch: *Cuba on the Brink: Castro, The Missile Crisis & the Soviet Collapse*, Pantheon, New York, pp. 108–11.
23. Ibid, p. 481.
24. Nikita S. Khrushchev: *Khrushchev Remembers*, translated by Jerrold Schecter & Vyacheslav Luchkov, Little, Brown, Boston, 1990.
25. *Cuba on the Brink*, p. 360.
26. PRO, DEFE 32/7 Record of a conversation between the chief of air staff, first sea lord and chief of the imperial general staff held in Ministry of Defence, 2.30pm, Saturday, 27 October 1962.
27. Jim Wilson: *Launch Pad UK: Britain and the Cuban Missile Crisis*, Pen & Sword, 2008, p. 150 (RAF Historical Society seminar 2001).
28. Ibid, p. 138 (Letter Gp Capt Roy Boast 1998).
29. Sir Kenneth Cross' recollections recorded by Group Captain, Ian Madelin, September 1993.
30. PRO Air 20/11371: Letter from Commander in Chief Bomber Command to Air Marshal, Sir Wallace Kyle, 31 October 1962.
31. Stewart Menaul: *Countdown: Britain's Strategic Nuclear Forces*, Robert Hale, 1980.

32. PRO, Air 25/1703 Operational Record Book, Headquarters No. 1 Group, October 1962.
33. PRO, COS 1546/29/10/62: Record of chiefs of staff meeting in Ministry of Defence, 27 October 1962.
34. *The Macmillan Diaries Vol. II*, pp. 513–14.
35. Peter Hennessy: *The Secret State: Preparing for the Worst 1945–2010*. Penguin Books, 2010.

Chapter 12

Burlington 'Berties'

The location of the headquarters and the check-point through which you pass are of the utmost secrecy, and must not be revealed to anyone at all.

1962 government *War Book* instructions,
'Manning Burlington'

The government's top secret *War Book* for 1962,[1] now declassified, sets out very clearly the steps that would have been triggered once the cabinet had taken the decision to institute a 'precautionary stage' in the lead up to global war, the point that was almost reached on Sunday, 28 October 1962.

The code-word 'Shadwell' would have been immediately flashed to all government departments putting them on a twenty-four hour watch, and reminding them urgently to bring up to date departmental plans for the transition to war. The decision would also have authorised the creation of a transition to war committee with responsibility to advise the cabinet on authorisation of the further precautionary steps the *War Book* laid out. But all this would have happened without any public announcement, or indeed any official statement in parliament. As the *War Book*, dated April 1962, states: 'The primary purpose of government in an international crisis must be to avert war, and they must take account of the danger that premature resort to dramatic preparatory measures or to actions (which although defensive in intent) would appear threatening to a potential enemy, might be misinterpreted, and so precipitate the outbreak of war.'[2]

The 1962 *War Book* justifies keeping the declaration of a 'precautionary stage' confidential by saying: 'The danger that action authorised by the government to prepare for war might lead the general public to the conclusion that war was inevitable and imminent could have unpredictable effects on public morale and on law and order.' Ministers and senior civil servants were very aware of the undesirability of disrupting the day to day life of the country except in the last resort. But as the Cuban Missile Crisis proved, the last resort could have been too late.

However, there were no such considerations about disrupting the lives of several thousand civil servants across Whitehall and key communications technicians from the GPO, the General Post Office which was responsible for telephone communications. The declaration by cabinet of a 'precautionary stage' would have resulted in these key government employees being warned they were required for service in the British Government's final redoubt, 'The Quarry' or as the *War Book* refers to it in the code of the time 'Burlington'. The secret of the extensive central government bunker at Corsham, in Wiltshire – during the Cold War one of the most closely protected *War Book* secrets of all – was not de-classified until 2004, although it is fairly certain the Soviet authorities knew of its location and existence well before the Cold War ended.

A whole chapter of the 1962 *War Book* sets out in precise detail what would have happened. It even provides examples of pre-printed forms which would have been issued to people to warn them – in far from clear terms – of their fate. The initial form those across Whitehall, whose names appeared on departmental lists, would have received, gave no clear details of the destination or the duties expected of the individual. Security demanded it should be shrouded in secrecy. Even though at this stage no public announcements would have been made by government, people would have been aware of a growing threat from a deteriorating international situation, so the instructions would have been daunting. 'You are one of a number of key personnel selected for duty at an important war-time head-quarters for the department. So far as anyone can say at the moment you may be there for about one month. You should return home, pick up the personal effects you wish to take with you, make whatever pay arrangements you wish and return immediately to this office. You should not reveal to anyone beyond your immediate family that you are going to the headquarters, and you should not be drawn into speculation about your future whereabouts. Your baggage will be subject to examination. You will not be allowed to take a wireless set or camera. Your baggage must be limited to one bag or suitcase which you can carry by hand. Clothing may be informal. Food cannot be provided on the journey, and you are advised to take something to eat such as chocolate or biscuits with you. As you will be away from your normal office and home for some time you will need to make arrangements for money for your family. If you complete the attached form your pay officer will deal with your salary as you direct. You will need only pocket money while you are away, but you will find it convenient to start off with a few pounds in your pocket to cover unforeseen needs on your journey. You may draw up to £25 now as advance payment of your salary or wages, and your pay officer will issue this sum against the authority of form "B" attached.'

With each prospective Burlington 'Bertie' by now wondering what fate he or she was destined for, the instructions ended: 'You will be able to communicate with your family by post, using the address BFPO 4000.'[3] Finally, with a bizarre twist, given the destination they were headed for and the grim circumstances that had precipitated it, the instructions ended: 'Facilities for entertainment will be limited. It is therefore suggested that you take a book or so with you.' Had these instructions ever been issued across Whitehall what personal concerns would have been raised that secrecy would have prohibited being answered? Would those receiving them have happily abandoned their families at such a time? And since the location and purpose of the mysterious 'headquarters' was a closely guarded secret known to very few at the top of government, there was no one who could explain where those selected would be going or why.

The *War Book* acknowledges the problems. 'It is impossible to forecast what conditions would be like in the precautionary stage: they might be anything from virtual normalcy to a high degree of panic and disorganisation ... We would not only have to man Burlington in a hurry, but also to do it without risking its security. It may get manned several days before an attack and within this period it would still be supremely important that its existence and whereabouts should not become known to the enemy.'[4]

Having been initially warned, collected their suitcase, and made their peace with their families, the future occupants of Burlington would have waited for the order to man the government's secret headquarters. The *War Book* reveals this would have been signalled by the use of the innocent sounding codeword 'Orangeade'! That was the code that would have enabled an identified civil servant in London to be put through to the caretaker staff at Burlington, with the warning that the British Government was about to move to its last bastion. At that point those chosen to staff it would have received their second information slip, marked very firmly 'Top Secret'.

'The location of the headquarters and the check-point through which you will pass are of the utmost secrecy and must not be revealed to anyone at all during or after the emergency. It is also most important that your journey to the headquarters and that of the others with whom you will travel should be as inconspicuous as possible and you are asked to co-operate by doing everything you can to ensure this.'[5]

The instructions then provided details of eight pick-up points around London where buses would convey them to a designated station. 'To avoid attracting unnecessary attention staff should, so far as possible, not carry their luggage from their offices through the street to pick-up points. Departments should use their own transport to convey luggage.'[6]

The station London staff were headed for was Kensington Olympia, adjacent to the Olympia Exhibition Centre. From there, though they would not know it until they were on their journey, special trains would take them west to Warminster. From Warminster, buses would ferry them to an army base on the edge of Salisbury Plain. Then the Burlington 'Berties' would be taken inconspicuously by army lorry up the country roads and lanes to Corsham to descend underground into their new home and workplace. They would hardly have found the Spartan accommodation waiting for them a comfortable 'home from home'. Its purpose and probable final fate is summed up in a doom-laden piece of graffiti scrawled on the wall near the entry to the Burlington bunker which reads gloomily 'Stuck Here 4 Eternity'!

Those civil servants not selected for duty in the supposed security of the quarry at Burlington were not let off the hook. According to *War Book* instructions they were to be informed they were expected to continue to work normally. If after an attack their normal place of work was inaccessible or destroyed, they would be expected to report to the nearest employment exchange 'in order that they may be called to duty as required!'[7] Quite a tall order when the country is under threat of nuclear bombardment and you have a wife and children at home in fear of their lives.

The Burlington bunker was massive. It was literally a Cold War city covering some thirty-four acres underground. Supposedly blast proof, but almost certainly not proof against a thermo-nuclear direct hit or close by, it was completely self-sufficient and able to accommodate as many as 4,000 people in total isolation for up to three months. It was equipped with all the facilities to keep its occupants catered for, from medical facilities to canteens, dormitories, laundries, and from offices to food stockpiles and supplies. An underground lake and treatment plant provided all the drinking water that would be required, and storage tanks held sufficient fuel to keep four generators running in Burlington's own power station for at least three months. The bunker was equipped with the second largest telephone exchange in Britain and with a BBC studio from which the Prime Minister could address what was left of the nation following a nuclear attack.

There was private accommodation for the Prime Minister and his close advisers and colleagues.

Burlington was cavernous, surrounded by 100 foot deep reinforced concrete walls inside a subterranean 240 acre limestone quarry which had once produced Bath stone. During the Second World War part of the area known as Spring Quarry housed an underground aircraft engine factory. Planning for Burlington did not start until 1957 and it was not ready for occupation until 1961, about a year before the Cuban crisis.

Steve Boggan, a *Guardian* journalist was given a guided tour of the declassified bunker in 2007 and described the underground scene as he witnessed it then:[8] 'Burlington is divided into twenty-four areas branching off concrete routes with names like West Main Road and North West Ring Road. There are vast stores with chairs still wrapped in brown paper, crates of loo rolls, mountains of stationery – some bearing the words "top secret", and thousands of chunky black telephones from the 1960s still in dusty cardboard boxes.'

'There are pots, pan scrubs, stacks of beds, and row upon row of dour metal wardrobes that would have filled dormitories where civil servants, typists, telephonists and maintenance workers would have lain, wondering what had become of their families above.'

'On an electric buggy that would not look out of place in the lair of a James Bond villain, Andy Quinn, the complex manager takes me to visit the bunker's hospital in area ten, where limestone is painted pastel green and pale yellow. There are canteens with cups and saucers that have never been used. Ornate coffee machines, still bearing their labels, sit, still shining, in a troglodytic cafe.'

'In area six is an industrial-sized bakery. In area sixteen, a BBC broadcasting studio. In area twenty-one, five communication centres for the intelligence services. In area eight, off East Main Road, is the communications centre run by the civilians of the GPO – the nationalised General Post Office – where bank upon bank of telephone exchanges stand like dominoes waiting to be pushed over.'

'There are enormous kitchens with squat iron stoves, labels still on their control buttons, walk-in fridges and row upon row of knives.'

'And at the centre of it, like the lair of a queen bee in a hive, is area seventeen, with its smaller rooms, bricked from floor to ceiling. Here there are buttons on the walls to summon staff and what appears to be an en-suite bedroom, the only one in the complex. No one knows for sure, but the assumption is that this is where the Prime Minister would stay. There was no provision for his family.'

This was where Harold Macmillan would have taken the core of the British Government had the Cuban crisis escalated further and the cabinet that Sunday afternoon had triggered the precautionary stage of the government's *War Book*.

The 1962 *War Book* recognised that with the advent of strategic missiles, there was the possibility that a potential enemy might launch a full-scale attack on the UK without any readily detectable preparation – the 'nightmare' scenario. 'We might thus (if the attack were to be launched at a time when there had been no obvious worsening of the international situation to put us on guard) have very little time – probably less than an hour – to make preparations,' the war planners noted. But they felt that 'a more likely hypothesis is that an attack on this country would be preceded by a period of progressive deterioration in the international situation – at some point in which it would become apparent that global war was an imminent possibility.'[9]

The Cuban crisis fell somewhere between the two; it appears to have left the Prime Minister, his colleagues and senior civil servants wrong footed and in something of a dilemma in their apparent reluctance to initiate any of the *War Book* stages until almost the last minute. In the event no 'precautionary stage' was called. There was no request from the Prime Minister to the chiefs of staff to bring the armed forces to a state of readiness in any but the most covert fashion, or for Burlington to be prepared. If Sir Norman Brook, the Cabinet Secretary and a man well-versed in the step by step guidance contained in the government's *War Book* had not been off ill at the time of the crisis it is possible that his advice might have steered Macmillan earlier onto the path the *War Book* advised. Had Khrushchev and Kennedy not reached an agreement, it may well have been too late on that crucial weekend for the cabinet to be called to institute the necessary steps to protect the country. That, of course, remains speculation; but what is not speculation is that after the crisis was over, Macmillan did have second thoughts, which is why he quite rapidly called for a post-Cuba review and a need for more flexibility in the *War Book*'s implementation.

The 1962 *War Book* indicated that after the establishment of a precautionary stage, as well as triggering the manning of the government's central bunker, it would also require consultation between the Prime Minister and the Home Secretary on the appointment of regional commissioners and their deputies – so that steps to activate the twelve regional seats of government could also be implemented. Regional commissioners would have been either ministers or persons of ministerial rank. Warrants of their appointment would have had to be submitted to the Queen for signature, so however dire the circumstances, the convention of adhering to the constitution was to be retained. What that would have meant to the safety of the head of state is never referred to in the plans.

The government *War Book* was certainly a comprehensive manual. Its many chapters cover in fine detail the process that virtually every department of government across Whitehall would have been required to undertake, as it prepared the country to face nuclear war. From the stock-piling and distribution of food, to the protection of water supplies, the preparation of medical and hospital services, civil defence, communications, it is all there. And one of the puzzling aspects of Macmillan's apparent rejection of this mass of intensive pre-planning during the Cuban crisis, is that just a month before the crisis broke, the entire *War Book* had been rehearsed in a paper-exercise conducted throughout Whitehall under the code-name Exercise Felstead. The rehearsal took place between 12 and 21 September 1962 and coincided with a large scale NATO exercise, Fallex, which was designed to test policies, plans and procedures for the transition to and conduct of nuclear war.[10] It was as part of Fallex that the V-Force and the Thor squadrons had been placed on full alert in the Micky Finn exercise across Bomber Command on 20 and 21 September. The *War Book* exercise was conducted at civil service level – the principals, Prime Minister, ministers, and chiefs of staff were not involved. Nevertheless, from the substantial reports of the lessons learned, which came in from every government department, it was regarded as a useful test of the *War Book*'s guidance. It seems strange, therefore, that when a real crisis, which might well have led to global war, surfaced less than a month later, all the guidance contained in the *War Book*, appears to have been sidelined.

Notes

1. PRO, CAB 175/3 Government *War Book* Volumes 1 & 2, April 1962.
2. Ibid.
3. Ibid.
4. Ibid: Chapter on Manning of Burlington.
5. Ibid.
6. Ibid.
7. PRO, CAB 175/13 Departmental Reports on Exercise Felstead.
8. *The Guardian*, 5 February 2007.
9. PRO, CAB 175/3.
10. PRO, CAB 175/13.

Chapter 13

Britain's 'Gods' of War

In the last resort to authorise on his own responsibility, retaliation by all means at his disposal.

Instructions to Commander in Chief, Bomber Command, 1962 government *War Book*, Appendix 'Z'

The British nuclear deterrent, poised at its highest alert of the Cold War, that weekend in October 1962, represented a considerable threat to the Soviet Union. One only has to look at the numbers of weapons lined up on each side of the Iron Curtain in 1962, to appreciate just how significant the British strike force was. The horrific manifest of nuclear destructive power says it all. The UK had no inter-continental ballistic missiles in its armoury – we had no need to reach distant targets half way across the world. The threat to the UK was closer to home. The Americans possessed 172 ICBMs (Atlas, Titan and Minuteman rockets) and they were manufacturing more as fast as the weapons industry could produce them; the USSR had only around twenty-four operational ICBMs, although Khrushchev boasted that he had many more. The UK had sixty American intermediate missiles based in England, the Thors under a dual-key agreement with the American Government, and the Americans had forty-five Jupiter missiles under similar dual-key arrangements on launch pads in Turkey and Italy. The USSR had significant numbers of intermediate and medium range missiles. America had 112 submarine based missiles, compared to ninety-seven in the USSR's fleet. In October 1962 the UK had none – the time when the UK would rely on submarine based missiles for its defence was yet to come. As far as long-range nuclear bombers were concerned, the Americans controlled a formidable fleet of 1,450 (B-47s and B-52s) many stationed at forward bases in the UK. During the crisis they deployed additional medium range B-47s to bases in the UK and in Spain to give them shorter-range advantage. The UK had the British V-Force of just over 140 aircraft, and the USSR had 155 operational nuclear bombers.[1]

Had the Cuban crisis resulted in a nuclear exchange, the British would have provided a significant element of any nuclear attack on the USSR, assuming the UK military got its strike away early enough. The Soviet Union would have had to deliver a massive blow against the UK to counter the severe attack it could expect to suffer from the British nuclear deterrent. It was this factor that would have ensured Britain would have rapidly been drawn into nuclear conflict over Cuba, whether we liked it or not, or whether or not we felt the issue was sufficiently crucial to risk a global war that would threaten human life across the planet. It was also the factor that might logically have persuaded Khrushchev that his best defence was a 'bolt from the blue' first strike against the UK – a nightmare scenario that weighed heavily with Macmillan, the British chiefs of staff, and those civil servants deep in Whitehall who had the task of planning national survival. Conversely, the terrible consequences to the USSR from UK based nuclear weapons so relatively close to the Russian homeland, if the Soviets engaged in nuclear war, obviously could not be ignored by the Soviet leaders as they wrestled with the arguments between diplomatic and military solutions to the Cuban crisis. In the six years of the Second World War the combined allied bomber forces dropped more than two million tons of bombs on Germany, devastating virtually every major town and industrial complex from the Rhine to Berlin and from the Baltic to the Swiss border. In 1962 Bomber Command on its own could have delivered the equivalent of 230 million tons in just a single raid: a terrible statistic to contemplate.

The V-Force in October 1962[2] consisted of twenty-two front-line bomber squadrons divided between two groups. No. 1 Group, with headquarters at RAF Bawtry controlled eight Vulcan squadrons based at RAF Waddington, RAF Scampton and RAF Coningsby. No. 3 Group, with its headquarters at RAF Mildenhall, consisted of six Victor squadrons based at RAF Cottesmore, RAF Honington and RAF Wittering. In addition there were three Valiant squadrons based at RAF Marham which were armed with American nuclear weapons under dual key arrangements, the so-called Project E agreement, assigned to operational control of the supreme allied commander Europe.

All these squadrons were supported by a number of specialist squadrons. At RAF Finningley, a squadron of Valiants was fitted out for a counter electronic measures role. Another squadron of Valiants based at RAF Honington fulfilled a tanker role, and similarly a further squadron of Valiants undertook a tanker role based at RAF Marham. Two squadrons of Canberras and one of Valiants undertook specialist reconnaissance missions from RAF Wyton. At any one time Bomber Command reckoned to be able to muster approximately 120 aircraft carrying nuclear weapons, allowing for some aircraft on routine maintenance or on detachment abroad.

Routinely, in peacetime, around the clock under the quick reaction alert programme, in October 1962, Bomber Command had sixty-eight nuclear weapons systems permanently armed and held at fifteen minutes readiness. They consisted of fifty-four Thor strategic ballistic missiles and fourteen V-bombers. Readiness State 'One-Five' – fifteen minutes – could rapidly be increased to 'Zero-Five', which meant cockpit readiness, five minutes from take-off. 'Zero-Five' could be held for up to four hours. The next escalation to 'Zero-Two' called for the starting of engines and taxing to take-off positions to await further instructions.

Recollections of former V-bomber crew, and of Marshal of the Royal Air Force, Sir Michael Beetham who was in the Bomber Command headquarters operations room during the crisis, indicate that over the weekend of 27 and 28 October a proportion of aircraft were ordered to 'Zero-Five' readiness. The operational record books of the two bomber groups also show that there was rapid generation of armed aircraft, and a marked increase in the number of aircraft fitted with nuclear weapons and ready for take-off.

But Soviet missiles and bombs targeted on cities and military facilities in the UK were equally horrifying to envisage. The planners in Whitehall listed the probable targets and the weapons likely to be targeted on them in an alarming and highly secret paper sent to government in 1967. Entitled 'Probable Nuclear Targets in the United Kingdom: Assumptions for Planning'.[3] It envisaged eight, one megaton missile air bursts over London plus two, 2,500 kiloton ones delivered by aircraft. The civil servants and scientists contemplating a Third World War forecast that seventeen other major UK cities would each be hit by two, one megaton missile air bursts and two, 2,500 kiloton nuclear bombs. Glasgow, Birmingham and Liverpool it was thought would each be destined to suffer four missile and two aircraft attacks, and the planners identified between sixty-five and seventy military targets they expected to feature on the Soviet attack lists. These included all the V-Force bases, the missile launch pads, all the American bases in the UK, and all the control and communications centres. It is probable that the Soviet targeting would have been very similar at the time of Cuba. Survival of anything was hard to imagine in the long dark nuclear winter which would follow such a blitz.

From November 1957 RAF Bomber Command and America's Strategic Air Command had agreed to work together to produce a fully integrated target policy. From joint RAF/USAF discussions it was clear that by pursuing separate strategies the two air forces would reduce their joint impact, because each planned to strike many of the same targets. A strategy was agreed which would maximise the strike forces available to the two commands, taking into account the RAF's ability to be on target first in the initial wave of bombing, several hours before the main Strategic Air Command aircraft could reach targets in the Soviet Union and Warsaw Pact countries from their home bases in the US. The joint plan also took into account the fleet of nuclear-armed American aircraft operating from UK bases.

A confidential memorandum from the chief of the air staff summed up the RAF's share of targets: 'Under the combined plan, the total strategic air forces disposed by the Allies are sufficient to cover all Soviet targets, including airfields and air defences. Bomber Command's contribution has been given as ninety-two aircraft by October 1958, increasing to 108 by June 1959; 106 targets have been allocated as follows: sixty-nine cities, which are centres of government or of other military significance; seventeen long-range air force airfields which constitute part of the nuclear threat, and twenty elements of the Soviet air defence system. It is intended that a third meeting will be held this month to co-ordinate the actual routes, timing and tactics of the aircraft attacking the targets selected. Full tactical co-ordination of operations will thus be achieved. In addition to the co-ordination of war plans, Bomber Command and SAC are also studying such measures as the use of each other's bases, the integration of intelligence, warning, and post strike recovery. Arrangements have also been agreed between the RAF and USAF to co-ordinate the Thor strike capability as this becomes effective. This, of course, is particularly important in view of the very short time of flight of these weapons.'[4]

From January 1962 Bomber Command introduced its quick reaction alert programme. One V-bomber per squadron was always standing by on QRA. That meant, in total, fifteen aircraft were permanently on fifteen minutes readiness or less, to take off fully armed with nuclear weapons. Also four RAF Valiants were permanently at fifteen minutes readiness at RAF Marham in Norfolk, attached to squadrons assigned to the supreme allied commander Europe. On the twenty Thor missile bases in eastern England a proportion of the Thor force worked on a similar readiness footing round the clock 365 days a year. That gave a total of sixty-nine nuclear weapons systems always at the very highest point of readiness on UK RAF bases, ready for launch when the Prime Minister pressed the 'nuclear button'. In the words of Air Marshal Sir Kenneth Cross, Commander in Chief of Bomber Command, the

124

introduction of QRA changed the relationship between his command and the American Strategic Air Command, from 'one of co-operation to one of integration'. It reinforced the morale of the operating crews and staffs throughout his command.

For the V-bomber squadrons QRA meant adopting a whole new routine. Crews on QRA ate and slept close to their aircraft. Each crew had a war bag, or go-bag, which contained the details of their target, their route, their tactics and intelligence on Soviet air defences. A considerable part of the crews' time was spent on target studies and learning in minute detail the planned approach and exit strategy, to ensure that if the order was given 'for real' they were thoroughly prepared. There was little else to do, while on fifteen minutes readiness, than eat, sleep, do target study and rehearse safety and escape drills. If the alert of an in-coming Soviet attack had been given, take-off would have been swift and automatic. Once the aircraft reached the 'Go/No-go' line over Norway the last order the crew would have received would have been a command signal from the Bomber Command headquarters bunker giving them authorisation to proceed. This would have taken the form of a coded message which three members of the crew had to verify independently of one another. The V-bomber crews knew that their role was to deliver their weapons with little hope of returning to their homes and families. Indeed it was debatable whether there would be any airfield left in the UK to return to. Some crews considered their best hope of survival might be to conserve fuel by turning off two engines and pray they could reach British bases in the Mediterranean area or elsewhere.

Peter West, was an air electronics officer in the crew of the CO of a Vulcan Squadron based at Coningsby in Lincolnshire at the time of the Cuban crisis. He recalled, as he and his colleagues were ordered to quick reaction alert under alert three, 'a not unnatural feeling of tension. We knew with certainty that should the policy of deterrence fail, then not only would we almost certainly not survive (our chances of getting back in one piece were assessed at only twenty per cent) but more importantly our wives and children would also be dead, as the airfields were high-priority targets for Soviet attack'.[5]

The British system of QRA was different from the Americans. A proportion of their nuclear-armed bombers was always in the air maintaining a vigil around the clock. V-bombers could not carry a second crew, as the American aircraft did, so long hours airborne, kept aloft by regular re-fuelling, was impractical for the RAF. Trials at RAF Waddington aimed at retaining a credible airborne deterrent by changing over aircraft every six hours, also proved to be impossible to sustain. The only realistic solution for Britain's V-Force was the QRA concept. It was improved upon with the introduction of on-line tele-talk communications from the Bomber Command controller at HQ, direct to the crews in the cockpit, and by modification of air-craft to allow simultaneous four-engine starts. This reduced the time from the order to 'scramble' and being airborne, to four minutes, the anticipated maximum warning time of a missile attack once the American ballistic missile early warning system became operational in the UK in 1963. In time of tension, as during the Cuban crisis, in theory the whole V-Force could be airborne within this timescale. QRA became the most prominent feature in the day-to-day existence of the V-Force crews. At the time of the Cuban crisis, when QRA was ordered on a much wider basis than normal and crews were well aware that this time it was 'for real', the nerve racking routine of being available for take-off for war at any minute built tensions well beyond the strains of routine training exercises.

The Thor ballistic missiles sitting on launch pads in the east of England, nominally with a range of 1,500 nautical miles, were capable of hitting sixty-four of the 131 city targets in the Soviet Union con-sidered to be the most important from a strategic point of view. These included Moscow, at a range of 1,350 nautical miles. The ambition was to increase Thor's range to 2,000 nautical miles or more by technical modifications, at which point the missile would be able to strike at 100 per cent of the targets considered the most strategic.[6] Each missile had two alternative targets allocated to it, and the crew had to be able to alter a target setting in five minutes. A third 'target of opportunity' was available to be entered if the order was given, but this took longer to feed into the guidance system. Targets were related to the pre-set angle at which the launch pad was orientated and the missile was aimed using two short–range electro-theodolites mounted inside the missile shelter when the rocket was horizontal. When it was erect for launch, aiming was maintained through the long-range theodolite housed in a small brick building some 400 feet from the launch pad. Unlike crew of the V-bombers, none of the RAF launch crew knew the target their missile was aimed at. Nor indeed was the group captain in charge of each complex of fifteen missiles aware of the destination of the missile's under his command. One group captain commented: 'It was not politically a good idea we should know.'[7]

All the RAF's nuclear targets were decided by the Joint Strategic Planning Staff based at Offutt Air Force Base in Omaha, a unit with representatives of the Strategic Air Command, the RAF and NATO.

Their targeting plan was known, with the Americans' fondness for initials, as the Strategic Integrated Operational Plan, or simply SIOP. There was a separate target list for the V-Force in the extremely unlikely event that Britain's deterrent was to be used entirely independently, in other words to defend the UK's vital national interests where neither America nor NATO were involved. This included strategic targets of such distance from UK bases that crews would have little or no chance of return. These one-way missions were real, studied by the crews and exercised in the same way as the SIOP targets. It was politically important that the UK could claim to have a totally independent nuclear deterrent, but as Cuba showed, in the Cold War there was little chance of Britain either being in a position of operating its nuclear deterrent in isolation, or not being drawn into a nuclear conflict even when the epicentre was as distant as it was in the Cuban crisis.

While Britain's Prime Minister and his close colleagues, service chiefs and special advisers would have been accommodated in hardened but vulnerable bunkers, as it seems they came close to doing on that Sunday in October 1962, the American command and control plan was rather more secure. America ensured its capability to survive a nuclear attack, and then respond and sustain a nuclear war, by putting its top commanders in airborne war control centres. This strategy was introduced in 1961 and given the odd code name of 'Silk Purse'. In the early sixties the United States had seven such units available at bases around the world, with at least one airborne twenty-four hours a day. The 'Silk Purse' flying command posts had direct communications with all parts of the US nuclear arsenal, their bases in the UK, and were in constant touch with the President himself.

There was, however, a very closely guarded UK secret fall-back process in the event that neither the British Prime Minister nor either of his deputies authorised to sanction nuclear retaliation, could be reached. It was contained in a highly restricted annexe to the 1962 government *War Book*, annex Z, circulated to a very few senior ministers, civil servants and high level military commanders.[8] Headlined 'Action to be taken should the country be attacked with nuclear weapons before Bomber Command has received instructions to retaliate', it instructs the air officer in chief of Bomber Command to:

1. If not already done, order all bombers to become airborne under positive control.
2. If unable to obtain instructions from the Prime Minister or his deputy in London or Burlington, confer with the nominated

127

United States commander to ascertain what instructions he has received and to obtain the release of nuclear weapons under joint control.

3. In the last resort, to authorise on his own responsibility retaliation by all means at his disposal.

So as a final position, if the UK was under nuclear attack and ministerial authorisation could not be obtained, the *War Book* explicitly provided for a solely military decision to launch Britain's nuclear retaliation. It placed huge responsibility on the shoulders of an air marshal some way below the level of the chiefs of staff to whom, nominally, he was answerable. But given the realities of the Cold War threat, particularly in the early 1960s, this was a practical acknowledgement that such a situation could arise, where a 'bolt from the blue' negated all the careful planning of the transition to war scenarios.

Notes

1. Len Scott: *Kennedy, Macmillan, and the Cuban Missile Crisis*, p. 190.
2. RAF Historical Society Journal 42, 'RAF Bomber Command and the Cuban Missile Crisis', Clive Richards.
3. PRO, DEFE 4/224 'Probable Nuclear Targets in the United Kingdom: Assumptions for Planning', 11 February 1967.
4. Chiefs of air staff's memorandum following joint RAF/USAF meetings, 14–16 November 1957.
5. Email exchange with author, April 2007.
6. John Boyes: *Project Emily: Thor IRBM and the RAF*, Tempus Publishing 2008, Appendix, p. 116.
7. *Launch Pad UK: Britain and the Cuban Missile Crisis*, p. 116 (Interview with Group Captain, Kenneth Pugh AFC, 2007).
8. PRO, CAB 175/3 Government *War Book* 1962, Vols 1 & 2.

Chapter 14

Looking Back

Cuba was certainly a very traumatic experience for those involved, but strangely enough the rest of the nation seemed to be quite unaware there was a crisis at all.

Marshal of the Royal Air Force, Sir Michael Beetham, in 1962 Group Captain Operations at Bomber Command Headquarters

From me downwards everything worked perfectly. From me upwards, nothing worked at all

Air Marshal Sir Kenneth Cross, Commander in Chief Bomber Command, 1962

The general public in the UK may not have realised how terrifyingly close the UK was to nuclear conflict during that weekend in October 1962, but those who had trained extensively to launch the British nuclear deterrent, remember the hours and days of tension all too well.

Jim Giblen was a Flying Officer AEO (Air Electronics Officer) with 27 Squadron based at RAF Scampton. He recalls sitting in the back of a Vulcan on Black Saturday, after Bomber Command had issued its alert three, with a live nuclear bomb in the bomb bay, engines running, waiting at five minutes readiness, for orders on the hot line from the bomber controller. 'I do not remember how long we were at this readiness state, but it would not have been long as we were fuel critical for the mission. We had insufficient fuel to return to the UK and planned to recover to Cyprus after the strike. Considering that we would not get to Cyprus until some six hours after general alert, I imagine that all we would have found where Cyprus used to be would have been an area of disturbed water!'[1]

Jim Giblen remembers the readiness state eventually being relaxed and he and his colleagues leaving the aircraft with much relief.

Flight Lieutenant Ray Dodkin was a radar navigator, with responsibility for the nuclear weapons, in a Victor crew of 139 Squadron based at RAF Wittering. On Saturday, 27 October, when the alert three was ordered, all crews were recalled to the station, briefed and issued with their war target folders. All available aircraft were serviced, fuelled, armed and moved to dispersals as close to the take-off point as possible. All crews were in flying kit at fifteen minutes readiness, and those allocated to QRA (Quick Readiness Alert) were with their aircraft.

'On Sunday, 28 October, all available aircraft were armed, some sixteen in all if my memory is correct, and crews were allocated to specific airframes. At various times of the day and evening, crews were brought to cockpit readiness for a fast engine start. At this point most people thought they would be on a mission of "no return" if the order to scramble was given.'[2]

'Knowledge of the progress of the crisis was obtained from watching TV, plus certain information given at briefings. However, I believe that our families, and the general public, thought that we were on a NATO exercise. The overall sense of calm was unreal.'

At the time of the crisis some aircraft of the V-Force were in Malta on annual exercise in the Mediterranean theatre. Having carried out a simulated attack on RAF Akrotiri, Cyprus, eight Vulcans from 50 Squadron, normally based at RAF Waddington, flew to RAF Luqa in Malta for a ten day exercise. Mike Pharaoh was pilot of one of the Vulcans. 'On 28 October', he recalled, 'I was the 50 Squadron duty officer. The rest of the squadron were having a party in the "Gut" in down-town Valetta. At about 21.00 hours I was handed a signal from No. 1 Group in Bawtry with the code-name "Whitecliffs" in it. When I checked the meaning of the code I was horrified as it was an immediate recall of all aircraft and crews, but most of the aircrew and ground-crew, apart from a handful of duty personnel were in the "Gut" many miles away and having a party!'[3]

'I went into town in the squadron land-rover and found personnel of all ranks all fairly intoxicated as I expected. It was not an easy job trying to convince them that they had to return to base immediately in the coaches provided, to get ready for flights back to the UK the following morning. By some miracle all the aircraft left RAF Lucqa on schedule and I was probably the only pilot without a hangover for the four hour flight to RAF Waddington!' Of course, by the time the crews landed back at their home station, Khrushchev had 'climbed down' and the tensions had been lowered. Nevertheless the V-Force remained at alert three with a proportion of the V-Force on quick reaction alert.

Barry Davies was an armourer on Vulcans. He had only completed his training some six months earlier. At the time of the Cuban crisis he was detached to RAF Waddington to complete the Bomber Command Vulcan servicing course for his trade. He recalls the hooter went off in the early hours of the morning and a tannoy message gave the signal for all aircraft to be made ready and armed. 'We grabbed our clothes and dressed as we ran to the armoury. The whole station appeared to be racing to their sections. On arrival we were immediately put into aircraft loading teams, even though we had not trained as teams. We were shipped out to the airfield and told to start loading the weapons as soon as they were delivered and the aircraft was cleared by the crew chief as serviceable. The nuclear weapons were being shuttled out to each aircraft and left nearby with an armed RAF policeman on guard. Each team just went from aircraft to aircraft loading the "beasties" as fast as possible with due regard for the safety aspects. The armament officer was supervising and flitting from team to team like a scalded cat. After my team had loaded six or seven weapons, and the majority of the aircraft on the station were armed and ready for Armageddon, we were taken back to the armoury for a meal and some sleep. Just sitting around until we knew what was going on. Time meant little as we were exhausted from physical and nervous exhaustion. I think we achieved a record for generating aircraft ready to go that was never beaten! During my service, nothing compares to the sense of purpose around that day.'[4]

It was the same sense of purpose and tension that was felt at the Thor ballistic missile launch sites manned by RAF crews on scattered and largely isolated bases down the east of England from Yorkshire to Suffolk. The twenty Thor missile launch sites, each accommodating three missiles, were grouped in four complexes, or wings, each made up of five squadrons. The CO of the Hemswell wing, the late Group Captain Roy Boast, recalled what happened when the alert three was called by Bomber Command with instructions that the move to a greatly enhanced operational readiness should be kept as covert as possible: 'I was advised by the air officer commanding group early on the Saturday morning, 27 October, that we were on stand-by for the "real thing".' The Thor missiles were routinely kept at a high state of alert and it would take just fifteen minutes to have brought them all to the point at which they could have been launched.

At another Thor launch site, a launch-control officer, the person whose action in turning the war key would have launched the nuclear tipped rocket, reflected 'We did very little, but we thought a lot.'

A member of a launch crew based at North Pickenham in Norfolk, one of the Thor missile bases in the Feltwell strategic missile complex, recalls: 'I was allocated to pad thirteen (lucky for some!). After carrying out initial checks on our missile like all the other pads, we carried out a countdown to the end of phase two, which in effect checked out all the basic systems. We retracted the shelter in which the missile was housed, erected it on its launch mount securely locked it in place. It was now vertical to a height of nearly seventy feet. At this point the countdown was put on hold. The only thing left to do was to fuel the missile, which would take approximately three minutes and from then on she would be ready to launch. After carrying out a further check on the targeting of the missile, we retired to the electrical equipment trailer, from where we could monitor the power systems and carry out retargeting if called upon to do so. At frequent intervals further checks were undertaken on pneumatic and hydraulic systems housed in various trailers around the launch pad. I seem to remember a calmness about it all, with everyone doing their duties in an air of normality which belied the seriousness of our situation.'[5]

A memorandum to Air Marshal, Sir Kenneth Cross, in May 1960 set out how the V-Force and Bomber Command's other lethal component the Thor force would be co-ordinated in operational conditions – the situation that developed as the command went to alert three during the critical weekend of the crisis.

'The Air Ministry now have under urgent consideration the steps which are required to bring the political machinery into line with the readiness of the weapon,' the memorandum stated. 'It is considered, however, that when the V-Force are despatched on 'positive control missions' the Thor force should be brought to T-8 (eight minutes to firing) and should current research and development studies prove it to be practicable, a proportion of the force should be brought to T-2 (two minutes from firing and loaded with fuel). There is in fact no difference in the problems with the two forces; when the decision is made not to recall the manned bombers, we must simultaneously commit the Thor force. It is one and the same decision.'

The RAF missile launch crews, unlike their counterparts manning the V-bombers, were unaware of the actual targets their missiles were aimed at. Squadron Leader, Frank Leatherdale, who was CO at RAF North Pickenham in Norfolk, and had flown many bomber raids during the Second World War, felt there were several strange psychological issues commanding a Thor squadron.

'Not least of these was not knowing your target. During the war I had been used to being well briefed on precisely what our target was and why we were attacking it; but with missiles, all you knew was a series of digits which had to be fed into the inertial guidance system very accurately and which had to be checked and re-checked several times a day. The checking was always done by the on-coming and off-going flight commanders together at every shift change, and was also done by other specialist personnel at other times in between. Another odd feeling we had was that we were working all the time to perfect our technique, but if ever we had to launch this deterrent weapon we knew we would have failed in our primary duty. Of course, being responsible for the safety of three nuclear warheads and all the expensive technical equipment was a continual mental burden. But I was not alone, for while I held ultimate responsibility I had very good support from my flight commanders, and they in turn were supported by their men. If ever the words "a team effort" meant anything, they certainly did in a Thor squadron. Our watchword was continual vigilance and strict adherence to the check lists and manuals at all times.'[6]

Squadron Leader, Bill Young, in command of the Shepherd's Grove launch pads in Suffolk, recalls the activity that October week-end. 'At the time of the Cuban crisis, all the missiles were brought to readiness and to save launch time, kept fuelled and "on hold" at the end of phase three of the launch process. This meant that the individual missile hangers were rolled back, the missile target system "captured", the launcher retracted, and liquid oxygen allowed to boil off through a safety valve. It would have taken only another two or three minutes to complete phases four and five, ending with ignition and lift-off. It was a very tense and nerve-racking time indeed. As the squadrons were only too well aware, the missile sites stretching from Suffolk to Yorkshire would be prime and essential targets in any "shooting war".'[7]

On the Thor bases a somewhat bizarre situation existed. The American USAF personnel responsible for the nuclear warheads, had been on a higher alert than the RAF launch crews responsible for firing the missiles if the order was given. The Americans had been ordered to DEFCON two with the rest of Strategic Air Command on Wednesday, 24 October. RAF Bomber Command did not issue its alert three until Saturday, 27 October. So for three days, those whose job it was to maintain and arm the Thor nuclear warheads, were on a considerably higher state of alert than those responsible for actually launching the missiles. It took two keys to arm and launch a Thor missile. One, carried by an American authentication officer, armed the weapon. The other, carried by an RAF officer, initiated the launch countdown. In a war situation it required the authority of both the President and the Prime Minister to authorise the arming and the launch. How smoothly such a complex procedure would have worked under conditions of war was mercifully never tested. The mechanics of it were of course routinely practised under exercise conditions which did not require the co-ordination at head of government level for official authorisation to press the button, or in this case turn the keys in the launch console. Normally the American authentication officers kept the war/peace key securely locked in a safe. After the DEFCON two order had been given, they wore it readily available on a chain round their necks. At all the Thor bases the nuclear warheads were stored solely under American control. No RAF personnel, however high-ranking, were allowed into the secure compounds in which the warheads were kept and maintained under armed guard.

A similar situation was in force at those RAF bases which fell under the control of the NATO supreme commander where American nuclear bombs were used on RAF V-bombers under an agreement known as Project E. The NATO Commander, General Lauris Norstad, after dining with Macmillan on the evening of 22 October, when the British Prime Minister urged on him not to order a full NATO alert because he feared overt provocative action would inflame the situation, gained President Kennedy's approval for NATO to move to an increased degree of vigilance short of full mobilisation. Norstad's directive to his subordinate commanders ended with the following caution: 'No measures will be taken which could be considered provocative or which might disclose operational plans. Actions should be taken without public notice if possible.' However, not all Norstad's commanders followed his orders to the letter. General Truman Landon, the Commander of United States Air Forces Europe (CINCUSAFE), while not imposing a formal DEFCON three state of readiness, did allow some of the features of such an alert to be implemented. He independently ordered a discreet increase in the overall capability of his forces to be effected in a gradual, unobtrusive way. Significantly, this included an increase in the number of nuclear-armed aircraft placed on quick reaction alert. It also called for them being loaded with high-yield thermonuclear weapons, in place of less destructive, lower-yield nuclear bombs. Some of these changes of the alert stance involved RAF V-bombers under NATO command at bases in East Anglia, notably RAF Marham in Norfolk. This prompted exceptional activity at the base. The American Mark 5 nuclear weapons were exclusively held under control of USAF personnel. US law insisted loading of American nuclear weapons had to be supervised by American officers, as was the case on the Thor missile bases. Normally this represented no particular problem. Whenever a Valiant of one of three RAF squadrons based at Marham under NATO control was armed and on fifteen minutes QRA, it was held in a secure compound and only released after the Americans had received an authenticated order on their own dedicated channels. However, during the missile crisis orders came through to arm all available aircraft. It was impossible with the relatively small number of Americans on the base to maintain the strict custody-and-control protocol demanded by US law. So the control of the weapons had to be handed over to the RAF base commander. A total of twenty-four Valiant bombers, each armed with two American nuclear weapons, were put under the effective control of Bomber Command, although legally the agreement between the US and UK governments meant they had to be regarded as still under the ownership of the USA.

Co-ordination of targets between RAF Bomber Command and the United States' Strategic Air Command appears to have extended to some cross-targeting involving F100 and F105 dual-capable aircraft (both bomber and fighter roles) of the American Tactical Fighter Wings based in East Anglia at Lakenheath, Bentwaters and Wethersfield, and the RAF's Thor missiles. According to a USAF NCO who served in the tactical alert section of the 48th Fighter Wing at Lakenheath, one pilot knew that he had to time his bombing run onto his target with extreme accuracy because he would be followed a minute later by a Thor missile aimed at the same area he was targeting. If he got the timing wrong he stood a good chance of being blown to bits by the Thor missile behind him. Another pilot was in an even more hazardous position. He was required to make his bombing run after one Thor and before another. The NCO recalled not surprisingly he was the pilot who appeared most nervous when on cockpit alert![8]

Peter West was a Flying Officer AEO serving with a Vulcan crew of 12 Squadron based at RAF Coningsby. He and his fellow crew members had formed up as a Vulcan crew only six months before the Cuban crisis. 'We were, I believe, a very competent, well motivated and happy bunch who from the start hit it off with one another. What we did not realise on forming up as a crew, an arbitrary procedure following the pattern of the Second World War bomber crews, was that each, came from a different Commonwealth country, as many of our 1939–45 forbears had done. Phil Largeson (pilot) was a South African who had flown with the South African Air Force as a bomber pilot during the Second World War; Cyril Parker (co-pilot) was a young New Zealander; Paul Berkley (navigator) was born in Melbourne, and although having spent the bulk of his life in England, still had an Australian passport; Gerry Taylor (navigator plotter) had come to us from the Royal Canadian Air Force having lived for five or six years in Canada, and I was the sole Briton, variously called Pommie Bastard and Limey!'[9]

'The Cuban missile crisis started, for us, with a call out from our homes one weekend evening in October – all of us lived either on the station or very nearby. Trained and ready to respond very quickly to any call-out, we assembled at "Ops" within a short time where we were briefed by senior staff, changed into flying kit and bussed out to the waiting aircraft. We had been warned that we would have to remain at readiness state fifteen, indefinitely, which meant that we would sleep and eat beside our aircraft. This was the first time that all of us on the three squadrons, 9, 11 and 35, were called to such a high state of readiness, and it was awesome to see all our aircraft "bombed up" with nuclear weapons. The bomb doors of each aircraft were left open so that the bombs could be attached to the "fish fryers". The "fish fryer" was an item of ground equipment which looked uncannily like frying machines in fish and chip shops, hence their sobriquet. The purpose of this gear was to keep the weapon primed and heated, an essential operation if they were loaded up with the aircraft ready to fly.'

'I should emphasise that we never flew with live nuclear weapons on board. These were only loaded for QRA or at a time of real crisis, and this was just such a time, indeed the only time it was believed to be necessary.'

'There was no tedium during our long wait. We were friends and there was plenty of banter, conversation and, when that faded, reading material. I can honestly say that I detected no fear or foreboding. This was not bravado or misplaced courage, simply that we all had total confidence in the policy of deterrence which we had discussed often. It was our belief then, and remains to this day, that provided we would not hesitate to retaliate in kind to any nuclear threat, these awful weapons would never have to be used. To illustrate this point, on the second day of stand-by, Paul and I were sitting together reading when he put down his newspaper, slowly rose from his seat, strolled over to the aircraft and, pulling a chinagraph pencil from his pocket, drew a large CND symbol on the side of the bomb. When he returned to his seat I asked him why on earth he had done this. His reply has remained with me over all of the intervening years: "If we drop 'the beast' those CND bastards were right." We never did have to drop "the beast", those CND bastards were wrong! You may have gathered from the foregoing that all of us considered that we had to combat two enemies. One was the recognisable and obvious opponent, the USSR. The other, more disturbing and disheartening was the CND movement.'

Peter West recalled that during the period of heightened alert he remembers being called to cockpit readiness on several occasions. 'At these times we had a not unnatural feeling of tension, but nothing serious. We knew with certainty that should the policy of deterrence fail, then not only we would almost certainly not survive (our chances of getting back in one piece were assessed as only twenty per cent) but more importantly our wives and children would be dead as the airfields were high priority targets for Soviet attack.'

'Each V-Bomber crew had a dedicated target throughout its tour of three years. The details of the targets were kept in a room at "Ops" called "The Vault" which was windowless, sealed and guarded by armed RAF police. The target details were kept in a special safe by a dedicated ops officer. Each crew member had his own target folder containing everything he needed to know. For example, as the AEO I needed to know the ground to air and air to air threats which I would have to combat with electronic warfare devices. Command and control was in the hands of the bomber controller at Headquarters Bomber Command. He was in radio contact with every crew. Nuclear release was a very tightly controlled system. Once one took off the aircraft headed for a "go, no-go" line on longitude prior to which an authorisation had to be received by Morse code and voice. This was a coded message and three members of the crew had each to verify it independently of one another. If the aircraft reached the "go, no-go" line without receiving the authorisation message then the aircraft returned to base. The system was as safe as was humanly possible.'[10]

The almost certain fate of wives and children, had the V-Force been launched to deliver retaliatory strikes, weighed heavily with V-bomber crews. Some arranged to leave cars for their families for them to make a dash for the relative safety of remoter parts of the UK, perhaps Wales, the Lake District or the west of Scotland.

At RAF Wittering the alert three was called as the station was celebrating the award of 'Freedom of the Town' granted by the nearby ancient town of Stamford. Ron Banks together with fellow officer Stan Blackwell were running the supplementary storage area on the base. On the Saturday morning they had both been involved in the 'freedom' parade through the town and were preparing to entertain the Mayor of Stamford and other civic guests in the officers' mess. Ron recalls that that afternoon his OC armament called round at his married quarters on base and asked his wife if he could have a quiet word with her husband. 'I took him into the dining room as the lounge was already occupied by my children. He explained that the Kennedy/Cuba face to face had reached crisis point, that command had ordered an alert and all aircraft were to be loaded with nukes reinforcing those few at QRA and already on stand-by. However, no general alert was to be sounded as we would have expected and only our airmen available on camp were to be used in strict secrecy so as to avoid possible civilian panic. My wife overheard some of the conversation and learned for the first time in two years what my actual job was – nursemaid to some twenty-odd nuclear bombs! She didn't panic.'[11]

'Stan and I went to the SSA where we found procedures already running smoothly under our stand-by team. All we had to do was a little supervision over a well drilled exercise and call in an extra few men to cope with the workload. Bombing up the aircraft went on smoothly through the rest of the day and night, albeit rather sombrely and with an air of apprehension. This was no exercise or "Micky Finn", but the real thing.'

'Meanwhile Stan and I took turns in the mess to entertain our Stamford guests, nipping back to the SSA occasionally to check all was well. Needless to say all other officers were going through similar drills in their own fields, ensuring maximum effort to get as many machines ready as possible. We were all on soft drinks, while the guests piled into the hard stuff! I must say I have never seen such a sober bunch at a mess party. We must have seemed cheerful enough, because weeks later I discovered that none of our guests ever suspected that anything unusual was going on – I doubt if they ever knew just how close to the brink it had gone.'

The routine system of QRA in the V-Force was that each squadron had to provide one aircraft on immediate standby round the clock. When the alert three was issued that situation was ratcheted up considerably, to a point where all serviceable aircraft and combat crews were involved. On QRA the aircraft were fitted with a rapid, simultaneous, four-engine start system called Simstart.

Ted Gregory an AEO on a Victor squadron based at RAF Honington in Suffolk recalls: 'On call out the ground crew would be at the aircraft first and have the electrical power connected. Once the crew were inside and had connected their intercom the crew chief, connected to intercom on an external lead, would initiate the Simstart. It always worked well, I remember, but on one frightening occasion it went badly wrong. One or more engines failed to ignite properly and we got a very wet start with burning fuel pouring onto the concrete beneath the aircraft. It was not a pleasant moment to be sitting on top of a pool of fire, strapped to an airframe containing a live "Red Beard" nuclear bomb. The attendant fire engine worked overtime!'[12]

Ted Gregory adds: 'My crew were on QRA on 22 October, 1962 at the time of the Cuban Missile Crisis. Early that evening on the TV news bulletin, we learned that President Kennedy would be making an important announcement to the American nation on TV and radio, and that the UK networks would be transmitting his speech live. We crowded into the TV room in the mess to see and hear it at the allotted time, and learned that there was a military blockade to intercept the Soviet Bloc ships approaching Cuba. To us it all sounded like the start of a Third World War. That night I went to bed in my flying kit fully expecting to be called to cockpit readiness for the real thing, or worse, getting airborne to attack. Somehow I slept, and was surprised to awake the following morning to find life going on as normal.'

But a great many RAF personnel within Bomber Command remember life was far from normal that crisis weekend. Brian Carlin was a Junior Tech Electrical Fitter at RAF Finningley working on Vulcan Mk B2s. Like others stationed at V-Force operational front-line bases, he was used to the fairly frequent tannoy broadcasts from Bomber Command headquarters at High Wycombe, announcing an immediate exercise, which brought the entire station to fifteen minutes readiness.

'On this occasion,' he wrote in a memoir of that crisis weekend:[13] 'the klaxon blared from the tannoy to notify all within earshot of the alert condition, but this time it was not preceded by the word "exercise". Instead, during the broadcast, the bomber controller specifically stated several times that "this is not an exercise". Nevertheless the well-practiced "Exercise Mick" procedures went into full swing, ordering all personnel to their place of duty. It involved about everyone on a bomber station. Aircraft servicing personnel, of course, commenced generating aircraft, but others had their roles to play. The service police increased the already tight security. The MT section mobilised for dispersal. Stores prepared for the task of issuing aircraft service parts. Even the catering staff made ready to ship out with the dispersed crews to man field kitchens at the dispersal airfields. Transport Command also got involved, by making their

Hercules aircraft immediately available to whisk ground crews and equipment to far-flung dispersal airfields.'

'Most people in the V-Force knew what to do when an alert was declared, but for yours truly, having only just arrived on an operational station a few weeks previously, this was my first experience of the station going to operational readiness. And wasn't it just my fantastic luck that, instead of it being an exercise, this was the real thing! On the first day I worked with others to help bring all aircraft up to full serviceability, at the same time being somewhat awe-struck at seeing armourers and riggers winching real nuclear weapons up into the Vulcan bomb bays. The nukes were massive, each filling the entire bomb bay of a Vulcan. We all knew that the flap had something to do with the Cuban missile situation but in typical service fashion no one was telling us anything.'

'By the end of the first day most aircraft had been "recovered", the first four of which were towed to the ORP – Operational Readiness Pan – a concrete apron adjoining the left-hand side of the runway at its extreme end, angled towards the runway for a rapid take-off. Very soon I joined them as a member of one of the starter ground crews. Typically, a Vulcan starter crew consisted of four or five erks, in addition to the crew chief. One ground crew member took up position at each main wheel to manhandle the heavy chocks, whilst the others dealt with disconnecting power cables from the ground power unit, and operating the Palouste starter trolley. For the duration of the alert we were housed in several caravans that had been towed to the ORP. Most of the caravans were divided into individual sleeping compartments containing bunk beds, except for one which was larger and served as an office/crew-room.'

'The question on everyone's mind was why weren't the aircraft being dispersed in keeping with the often practised strategy. Having all our V-bombers concentrated at a few stations made them (and us) sitting ducks for a first strike by the Russians. Many years later it was learned that Macmillan had deliberately ordered the air chiefs not to disperse the aircraft.'

'We remained at fifteen minute readiness all through the day, but on the following day the tannoy at the ORP crackled into life with the announcement, "this is the bomber controller, readiness condition zero-five, I repeat readiness condition zero-five". Chairs were knocked aside as we tumbled out of the crew room and ran to our assigned Vulcans in response to the newly announced five minute readiness condition. The crew chief was already there. He had opened the aircraft entrance hatch ready for the crew to climb inside. One of the engine lads fired up the Palouste, as the rest of us waited by our stations for the aircrew to arrive. Electrical power was already on to the aircraft as a condition of the prior fifteen minute readiness state. Within a few minutes four crew coaches came tearing around the peri-track, one behind the other, and heading in our direction. On reaching the ORP they split up and each made for an individual aircraft, screeching to a halt alongside the nose section. The folding doors of the coach were thrown open by a grim-faced crew member who then sprinted for the entrance hatch followed by his other four crew colleagues. The men quickly ascended into the bowels of the Vulcan crew compartment and shortly afterwards the AEO started the auxiliary power unit (APU) from his position on the port side of the crew compartment. The APU was used to rapidly start the engines, almost simultaneously, in the event that the readiness state was ratcheted up to the next level, which would have been zero-two – start engines. At that point we would be moments away from launching the aircraft on a one-way trip to Russia.'

'The crew chief signalled for the ground crew manning the external twenty-four volt and 200 volt ground power cables to pull them out of the sockets that connected the electrical power to the aircraft. He also indicated that the Palouste be shut down, disconnected and moved out of the way. The Vulcan was now independent of ground power and capable of starting its own engines from compressed air supplied by the APU. Meanwhile, those of us standing by the chocks watched the crew chief's every move, since an engine start would have also been accompanied by the "chocks away" hand signal. The moment was tense, but all thoughts of the seriousness of the situation were distant as we concentrated on doing our jobs. The question of what would happen afterwards, should the Vulcans take off, was hardly dwelt upon. In fact no one had told us what we should do afterwards. As a 21 year old, I was imbued with the strong sense of immortality common to most young people, and had no doubts about coming through unscathed whatever happened. In retrospect, I wonder what actually would have happened, and just hope that there was some kind of contingency plan to get everyone remaining behind into some form of shelter, perhaps the hardened bunkers where the nuclear weapons had, until very recently, been stored.'

'Although an attack on the station, after the Vulcans had departed, had to be futile from the Russian strategic point of view, it was a very real possibility in the fog of war. As for the Vulcans, the aircrew had their standing orders that after delivering their weapons on their target, they were on their own. Chances were that there would be no

141

base to return to, so they should seek a safe haven wherever they could find it.'

'We stood underneath the Vulcan for what seemed an eternity, and then suddenly the crew chief indicated that ground power should be restored. The Vulcan crew door unlatched and swung downwards in readiness for the crew to de-plane. A visible look of relief swept over us – we were back to fifteen minutes readiness. No one there was in any position to know if and when the alert level would increase again.'

'Looking back, it seems more frightening that we all came so close to be wiped out in a nuclear holocaust, with the majority of people in the British Isles never knowing what would have hit them until the bombs and ballistic missiles came raining in. But by then it wouldn't have mattered.'

Had the call been transmitted from the bomber controller for an operational take-off to head for the targets in the Soviet Union the crews had so long been preparing themselves to attack, there would have been no hesitation.

Jim Giblen recalls: 'We trained so long and hard for this situation that, when it happened for real, we just carried on as though it was yet another exercise. There were certainly no dramatic goodbyes. Each crew member had a job to do which required total concentration. The only fear was of letting the side down, making a mistake that would endanger the crew. Soldiers do not fight for Queen and country, or even service or regiment or squadron. They fight for the small group, company, squad or, in this case crew with whom they had lived and trained for this moment.'[14]

The public was largely ignorant that the crisis they were watching unfolding on their television screens, or being informed about via newspapers and radio, had brought British nuclear forces across the UK to a level of alert unprecedented since the end of the Second World War. Outside the fairly closed circles of operational V-bomber and Thor missile bases, the British people were going about their business unaware that RAF crews were at the brink of operational readiness, with nuclear weapons ready and loaded. What is still not clear is whether ministers, and indeed the Prime Minister himself, grasped the full implications of what was happening on operational stations.

These questions became clear in an important and revealing debate about the October 1962 crisis that took place in April 2001 at the RAF Historical Society seminar on 'The RAF and Nuclear Weapons 1960–98'. The seminar heard some fascinating reminiscences of the crisis at HQ

Bomber Command and at RAF station level by senior officers and civil servants who were involved.

Their comments were recorded in the proceedings of the seminar. Among those present was Marshal of the Royal Air Force, Sir Michael Beetham, who was Group Captain (ops) at Bomber Command, alongside the Commander in Chief, Air Marshal Sir Kenneth Cross. Sir Michael said he did not think many politicians fully understood all the implications of, or indeed were even aware of, the very high states of readiness which nuclear forces regularly maintained. The only Prime Minister he could recall, during his time as chief of air staff, to take a deep interest in a major deterrent exercise was Margaret Thatcher. 'She demanded to know what was going on and attended the exercise; I think the experience taught her a great deal. Then again Jim Callaghan had been Prime Minister when I was commander in chief in Germany. He paid us a visit and we took him to Bruggen where we showed him the QRA force on standby with live weapons. He was quite taken aback; could hardly believe it. He was very thoughtful at dinner that evening as, I think, the realities of what we had been saying to him during the day began to sink in, that, as Prime Minister, he might have to make some very difficult decisions – and make them at very short notice.'[15]

Sir Michael said he thought the Cuban crisis had served to focus the minds of people who were in the front-line. 'Until then they had gone through the motions of loading weapons on exercises but it suddenly became very apparent that they just might really have to use them.'

'As soon as the missile crisis began to develop we got the message from the government, from Macmillan, that no overt action was to be taken. So, anything we did decide to do had to be done quietly. We couldn't, for instance, use the BBC to recall people from leave as we would have liked to have done. In fact, we were so successful that nothing ever seemed to appear in the press, despite the fact that we had generated the entire V-Force to a very high state of readiness. We even put the crews in their cockpits at one stage but basically they were held at fifteen minutes' notice. Ideally, once the bombs were on board, what we wanted to do was move on the next stage of our pre-planned alert procedures which would have dispersed the force. We were forbidden to do this, however, so the aircraft had to stay on their main bases.'

Sir Michael said he was quite sure that Cross never exceeded his authority. He gave his staff no indication that he ever did. 'We were with him all the time and he was constantly in touch with Whitehall.'

On the other hand Sir Michael said he was surprised at suggestions that Cross was not in contact with the American Strategic Air Command. 'I was never present when he had any conversation with CINCSAC but they were very close personal friends and Cross dealt with General Power on a regular basis. We were fully aware of the state of DEFCON, of course, and of the state of SAC's airborne alert but I cannot actually say whether or not the commander in chiefs were talking. I have a feeling that Cross would have told his staff, or at least SASO and me, if he had been having difficulty with the Americans.'[16]

'Looking back, Cuba was certainly a very traumatic experience for those involved, both at station level and at headquarters. But, strangely enough, the rest of the nation seemed to be quite unaware that there was a crisis at all. When we went for a meal or took a break outside, the sun was shining and the media was obsessed with some football match! It all seemed quite unreal.'

Group Captain, Ian Madelin, of the RAF Historical Society said there were questions, that forty years after the Cuban crisis, had still not been answered. Some that would never be answered. 'With the advent of the nuclear age someone coined the phrase "thinking the unthinkable". That's about it. We've heard from people in this room about Russian cities whose street plans they knew by heart and which, had they completed their missions in a nuclear war, simply would not be there any more. Nor, afterwards would there have been anywhere for them to return to. It is impossible to comprehend that in any rational way. It is hard to get one's mind round Armageddon. So it is not surprising politicians and their like, even if they had had more knowledge of the details, should have shown an unsure grasp of the implications. But the trouble is that, for nuclear deterrence to work, the politician's grasp of the matter needed to be as intimate and responsive as the readiness states themselves, and my reading of this in the documents now released in the public records office is that Macmillan's – and even that of the air staff in Whitehall – fell a long way short of that.'[17]

Group Captain Madelin, whose involvement with the air historical branch, had meant that he had made a particular study of the Cuban crisis, went on to say that some time afterwards Macmillan had told his grandson that, looking back, 'it all seemed like a dream.'

'I reckon that is probably truer than he'd meant it to be – and it aptly fits Mac's character don't you think? Despite all that one reads of very statesmanlike manoeuvrings, there is no corresponding evidence of this in any of the cabinet minutes. Macmillan was

144

first informed of the crisis by Kennedy on Sunday, 21 October; Khrushchev capitulated on 28 Sunday. So we are talking about just one week. There were two cabinet meetings in that week. There was no discussion of alert states or indeed of specifically military matters at either. Peter Thorneycroft, Secretary of State for Defence, was present at both but made no submissions at either. Hugh Fraser, Air Minister, was not present at either meeting. The Prime Minister reported to the cabinet that he had offered President Kennedy our support, both legal and in the UN. We had to be alert to possible Soviet counter measures in Europe, for example, by Khrushchev engineering a crisis in Berlin. There was a feeling that the US was perhaps overreacting to the fact of finding itself within range of Soviet missiles. After all, that had been the state of affairs in western Europe for years and we had got used to it.'

Group Captain Madelin added that he had checked the meetings of the defence committee, of which there was one during the crisis week on 24 October attended by Thorneycroft, Fraser and Sir Thomas Pike, Chief of the Air Staff. Astonishingly there had been no reference to Cuba at that meeting at all. Indeed Cuba does not appear in the subject index for that committee's minutes for the whole of 1962.[18]

One might conclude from all of this that there was an alarming disconnect, a mystifying gap between ministers, Whitehall and the military commanders in their headquarters. That is confirmed in Air Marshal Kenneth Cross' own words. Commenting on the Cuba experience he said: 'From me downwards, everything worked perfectly. From me upwards, nothing worked at all.'[19]

Notes

1. Exchange of emails with author, November 2011.
2. Letter to author, August 2011.
3. Published in Ilminster & Chard RAFA Branch Newsletter, September 2009.
4. Exchange of emails with author, October 2011.
5. Exchange of emails with author, April 2007.
6. Discussion with author, April 2007.
7. Bill Young published his recollections in 2000.
8. 'Britain and the Cuban Missile Crisis, 1962: Political, Military and Intelligence Dimensions'. Chapter Eight: Dr L V Scott.
9. Exchange of emails with author, April 2007.
10. Ibid.
11. Exchange of emails with author, November 2011.
12. Letter, October 2011.
13. http://www.rafbea.org/stories/brian_carlin/vulcan.htm (Website of RAF Boy Entrants Assoc.)

14. Exchange of emails with author, November 2011.
15. RAF Historical Society Journal No. 26, 2001.
16. Ibid.
17. Ibid.
18. Ibid.
19. From Group Captain Madelin's recorded conversation with Air Marshal Cross.

Chapter 15

Sunday, 28 October

This has been a battle in which everything was at stake.
Prime Minister, Harold Macmillan in his
personal diary, 4 November 1962

Moscow

Khrushchev was in no doubt by Sunday, 28 October that the Soviet
Union was facing the danger of nuclear war and that a tipping point
was approaching rapidly. He told his colleagues as much. They were
at the brink of Armageddon.

Because of the considerable time differences (Moscow was eleven
hours ahead of Washington), Khrushchev knew nothing about the
shooting down of the American U-2 spy-plane until he awoke that
Sunday morning. President Kennedy's letter was also awaiting his
attention. At noon a meeting of the Presidium was convened and the
atmosphere was tense. Troyanovsky, Khrushchev's foreign relations
adviser, recalled everyone present was visibly on edge. His boss was
practically the only one who spoke. The prevailing mood among all
the other Kremlin leaders seemed to be that Khrushchev had got the
Soviet Union in to this situation, 'now get us out'.[1]

The previous day (Black Saturday) the Soviet commanding general
in Cuba, General Pliyev, had informed Moscow of his determination to
'employ all available means of defence' if the Americans launched an
assault on the island. That meant using nuclear weapons. Khrushchev
and Malinovsky had initially agreed to that. When Khrushchev's
second message to the President was read out over Radio Moscow,
support for the use of nuclear weapons had been withdrawn and
Pliyev had been forbidden to use nuclear war-heads on his tactical
missiles or to arm planes with nuclear bombs unless expressly
authorised by Moscow. Now, on the Sunday, the Presidium decided
they had to allow Pliyev to fight back if he was attacked.

147

But again the Soviet leadership were having second thoughts. Khrushchev told his colleagues they were face to face with the danger of war and above all of nuclear catastrophe. 'In order to save the world,' he told his fellow members of the Presidium, 'we must retreat.' He then instructed Troyanovsky to read out President Kennedy's latest message. Before any of his colleagues could react, Troyanovsky was called to the telephone to receive Dobrynin's report from Washington on his meeting on the Saturday evening with the President's brother. Troyanovsky later recalled that the entire tenor of the meeting was clear: 'The time of reckoning had arrived.'[2] It did not take long for Khrushchev to decide he had no alternative but to accept President Kennedy's conditions: The Soviets to remove their offensive weapons, and the Americans to give a guarantee not to invade Cuba. The only remaining option was war.

What added urgency to the Soviet decision was the fact Soviet intelligence had warned the Kremlin, Kennedy was due to address the American nation later that day. The Soviet authorities assumed it was to announce an air strike, or more likely the invasion of Cuba. Soviet intelligence did not realise that the scheduled broadcast was not a new statement to the American people from the White House, it was in fact merely to be a re-run of the President's 22 October speech. On such relatively trivial details the fate of the world over the next few hours was decided.

Khrushchev immediately started to draft his reply. A copy was taken to the American Embassy in Moscow. Another was sent at speed through the Moscow streets to Moscow radio for immediate broadcast, with the object of getting it on the airwaves before the President's televised broadcast in the United States. Khrushchev's letter fulfilled all the demands Kennedy had made. The Soviet Union was backing down.

'I regard with respect and trust the statement you made in your message of 27 October that there would be no attack, no invasion of Cuba, and not only on the part of the United States, but also on the part of other nations of the western hemisphere,' Khrushchev wrote. 'Then the motives which induced us to render assistance of such kind to Cuba disappear. It is for this reason that we instructed our officers ... to take appropriate measures to discontinue construction of the aforementioned facilities, to dismantle them, and to return them to the Soviet Union. As I had informed you in the letter of 27 October, we are prepared to reach agreement to enable United Nations representatives to verify the dismantling of these means. Thus in view of the assurances you have given and our instructions on dismantling, there is every condition for eliminating the present conflict ...'

Khrushchev, however, was still angry about the violations of Soviet airspace, and he brought up the case of the U-2 which had intruded over Soviet borders in the Chukotka Peninsula on the previous day, an event he described as a 'dangerous case.' 'The question is, Mr President: How should we regard this? What is this: A provocation? ... Is it not a fact that an intruding American plane could be easily taken for a nuclear bomber, which might push us to a fateful step?'

'We value peace perhaps even more than other peoples because we went through a terrible war with Hitler. But our people will not falter in the face of any test. Our people trust their government, and we assure our people and world opinion that the Soviet Government will not allow itself to be provoked ... But we are confident that reason will triumph ...'[3]

Khrushchev had made no mention of America withdrawing its missiles based in Turkey, because Dobrynin had emphasised how strongly Robert Kennedy had insisted this part of the agreement had to be kept secret. Now he fretted over whether a key part of the agreement from the Soviet point of view needed some form of confirmation. Late at night he wrote a secret message to Kennedy insisting his earlier message had assumed that 'you had agreed to resolve the matter of your missile bases in Turkey, consistent with what I had said in my message of 27 October and what you stated through Robert Kennedy on the same day.'[4] Khrushchev wanted to see the President's Turkish concession put on the record.

Washington

When Dobrynin tried to present this new communication from Moscow to Robert Kennedy, the president's brother confirmed the Turkish part of the deal orally, but refused to accept the letter from Khrushchev in order to keep that part of the deal totally secret and unwritten. He told Dobrynin that the White House would not formalise the accord over the missiles in Turkey with any confidential letters, the matter was too sensitive. And it remained too sensitive for years afterwards. Several of the main characters in the United States prevaricated or avoided a direct answer when questioned about the deal. It is astounding Soviet leaders, who had so much to gain by making the deal public and thus emphasise how much the Kremlin had gained in the exchange, also never published the truth of the Turkish missile withdrawal.

The crisis was over. In Washington, Kennedy and his advisers were relieved, but cautious.

London

Macmillan was finishing lunch at Admiralty House with Rab Butler his deputy prime minister, Peter Thorneycroft, Defence Minister, Alec Douglas-Home, the Foreign Minister, and Edward Heath, Lord Privy Seal. It had been a sober affair, all of them were contemplating a grim but crucial cabinet meeting that afternoon and the genuine and terrifying possibility of not just war, but nuclear war. 'As we were finishing lunch together,' Macmillan wrote in his diary, 'the news came by radio that the Russians had given in! First, they admit to the ballistic missiles (hitherto denied by communists and doubted by all good fellow-travellers in every country). Then they said they would be packed up, crated and taken away – a complete climb-down (if they keep their word).' The Prime Minister had underlined the word 'if'.[5]

There is little doubt that the events of those tense days took their toll on the British politicians at the centre of events. Peter Thorneycroft recalled an unreal, almost sinister tranquillity as he crossed St James' Park on the Sunday morning of that fateful weekend. Whitehall was deserted. It was a very quiet but beautiful autumn morning. As he approached the Ministry of Defence he remembered thinking, 'My God, I wonder whether this really is it.'

Harold Evans, the Prime Minister's Press Secretary, described in his diary what he called 'the end of the Cuban crisis week, and in particular, a dramatic weekend.' He wrote that he felt 'jaded and worn' and that clearly Macmillan did too. Evans described the PM's relief: 'It's like a wedding,' said the PM 'when there is nothing left to do but drink the champagne and go to sleep. He had flopped down in a chair by the tape machine, with Tim (Bligh, his Principal Private Secretary) Philip de Zulueta (his Private Secretary) and my-self as audience. The captains and the kings had departed and this was the Number 10 family. The captains and the kings – Rab (Butler) and Alec Home in particular, plus Ted Heath, plus Harold Caccia (Permanent Under-Secretary at the Foreign Office), plus this morning, Thorneycroft – had spent most of the last twenty-four hours in and out of Admiralty House. I was summoned from Rottingdean at 6.30pm last night (Saturday) and got to Admiralty House at 8.40pm. The position then seemed to be that Kennedy had rejected a Cuba-Turkey deal and was hell-bent on destroying the missile sites. This carried the strong possibility of Soviet retaliation in Berlin or elsewhere, with the prospect of escalation into nuclear war.'[6]

Evans went on to say that during the long hours of the night waiting for news, Macmillan had favoured taking the initiative by proposing a summit meeting in London, but Caccia had argued strongly against anything which might be construed as 'the British being the first to crack. So we ended with a mouse-like message to Khrushchev, appealing to him to take the course proposed by Kennedy, and this went off at noon – just in time for us to be able to claim it had anticipated Khrushchev's caving-in reply.'

Macmillan himself in his memoirs described the strain and relief of that memorable Sunday rather differently. 'Almost with a sense of anti-climax,' he wrote, 'after days in which it was difficult to restrain yet necessary to conceal our emotions, on that Sunday afternoon my colleagues and I were able to share the feeling, if not of triumph, yet of relief and gratitude. We had been on the brink, almost over it; yet the world had been providentially saved at the last moment from the final plunge.'[7]

Sir Solly Zuckerman, Chief Scientific Adviser to the Ministry of Defence, also recalled that memorable Sunday lunchtime. He arrived to join the Minister of Defence, Peter Thorneycroft, to attend a meeting of the chiefs of the armed services, expecting to discuss an escalation of the stance of the British nuclear deterrent force. 'When I joined Peter Thorneycroft' he wrote later, 'I learnt that the crisis was over and that the Russians had accepted the American terms without loss of face. We sat around the table just looking at each other. Dickie Mountbatten (Lord Mountbatten, Chief of the Defence Staff) broke the silence. "Well what would we have done if the Russians had not pulled back? Do we know? We have got to work this out." No one knew, but he was the only one to put the question. To the best of my knowledge neither he nor anyone else has provided an answer. Perhaps there is none.'[8]

That meeting of the chiefs of staff with Thorneycroft recognised that the events of the past few days had exposed a significant weakness in the UK's planning of transition to war. There were detailed plans to be applied in the event of a NATO alert, a crisis which threatened the security of Berlin, or a raft of other situations that might have resulted in the UK being directly involved. But according to a record of the meeting: 'Little consideration had ... so far been given to the precautionary measures which it would be prudent for the United Kingdom to take in circumstances such as these when there was a confrontation between the United States and

Russia, in which the United Kingdom was not directly involved.'[9] Late in the day, it was clear recognition that events had overtaken the government's handling of the crisis. The confrontation might have been initially solely between the United States and the USSR. Had Khrushchev reacted differently to Kennedy's ultimatum, the UK would have inevitably been drawn into the conflict and on that very Sunday the country could have been under nuclear attack.

Throughout the days of crisis, and particularly during the crucial weekend, Macmillan and his Foreign Secretary, Alec Douglas-Home, between them exercised almost complete control. They never followed the steps set out in Britain's *War Book*. They didn't establish a war cabinet recommended by the cabinet secretary. Evidence that between them the two senior ministers had indeed taken management of the most dangerous crisis of the Cold War almost solely in their own hands came in a note written by the Queen's Private Secretary, Sir Michael Adeane. Sent on 31 October it read: 'I made a rough note of the various contacts which took place during the last weekend between the Queen on the one hand, and yourself and the foreign secretary on the other. These were numerous and as a result Her Majesty was fully and continuously informed of what was going on in the relations between this country, the United States and the USSR. The Queen knows very well what a heavy strain both you the foreign secretary and your staff were working under during these days and she wishes you to know how much she appreciates the trouble which was taken in your office and the Foreign Office to see that she was kept up to date with the rapidly changing news.'[10]

Somewhere in Whitehall there must have been officials, if not ministers, mindful that if Britain was headed for nuclear war, plans to get the Queen to safety would need to be put in hand swiftly and effectively. The royal yacht *Britannia* was regarded as one safe haven, but only if there was sufficient time to get Her Majesty on board and for *Britannia* to sail far enough from her island kingdom to escape the effects of a nuclear bombardment. A highly secret plan codenamed Operation Candid dealt step by step with the protection and evacuation of the Queen in the event of nuclear war. But none of this was set in motion in October 1962. Macmillan was taking a massive gamble that the crisis would not plunge over the brink – but the knowledge that he had chosen not to set in motion any of the carefully planned steps contained in the *War Book*, not even protection of the royal family, must have weighed heavily on his mind as he and Douglas-Home waited for the outcome of the crisis. The war planners had taken account of the special role of the Queen in the British constitution should war break out. It would have been folly to accommodate her in the same central government bunker at 'The Quarry', alongside the Prime Minister and other senior ministers. If the Prime Minister and his colleagues had all been killed the constitution demanded that the Queen appoint a successor. So it was vital to assure the safety of the monarch in a separate location, otherwise the continuity of government even under the horrific circumstances of a nuclear wasteland could not be assured.

Clearly Macmillan did not 'play the crisis' like the book – the *War Book*. Rightly or wrongly he kept the whole terrifying situation at a low profile. The risks he ran in doing this are clear. The benefit was the British public was not panicked, although a group of Sheffield students, as a rather tasteless practical joke, produced newspaper placards bearing the headline 'War Declared, Official'. They were suspended by the university authorities before too much harm was caused.[11] Widespread panic would certainly have taken hold had nuclear warfare broken out before any of the warnings or precautions for the protection of the public that the civil service and scientific advisers had planned were put into effect. Macmillan knew how futile precautions would be against a nuclear attack of the scale the government anticipated the Soviets would launch. But there are indications that he might have had 'second thoughts'. As the relief of the crisis being over hit home, the Prime Minister took immediate steps to revisit and revise the UK's preparations for putting the country on a nuclear-war footing.

Within days Macmillan ordered a post-Cuba review. He knew the crisis had exposed gaps in a situation where sudden international events plunged the country on a trajectory to nuclear war. As the Cabinet Secretary, Sir Burke Trend, appointed following the retirement of Sir Norman Brook, put in a note to the Minister of Defence, Thorneycroft some months later: 'After the Cuban crisis the Prime Minister directed that the home defence committee should review the state of government *War Book* planning in order to ensure that it was sufficiently flexible to enable us to react quickly and appropriately to a sudden emergency, in which we might have no more than two or three days' warning of the outbreak of war.'[12]

In his autobiography, Macmillan quoted President Kennedy's conduct of the Cuban crisis as evidence that the special relationship between the United States and the UK had worked. But some queried how well it had worked, and whether it had worked specifically in the UK's national interest. Certainly there were frequent conversations between the President and the Prime Minister on the trans-Atlantic 'hot-line'. But subsequently some British newspapers criticised what had happened and accused America of risking total war for a quarrel that did not concern Europe, and failing to consult their allies in Britain, despite substantial elements of Strategic Air Command being based in the UK. Macmillan accused these critics of 'ignorance of what really happened.' But Macmillan's own account and his diary, show that as the crisis deepened, President Kennedy and his officials ceased to seek British advice. In the last desperate thirty-six hours there was no communication between them. Kennedy's final phone call to the Prime Minister was on Friday, 26 October. In it Kennedy promised to be in touch the following day: 'I will also keep in touch with you tomorrow at this time, or,' he said, 'I will send you a message unless we get something immediate ... We will not take any further action until I have talked to you in any case. I will send you a message if there is anything new, in any case, I'll talk to you on the phone before we do anything of a drastic nature.'[13]

In fact Kennedy did none of that. The call never came, leaving Macmillan worrying and waiting. Kennedy despatched his final ultimatum to Moscow, two days later on the Sunday morning without either consulting or even informing the Prime Minister. In his private diary Macmillan describes any suggestion of a secret swap of Turkish-based US missiles for the Soviet missiles in Cuba as 'very dangerous.' He describes critical reports in the *Times* and the *Manchester Guardian* as 'particularly gullible,' and those in the *Sunday Times* and *Observer* as 'awful.' 'It was like Munich,' his diary notes, in reference to the press response to the outcome. And in justification for the role he had played, he wrote: 'We were "in on" and took full part in (and almost responsibility for) every American move. Our complete calm helped to keep the Europeans calm. The French were anyway contemptuous; the Germans very frightened, though pretending to want firmness; the Italians windy; the Scandinavians rather sour, as well as windy. But they said and did nothing to spoil the American playing of the hand.'

Later, in retrospect Macmillan wrote of that week and commented on: 'The frightful desire to do something, with the knowledge that not to do anything (except to talk to the President and keep Europe and the Commonwealth calm and firm) was probably the right answer. I still feel (with all the other work of the week) tired out. One longs for some days of continued rest, which is impossible. At 68 I am not as resilient as when I was a young officer. Yet this has been a battle in which everything was at stake.'[14]

On 1 November, Macmillan tried to assess in his diary what the crisis had meant and why Khrushchev had embarked on his risky adventure in the Caribbean. 'He hoped to finish the job; go to the United Nations at the end of November; threaten about Berlin, and then reveal his Cuban strength, pointing at the soft under-belly of the USA, three minutes warning instead of fifteen. Of course, to us who face nearly 500 of these missiles in Russia trained on Europe, there is something slightly ironical about these twenty to thirty in Cuba. But, as I told the President, when one lives on Vesuvius, one takes little account of the risk of eruptions!'[15]

Macmillan went on to record that the invasion of Cuba by American forces was timed for Monday, 29 October. 'This American invasion,' he wrote in his personal diary, 'could not be stopped by conventional means. Therefore the Russians would have had to use nuclear, in a "first fire" attack. This they would not face – and rightly. But if the Americans attacked they would do three things: i) destroy Castro and the communist regime; ii) deal a great blow to Russian prestige; iii) capture the missiles. So by his apparent cave-in, Khrushchev at least avoided all these disadvantages.' Then Macmillan summed up the strategic lessons of the crisis. 'May they not be that, under the cover of the terrible nuclear war, which nobody dares start, you can get away with anything you can do by conventional means. You can take Cuba. The enemy can only reply by all-out nuclear war. But this applies to Berlin. The Russians can take Berlin by conventional means. The Allies cannot defend or re-capture it by any conventional means. (The conclusion to be drawn is rather sinister).'[16]

Then Macmillan, who had been stung by some of press criticism directed at him and by the views of prominent Labour politicians, notably Hugh Gaitskell and Harold Wilson, committed to his diary a defence of his own role on behalf of the UK. 'Some,' he wrote 'have been making out that the Americans not only failed to consult us, but have treated us with contempt; that the "special relationship" no longer applies; that we have gained nothing from our position as a nuclear power; that America risked total war in a US/USSR quarrel without bothering about us or Europe. The reasons for this attitude are (a) ignorance of what really happened (b) desire to injure or denigrate me personally (c) argument against the deterrent (d) annoyance at the success – or comparative success of the Cuban enterprise (e) shame – for they let it be known that they would oppose force, or the threat of force. In fact, of course, the President and Rusk (Dean Rusk, US Secretary of State) and above all the President's chef de cabinet, McGeorge Bundy, were in continuous touch with Alec Home and me. David Gore (British Ambassador in Washington) was all the time in and out of the White House ...'[17]

That was Macmillan's view. The UK public, kept largely ignorant of the considerable threat they had been under may have had a different view had they realised the full truth of the events of that terrifying weekend.

Notes

1. *Khrushchev, The Man and his Era*, p. 574.
2. Ibid.
3. Foreign Relations of the United States, 1961–63, Vol. XI Cuban Missile Crisis and Aftermath: Doc. 102.
4. *Khrushchev, The Man and his Era*, p. 576.
5. Peter Catterell: *The Macmillan Diaries Vol. 2*, pp. 513–14.
6. Harold Evans: *Downing Street Diary: The Macmillan Years 1957–63*, Hodder & Stoughton. 1981, pp. 224–6.
7. Harold Macmillan: *At the End of the Day 1961–63*, pp. 214–15.
8. Sir S Zuckerman: *Monkeys, Men and Missiles'*, Collins, 1988, p. 303.
9. PRO, DEFE 13/212, Record of a meeting between the minister of defence and the chiefs of staff, Sunday, 28 October 1962.
10. PRO, PREM 11/3689, Adeane to Macmillan, 31 October 1962.
11. *The Times*. 30 October 1962.
12. PRO, DEFE 13/321, Trend to Thorneycroft, 21 May 1963.
13. *At the End of the Day*, p. 211.
14. Ibid 216 and *The Macmillan Diaries Vol. 2*, pp. 514–15.
15. *The Macmillan Diaries Vol. 2*, p. 515.
16. Ibid, p. 516.
17. Ibid, pp. 517–18.

Chapter 16

'Near the Edge'

The world has had a shock. We have been very near the edge.

Prime Minister, Harold Macmillan in the House of
Commons, 30 October 1962

Macmillan had little time for rest following the relief of hearing that tense Sunday lunch-time that the threat of war had lifted.

The cabinet meeting that it seemed so likely to be called that Sunday afternoon, thankfully never took place. The dramatic decisions it would have taken were no longer necessary. But the next day Macmillan did call a cabinet meeting to brief his fellow ministers on the outcome of that historic weekend.

He was anxious to dispel some of the criticisms that were being voiced on whether or not there had been close consultation between the two major allies in NATO. The Prime Minister told his cabinet colleagues, President Kennedy had played his hand with great skill. He had turned the usual communist methods against themselves by observing to the full the proprieties of international consultation in the United Nations, and showed at the same time an unwavering determination to attain his objective of securing the removal of the offensive missiles from Cuba with the implication that he would not shrink from using force if he had to as a last resort.

Macmillan said Kennedy had also dealt effectively with the pressures upon him from within the United States, where 'a strong body of opinion had been calling for violent measures.' The President had steered a difficult course between being driven into a premature use of force and not appearing to waver in his determination. While reluctant to authorise an invasion of Cuba he had shown great firmness in continuing to make preparations for it.

The President and his advisers had shown themselves ready to ask for and to consider advice. Despite the offer he had floated to Washington of de-commissioning the Thor ballistic missiles in England, the Prime Minister said it would have been wrong for him to have offered himself as a mediator. This would have meant a withdrawal from the British position of strong support for President

157

Kennedy's stance that no discussions could take place until the missiles had been withdrawn.[1]

Mr Macmillan said he had, in the concluding stages of the crisis, judged it right to send a message to Mr Khrushchev making clear Britain's support for the United States position that until the missiles went no negotiation could take place. It was unfortunate this message had reached Moscow at about the time Mr Khrushchev had given publicity to his final decision to withdraw his missiles under UN supervision.

The Prime Minister insisted Britain had played an active and helpful part in bringing matters to their present conclusion, but in public little had been said and the impression had been created that 'we had been playing purely a passive role.' Macmillan said there were now three tasks facing the government; to present the course of events and the government's part in them, to public opinion; to identify lessons to be learned from the negotiations both between the Allies and with the Soviet Government; and to consider how those lessons might be applied for the future.

Sir Alec Douglas-Home, the Foreign Secretary said that if the United States had attacked Cuba there could be little doubt the Soviet Government would have reacted in Berlin. There would then have been a real and immediate risk of nuclear war. The free world would have to take account of the fact that the communist powers had deliberately engaged in a policy of deception to further their strategic designs; and this underlined the need for measures of international verification to be included in any agreement on disarmament, whether it was nuclear or conventional. An agreement on missile bases, he added, would also present difficulties since all the Russian bases of any importance were on their own soil. In short it would be necessary to point out realistically that the chances of international agreement on major issues had not been improved by the crisis but might have become worse, because the west had more reason now to be suspicious of communist professions of good faith.

In the ensuing discussion, the cabinet agreed that when the Cuban affair was seen in perspective it appeared that Khrushchev had brought the world to the brink of war and had lost his nerve at the last moment. There was nothing in this on which to build great hopes for the future. Nevertheless the free world was entitled to enjoy a sense of relief without a sense of surrender: nothing had been given up and the mistake had not been made of feeding the aggressor's ambition by yielding to his demands little by little.

The following day, Tuesday, 30 October, a new session of parliament began with the traditional ceremony of the Queen's Speech. Back in the Commons, Macmillan made a major speech on the crisis which he said had 'boiled up very quickly.' Despite the rapidity with which the crisis had emerged, the American Government had not only preserved diplomatic propriety in the way it had informed allied governments but had also maintained the closest possible co-operation with its allies.

Macmillan told the House that Khrushchev's proposal that Soviet missiles would only be removed from Cuba provided the United States would remove their missiles from Turkey, was a 'public demand that we should sell out Turkey' and had been repudiated publicly by the White House spokesman. 'His decision was certainly supported by the British Government. You cannot avoid your own danger by making an ignoble bargain at the expense of an ally. Nor, in spite of a specious and superficial geographical parallel was there really any comparison to be made between the situation in Europe, where the two great armies of NATO and the Warsaw Pact have ranged and faced each other for many years, and the gratuitous and stealthy introduction of a new threat into the western hemisphere.'

So Macmillan appeared totally unaware that a bargain had been struck between the American president and the Soviet leader over the Jupiter missiles in Turkey. One may well wonder what the Prime Minister's attitude would have been had he known that there was a covert sub-text to the 'climb down' everyone thought Khrushchev had made.

Macmillan went on to read to the House the message he had sent to Khrushchev on behalf of the British Government at noon on Sunday, just as the crisis was about to be resolved. 'Dear Mr Chairman, I have had an opportunity to study your letter to President Kennedy and his reply. The essence of the position reached is that, once the problem posed by the offensive missile bases in Cuba has been dealt with under effective United Nations control and the situation in the area normalised, the way would be open for us all to work towards a more general arrangement regarding armaments. For instance we should be able to reach an early conclusion of an agreement about the banning of tests of nuclear weapons on which much progress has already been made, as well as to give firm directives to settle the main elements in the first stage of disarmament. I would hope that this might mark a new determination to resolve the problems from which the world is suffering. I therefore ask you to take the action necessary to make all this possible. This is an opportunity which we should seize.'

Macmillan said the purpose of his message to Moscow was to range the British Government squarely and publicly with the President and to support his demand that the missiles must be, by one means or another, taken away. 'What would peoples in distant parts of Europe bordering on Russia, whose soldiers, in Mr Khrushchev's words ... face each other day by day upon the frontier lines ... have thought of the value of a guarantee to people 3,000 miles away if the United States was not able to enforce its will ninety miles distant? How, they would think, can America defend us. She cannot even defend herself against such a threat. This would have been a kind of super Munich, and might easily have led to the collapse of defence of the free world.'[2]

'This seemed to me and my colleagues one of the great turning points of history, for, after sending this message which made it clear where Britain stood, one could not help wondering what would happen next. There was no more we could do except just wait and see what would happen. By a strange coincidence, with an extraordinary sense almost of anticlimax, just at that moment when our message was being delivered in Moscow, we hear on the wireless – not through diplomatic channels – Mr Khrushchev's public statement in which he accepted, in effect, the American proposals that the missiles would be, in his own words, "... packed up, crated, and returned to the Soviet Union under the supervision of the United Nations organisation".'

The Prime Minister added: 'We made our decision and sent our telegram, and I must ask how anyone who bore any responsibility – and I bear some – could not have had a sense of relief when that message came across the radio. It was a particular satisfaction to feel that on this occasion we could enjoy that sense of relief without a sense of shame, or the haunting fear that the relief would only be temporary and that worse might follow.'

'The world has had a shock. We have been very near the edge. Can we use this experience, not for recrimination or debate, not to expect one side or the other to obtain a narrow advantage, but for the common good? Can we use this for a renewed effort to rule out some of the dangers and resolve some of the problems that confront us all? ... One cannot live in a world which is just nothing but suspicion and fear the whole time – life becomes almost intolerable.'

What the Prime Minister failed to mention to parliament was the high readiness alert that the British nuclear deterrent forces had been ordered to – and were still at. That fact remained under public wraps for another three months before a newspaper report brought it to public attention and even then Macmillan refused to tell the public the whole truth.

There was a shock for Macmillan and his Foreign Secretary, Sir Alec Douglas-Home, three weeks after his statement to parliament. Major General Sir Kenneth Strong, director of the Joint Intelligence Bureau, who had been in Washington from 13 to 25 October, and had excellent contacts within the Kennedy administration, sent a top secret, four page memorandum to the Prime Minister. It reflected deep concern that Kennedy and his advisers had been prepared to 'go it alone' either without consulting their allies or irrespective of what their allies said, had the Russians reacted against the blockade of Cuba by launching an attack on West Berlin. General Strong thought the American Government was prepared for their action over Cuba to escalate into nuclear war. It seemed to him that the US administration were over-confident that they had pinpointed the position of all the main sites of inter-continental ballistic missiles in the Soviet Union and they hoped they would be able to take these out with a pre-emptive nuclear attack. Macmillan and Home were horrified that their allies, who had appeared to consult them from the early stages of the crisis, seemed to have only been paying lip-service to the idea. They worried that Strong's view indicated that America was dangerously 'gung-ho' about fighting a nuclear war, which the Pentagon assumed it could win. Realisation that the UK would have been the loser had America launched such a pre-emptive attack, made Strong's assessment even more alarming. The Prime Minister considered the report from his intelligence chief so significant, that he immediately sent a copy to the Queen.[3]

There were some senior American officers in October 1962 who believed America possessed a first-strike capacity sufficient to destroy the ability of the USSR to retaliate. They felt America's nuclear arsenal was so much greater than the weapons, particularly the inter-continental missiles, available to the Soviet Union that they had the means to wipe out the Soviet's nuclear capability with only a limited risk of retaliation.

Strong's startling memorandum was only released to the National Archives in Kew in April 2006. The Joint Intelligence Bureau director had been a well informed observer in Washington during the crisis. He was well connected and trusted, having been General Dwight D Eisenhower's intelligence chief at the time of D-Day and was receiving briefings from his friend John Alex McCone, director of the CIA. The unspoken factor, of course, was that it would have taken American aircraft operating from UK bases to achieve what Strong indicated the Americans had in mind. Could this really have happened without consulting the British Government? Are the protocols under which the Americans operate their British bases so imprecise? Strong's memo certainly made a powerful impact on the British Prime Minister. Did Macmillan subsequently raise this with President Kennedy? There is currently no evidence that he did.

Notes

1. Minutes of cabinet meeting, 29 October 1962.
2. Hansard, parliamentary proceedings, 30 October 1962 Vol. 666, cc4–142.
3. *Daily Telegraph*, 3 April 2006.

Chapter 17

The Penkovsky Factor

A future war will begin with a sudden nuclear strike against the enemy. There will be no declaration of war.

Colonel Oleg Penkovsky on the USSR's first-strike strategy

Britain can claim responsibility for one critical factor crucial to the resolution of the Cuban Missile Crisis. This was the recruitment by the UK's secret intelligence services of Colonel Oleg Penkovsky, a senior officer of the GRU (Glavnoye Razvedyvatelnoye Upravleniye), the Soviet military intelligence agency. Between 1960 and 1962 he provided invaluable information on the Soviet Union's nuclear rocket capabilities, which allowed the Americans positively to identify the launch sites in Cuba, and the types of missiles for which they were being constructed. It was priceless information and it gave President Kennedy and his advisers a head-start in understanding what Khrushchev was planning in Cuba.

Jerrold L Schechter, writing in June 1993, put Penkovsky's role into context. 'It was Penkovsky who was the catalyst for closing the missile gap and who provided the information that allowed President Kennedy to force Khrushchev to blink and back down during the Cuban missile crisis ... The manual that Penkovsky supplied for the SS-4 missiles, enabled Kennedy to calculate the amount of time needed to put the missiles in place and gave him a window to exchange letters with Khrushchev before the missiles became operational.'[1]

Penkovsky was a professional soldier who had fought in the Second World War after graduating in 1939 from the Kiev artillery academy. In 1955 he was appointed military attaché in Ankara, Turkey, as cover for his intelligence activities. Later he worked at the Soviet committee for scientific research where he gained expert knowledge of the ballistic missiles the Soviet Union was producing. A trusted officer, he was a personal friend of the head of the GRU, Ivan Serov and of Soviet Marshal, Sergei Varentsov.[2]

British intelligence first spotted him as a possible defector during his time in Turkey. He attempted to make contact with the Americans shortly after the trial in Moscow of the American U-2 pilot, Gary

Powers, but the CIA was wary and he was rebuffed. In November 1960 he met the British businessman and MI6 agent Greville Wynne and they became good friends. In April the following year he gave Wynne a resume of his career, together with a package of valuable information. Two weeks later Penkovsky was sent by his superiors to London, overtly as a member of a Soviet trade delegation, but in reality as a Soviet military intelligence agent. He used the opportunity to make further contact with British secret intelligence. Penkovsky passed vital information to SIS about Soviet missile development, nuclear plans, the locations of military headquarters, and the identities of KGB officers. The secrets he divulged included evidence that Khrushchev had been wildly exaggerating the number of nuclear missiles the Soviet Union possessed, its lack of warheads and of accurate guidance systems. The information he disclosed made it clear that what had previously been considered by the Americans as a serious 'missile gap' between United States and Soviet arsenals was patently not true.

Penkovsky's information was 'pure gold' to western intelligence. Over a period of fourteen months he passed photographs of some 5,000 secret papers to the SIS and the CIA. The significance of these disclosures can hardly be overstated. It gave the American administration a key insight into the limitations of Soviet power. It also provided them with operating instructions of the type of missile systems being installed in Cuba, and this knowledge gave Kennedy the confidence to wait and take time to debate the best course of action to challenge Khrushchev's plans for an offensive base on Cuba.

When, on 21 October 1961, just as the twenty-second communist party conference was taking place in Moscow, the United States Deputy Defence Secretary, Roswell Gilpatric, announced that the United States: 'Has a nuclear retaliatory force of such lethal power that an enemy move which brought it into play would be an act of self-destruction,' he based his speech on information Penkovsky had been supplying about Soviet nuclear capability. Gilpatric, on the evidence provided by Penkovsky, declared the United States had, 'a second strike capability which is at least as extensive as what the Soviets can deliver by striking first. Therefore, we are confident the Soviets will not provoke a major nuclear attack.'

Perhaps, Khrushchev's Cuban adventure was in answer to that challenge.

The manual for the SS-4 missiles, supplied by Penkovsky, enabled Kennedy to calculate the time required by Soviet technicians on Cuba to construct launch emplacements and bring the rockets to launch readiness. He knew he had a window of opportunity to negotiate with Khrushchev before the Soviet military were able make the missiles fully operational. Without that knowledge the United States may well have launched an early invasion leading to the use by defending Soviet troops of the tactical nuclear weapons with which they were equipped, and almost certainly triggering a Third World War.

In January 1962 Penkovsky realised that Mrs Janet Chisholm, wife of a British intelligence officer and Penkovsky's contact in Moscow, was under surveillance. He suggested they stop meeting in public places, but courageously continued to covertly deliver film and packages to her at diplomatic functions until Mrs Chisholm left Moscow to return to the UK in June 1962. The KGB, because of its rivalry with the GRU, needed an airtight case against Penkovsky before arresting him. They continued to keep him under surveillance to establish whether he was working alone or in a spy ring. Penkovsky was a senior officer with friends in high places, and it was probably this which delayed his arrest until October 1962 just as the missile crisis was breaking.

On 20 October Soviet intelligence officers raided Penkovsky's apartment and discovered a Minnox camera that he had used to photograph secret documents. Two days later – the day Kennedy broke the news of Khrushchev's infiltration of missiles into Cuba – Penkovsky was arrested. The Soviet counter-intelligence authorities were desperate to know as quickly as possible what information Penkovsky had passed to the UK and America. Under questioning, Penkovsky gave the name of Greville Wynne as his British contact. Wynne was arrested a few days later in Budapest, Hungary. In May 1963 the two men stood trial in Moscow for espionage. Wynne was sentenced to eight years imprisonment and Penkovsky, accused of treason, was sentenced to death. He was executed by firing squad on 16 May 1963. Wynne did not serve his full sentence in the Lubyanka Prison in Moscow and he was eventually exchanged for a group of Soviet spies who had been caught in the United Kingdom, Gordon Lonsdale and the Krogers.

The recruitment of Penkovsky was hailed in both Britain and the United States as the most successful penetration of Soviet intelligence since the Second World War, although some commentators, notably Peter Wright, an MI5 officer, in his book *Spycatcher*,[3] was convinced Penkovsky was a Soviet plant designed to lead the United States to the conclusion that the USSR's intercontinental missile capabilities were much less than they actually were. However, another GRU defector, Colonel Viktor Suvorov, was in no doubt of Penkovsky's value to the west. He wrote in his book *Soviet Military Intelligence*: 'Thanks to his priceless information the Cuban crisis was not transformed into a last World War.'[4]

What impelled such a trusted and senior Soviet intelligence officer to provide such valuable information to the British and American authorities? Penkovsky firmly believed that Khrushchev's leadership was taking the Soviet Union on a path towards inevitable nuclear war. In a document smuggled out of the Soviet Union to the west dubbed 'The Penkovsky Papers,'[5] he revealed his motives for frustrating the objectives of his own country by providing an immense amount of material of huge significance to the west. Some have questioned the authenticity of the 'papers', but in a personal comment associated with the book, Greville Wynne, who knew Penkovsky better than most, shared the dangers inherent in espionage with him, and was put on trial in Moscow at the same time as Penkovsky, wrote: 'He was willing to put up with the basic deceptions of spying and the tremendous strains of his lonely life because he believed in a cause. He believed simply that a free society should emerge in the Soviet Union, and that it could only come by toppling the only government he knew. He was a heroic figure.'[6] That does not sound like someone who doubts the veracity of the testament Penkovsky smuggled to the west.

Penkovsky revealed he was alarmed at the new military strategy emerging in the Soviet Union in the early sixties which had been disclosed in a top secret collection of articles devoted to a discussion of the problems of a future war and a new Soviet doctrine being championed by Khrushchev. The Soviet leader was re-orienting Soviet military policy in a direction more suitable to the nuclear-missile age, despite resistance from some quarters within the military. It went beyond deterrence and so-called 'peaceful co-existence', and advocated a 'first-strike' stance very close to preventive war. Penkovsky believed Khrushchev was committing the USSR to the dangerous 'automatic reflex' principle of 'strike first and ask questions after fall-out'. Within the Soviet Army, Khrushchev's displays of brinkmanship were regarded by some as careless to the point of folly, Penkovsky said. The Soviet leader was committing the cardinal military sin of threatening to use power that he did not possess and employing diplomacy that smacked too much of gambling. Penkovsky's assessment in 1960 presaged Khrushchev's Cuban adventure two years later.

Commenting in his testament smuggled to the west, on the new military policy being secretly expounded in the Soviet Union,

Penkovsky wrote: 'Virtually all the authors recognise the importance of a first thermonuclear strike. In the first place, to be the first one to deliver a nuclear strike is important not only as far as the initial stage of the war is concerned, but also because it concerns the entire course and the outcome of the war. Secondly, strategic nuclear missiles, which play a tremendous part in the initial stage of the war, will also make it possible to achieve the necessary strategic goals of the war within the shortest possible time.'

'All military men are perfectly aware that the final decision to attack rests with the political leadership, in this case with the Presidium of the central committee of the CPSU and with Khrushchev personally. This new military doctrine must become, or perhaps already has become a sort of guide for the Soviet state in preparing its armed forces for war, and it sets forth in detail where and how future military action should start.'

'A future war will begin with a sudden nuclear strike against the enemy. There will be no declaration of war. On the contrary every effort will be made to avoid a declaration of war. When circumstances are favourable for delivering the first nuclear strike, the Soviet Union will seize the initiative by delivering this strike under the pretence of defending herself from an aggressor. All operational plans for a future war are being developed on this assumption.'[7]

Penkovsky went on to say that the Soviet Union did not wish to wage a long war and could not achieve victory in a lengthy conflict because the country's economy and the people's morale would not endure a prolonged nuclear ordeal. 'I have tried to substantiate all I have said about the new Soviet military doctrine and Soviet plans for surprise attacks, with facts and documents which I saw by virtue of my official position ... Khrushchev's peculiar variety of "peaceful co-existence" has advanced so far that Khrushchev could decide by 1962–63 basically to complete production of the required number of strategic missiles with nuclear warheads, so that by adding them to the existing stock of weapons of mass destruction we could direct these weapons against all the NATO countries and their bases. Such missiles are already aimed at England, Italy and the USA; ballistic weapons are in a state of readiness.'[8]

Shortly after the 'Penkovsky Papers' were published, the claim Penkovsky had made that Khrushchev had been preparing a first-strike against the UK and the United States was raised in questions in the House or Lords. Lord Kennet asked the Parliamentary Under Secretary for Foreign Affairs, Lord Walstan, if the government was aware of Penkovsky's alarming claim, and whether it was credible.

167

Lord Walstan said the government was 'quite aware that that is what Colonel Penkovsky had said.' How incredible that may be is a matter on which noble lords and others must draw their own conclusions.' Lord Kennet then asked whether the government considered the papers a 'valid historical document.' To which the Foreign Office minister replied: 'If by a valid historical document he means an interesting contribution to contemporary history, the answer is, yes, certainly.'[9]

The Penkovsky case poses a puzzling mystery which still has historians and commentators arguing over exactly what took place. The British and American handlers of Colonel Penkovsky made elaborate arrangements, under the codename 'Distant', to ensure that the west received a direct warning if the Soviet nuclear first-strike that Penkovsky feared, was imminent. If he received information that the USSR was about to launch an attack he was told to ring one of two telephone numbers he had been supplied with and blow into the mouthpiece three times, wait one minute and then repeat the procedure. He was told not to speak on the phone but if at all possible to leave further detailed information in a secret dead-drop location. The telephone signal alone would be considered as a warning message of the highest importance; meaning either that the Soviet Union had decided to attack, or that an attack would take place if the west failed to take specific action. It was impressed on Penkovsky that the UK and US authorities would act on his warning immediately.

On 2 November, eleven days after he had been arrested (although neither MI6 nor the CIA knew of his arrest), the 'Distant' emergency procedure was activated. The two calls were received one minute apart and someone blew three times into the mouthpiece each time. When an agent was sent to see if anything had been left at the dead-drop point, KGB officers were there and the agent was arrested and interrogated. Clearly Penkovsky had told the KGB how to activate the 'Distant' warning. But had he told the KGB exactly what the signal meant? By activating it, the KGB had given the west the signal that a nuclear attack was imminent. Why? Was it that Penkovsky, knowing he would be put on trial and executed, let the KGB unknowingly, in effect, press the nuclear button in the hope that a military response from the UK and US would be his final revenge on the Soviet system he hated? Or was it that the KGB, aware that the period of highest crisis had passed, used the procedure to find out more about Penkovsky's contacts? It could have been disastrous, but his SIS controller in the British Embassay in Moscow, Gervase Cowell, was convinced the signal could not be genuine, and took the brave decision to do nothing, neither alerting the British Ambassador in Moscow nor his MI6 boss in London. He was certain Penkovsky had been captured and that information about the 'Distant' call sign had been extracted from him. One man's decision averted what might have led to horrific consequences. Three days later, on 5 November, Bomber Command's unprecedented alert three was withdrawn and the V-Force and Thor force in the United Kingdom reverted to their normal vigilance stance. However, the Americans maintained their blockade of Cuba and their peak alert stance until 20 November, when it became clear that Khrushchev had kept his side of the bargain.

Why did British nuclear forces stand down so much earlier? One theory that has been advanced links the decision to the activation of Penkovsky's 'Distant' code after the SIS's master spy had been arrested. Was it that Penkovsky, in a last throw, tricked the KGB into using the 'Distant' warning in the hope that it would trigger a nuclear attack on Russia? Could it be that the British Government lowered the alert status early, deliberately to reduce tension in Moscow?

Notes

1. Jerrold L Schechter: *New York Review of Books*, June 1993.
2. *KGB: The Inside Story*, Oleg Gordievsky and Christopher Andrew: Hodder & Stourton, 1990.
3. *Spy Catcher*, Peter Wright: William Heinemann, 1987.
4. *Soviet Military Intelligence*, Victor Suvorov: Grafton Books, 1986.
5. *The Penkovsky Papers*, Oleg Penkovsky: Collins, 1965.
6. Excerpt from articles by Greville Wynne published in the *Sunday Telegraph* and re-printed as a personal comment in *The Penkovsky Papers*.
7. *The Penkovsky Papers*, pp. 172–3.
8. Ibid, pp. 173–4.
9. Hansard, 1 February 1966, Vol. 272, cc 262–3.

Chapter 18

Post Cuba Review

*If the situation had deteriorated very rapidly, the chance of any-
thing effective being done in the home defence field would have
been slight.*

Home Office report on the Cuban crisis, November 1962

Had Khrushchev not struck a deal, to the evident relief of an
exhausted and clearly deeply worried Prime Minister that lunch-
time on Sunday, 28 October 1962 it is very clear the transition to war
committee would have been activated that afternoon. The endlessly
debated plans to take the UK on the path to probable nuclear war
would given the bleakness of the situation over the previous twenty-
four hours, belatedly have been put into operation. That much is
clear from a letter the cabinet secretariat drafted on Monday,
29 October for the cabinet secretary to send to permanent secretaries
across government departments in Whitehall.

With typical British understatement, it read: 'Fortunately we did
not need to disturb you over the weekend, but if the Cuban situation
had taken a sharp turn for the worse (as seemed likely at one time)
we might well have had to call a snap meeting of the transition to
war committee'.[1] The cabinet secretary's purpose in sending the
letter seems to have been to point out to some of the most senior
civil servants in Whitehall that the providential last minute escape
from the prospect of nuclear conflict should make them think hard
about the flexibility of the government's war-planning. Was it up to
meeting the needs of a fast-moving threat to world peace that came,
as the Cuban crisis had, without either weeks or months of darkening
clouds on the international sky-line in which to plan a response?

Macmillan swiftly ordered a post-Cuba review from the ministerial
committee on home defence. Undoubtedly he realised the world,
and particularly the UK, had had a lucky escape. His action in
demanding a re-think indicates he may have had second thoughts
about his handling of the Cuban crisis. The cabinet secretary, on
instructions from the Prime Minister let it be known that the review
should ensure that contingency planning was 'sufficiently flexible to

enable us to react quickly and appropriately to a sudden emergency, in which we might have no more than two or three days' warning of the outbreak of war.'

On 19 November 1962 a note from the home office to the home defence committee pulled few punches in its criticism of the lack of preparedness during the crisis and the chaos which would have followed had the cabinet met on the Sunday afternoon of that very dangerous weekend, and authorised the immediate implementation of 'Transition to War'.

'During the Cuban crisis (23–28 October) no general directions were given by ministers and no start was made on any general transition measures. If the situation had worsened and ministers had decided that home defence steps should be taken, it is unlikely departments would have had seven, or even five days, in which to implement their present plans. If the situation had deteriorated very rapidly, the chances of anything effective being done in the home defence field would have been slight.'[2]

Was this an implied criticism of the Prime Minister, as well as other responsible ministers in the cabinet? Was it criticism of civil servants who had not pushed hard enough for the formation of a war cabinet and the implementation of *War Book* plans? Whatever the reason it was recognition that had Cuba triggered nuclear war, the UK would have been caught trying desperately to catch up to implement all the necessary plans to try to ensure national survival.

During the review, civil servants strove to find ways of creating a time-table to war that would reduce the lead time from a week to perhaps two or three days. One of the outcomes was the decision to allow the Prime Minister to authorise calling a precautionary stage himself without the requirement to hold a cabinet meeting beforehand. Another was the drafting of an Emergency Power (Defence) Bill which could be rushed through both Houses of Parliament in the final days of peace. So massive were the powers the emergency bill would have granted to the regional commissioners, who would govern their own private fifedoms of the UK from protected bunkers, that its terms were kept secret for fear that had they been known, other than at a time when the country faced the dire prospect of nuclear war, they would have been regarded as wholly unacceptable. The bill, had it ever been implemented, would have given the twelve regional commissioners power over life and death, over property, food supplies, and finance so drastic as to amount to a voluntary abdication by parliament of the whole of their democratic functions for the period of the emergency. The bill would have made regulations that were imposed during the Second World War look tame by comparison. No one outside the group of planners responsible for the UK's *War Book* knew of its contents, until it was declassified and lodged in the National Archives in the late 1990s. It contained an all-embracing clause which related to 'special circumstances arising or likely to arise out of any war in which her majesty may be engaged or out of the threat of such a war' that could be interpreted to mean virtually anything a regional commissioner wished it to. It covered the administration of justice, the death penalty, maintenance of public order, and of supplies and services essential to the life of the community.[3]

Who would be appointed to the role of a regional commissioner would not be known until the moment of doom had arrived. Then those ministers selected to assume absolute power in their sectors of the country would learn of the huge responsibilities that would fall upon them. In a nice ceremonial and constitutional touch they would find out that their appointments were sanctioned by the Queen via a royal warrant, and that in preparation for such a terrible occurrence, warrants with the blanks ready to be filled with the names of the commissioners had already been printed and were held ready.

Peter (now Lord) Hennessy, in his book *The Secret State* quotes the very document: 'Elizabeth the Second, by the grace of God of the United Kingdom of Great Britain and Northern Ireland and of our other realms and territories, QUEEN, head of the Commonwealth, defender of the faith to our ... Greeting! In pursuance of regulation 4 (2) of the defence (machinery of government) regulations we hereby appoint you the said ... to be regional commissioner for the purposes of those regulations. Given at our court of Saint James's ... day of 19... In the year of our reign. By Her Majesty's command.[4]

What a nice touch. Nuclear war is about to commence. You have been informed you are to take almost absolute control of a region of the country, exercising powers over life and death in what will soon be a waste-land, and you receive greetings from the Queen!

The fault-line in the grand plan for government of nuclear war-time Britain by twelve regional commissioners, was that by 1963 it was pretty clear that the Soviets knew the location of all the bunkers where they and their staffs of advisers would be sheltering. Consequently the chances of survival for any of them was not great. The group campaigning against nuclear warfare under the name 'Spies for Peace' had distributed the list of locations publicly during the Aldermarston march in 1963.

The planners went about their gloomy task comprehensively and with a morbid eye to detail. Envisaging the actual period when the UK would be battered by multiple nuclear strikes, a government paper written six years after the Cuban crisis paints an horrific picture: 'Millions of homeless, bewildered people would need rudimentary shelter and sustenance. Looting of food stocks and other essential supplies, the blocking of essential routes by refugees, the seizing of property, all these problems on a mammoth scale could overwhelm the surviving police resources.'[5] The planners were presumably trying to look on the optimistic side, but it must have been very difficult to be up-beat about the chances of national survival in any meaningful form. Describing the post-attack period they paint, if anything, an even blacker picture: 'As the long term battle for survival progresses, crucial struggles are likely to arise over securing sources of food and other essential commodities, together with the means of transporting them by sea and air. We foresee the possibility of new threats developing, affecting both our overseas activities and our home base. Subversive organisations are likely to survive and the general chaos of the post-attack struggle could provide a better opportunity for them to succeed than anything which obtained pre-attack.'[6]

That secret nightmare vision of the civil servants and scientists had been graphically portrayed in a documentary made by BBC TV director Peter Watkins in April 1965, when the tensions of the Cuban crisis were still fresh in the public's mind. Watkins said he wanted to 'make the man in the street stop and think about himself and his future'. But his forty-seven minute film 'The War Game' was too realistic and too disturbing for the politicians and the broadcasters to allow it to be shown. The chairman of the BBC governors was Lord Normanbrook , the same man who as Sir Norman Brook had been cabinet secretary from 1947–1962 and been deeply involved in all the secret discussions in the depths of Whitehall around planning for a Third World War. He later said that he wished he had stopped the film being made in the first place. There was a widespread feeling in government that if anti-war sentiment was allowed to spread, it would pose a significant threat to the security of the country. 'The War Game' portrayed the effects of a nuclear war on a single town. It showed hospitals overwhelmed by the dead and dying; police shooting the seriously injured and the terminally ill; food riots; the collapse of civil order, and the imposition of martial law. Its final message was that it was more than possible that what had been shown in the film would take place before 1980. It was not until 1985 that the BBC finally agreed to show it to a mass audience

Now we know the twentieth century escaped the horrors, perhaps the demise of civilisation, even of life itself, a nuclear conflict would have brought. It is as well that the predictions and the precautions the Whitehall 'warriors', discussed in secret, never saw the light of day until well after the Cold War ended. The formal, logical reports and documents the civil servants prepared for government, outlining the dire consequences for everyone of nuclear apocalypse, were every bit as disturbing as the dramatic scenes portrayed in 'The War Game'.

Notes

1. PRO CAB 21/4888 'Revised Government *War Book*. Revision' May–Dec 1962. Leavett to Trend 29, October 1962.
2. PRO CAB 134/2021 'Home Defence Preparedness. Note by the Home Office'. 19 November 1962.
3. PRO DEFE 12/321 'Review of Government *War Book* Planning in the Light of the Cuba Crisis': 'Emergency Powers (Defence) Bill Draft 19 March 1963.
4. PRO, CAB 175/28.
5. PRO DEFE 4/232 'Military Aspects of the Home Defence of the United Kingdom' 1 October 1968.
6. Ibid.

Chapter 19

Last Word

The American imperialist beast was forced to swallow a hedgehog,
quills and all ... I'm proud of what we did.

Nikita S Khrushchev, *Khrushchev Remembers*

Following resolution of the crisis, one major mystery remains. Why did Khrushchev maintain his silence over the deal he had won in getting America's missiles out of Turkey. The whole truth of the bargain struck between the United States and the USSR never became public until the 1980s. To all appearances Kennedy had won 'hands down' and Khrushchev had 'backed down'. Some members of the Kennedy administration went to great lengths to conceal the fact that Robert Kennedy had agreed, with the knowledge of his brother as President, to remove the Jupiters threatening the Soviet Union, which had been a particularly sore point for the Russian leader. McGeorge Bundy, US National Security Adviser 1961–66, confessed in his memoirs published in 1988: 'There was no leak. As far as I know none of us told anyone else what had happened. We denied in every forum that there was any deal, and in the narrowest sense what we said was usually true, as far as it went.'[1]

Khrushchev could have gained prestige for himself had he revealed that in reality a 'swap' had been made. Russian missiles in Cuba traded for American missiles in Turkey. But, for whatever reason he chose not to.

As it was, Khrushchev persuaded himself that his missile gamble had been a success and not a humiliation. He had won his primary goal which was a United States promise not to invade Cuba. He stated in his memoirs, in a typically boasting phrase, that for the first time in history 'the American imperialist beast was forced to swallow a hedgehog, quills and all ... I'm proud of what we did.'[2] But spending what must have been the equivalent of a billion US dollars to move missiles, troops and related equipment in and out of Cuba was a high price to pay for Kennedy's pledge not to invade, a pledge that could have been revoked at any time, had the Cubans been caught smuggling arms to Latin America, or endeavouring to spread subversion, or threatening security elsewhere in the Caribbean or South American regions.

When the face-off ended on Sunday, 28 October one of America's more aggressive military chiefs of staff suggested that the President should still go ahead with a massive bombing raid on Cuba. 'The military are mad,' concluded Kennedy. His brother, the attorney general, recalled: 'Many times I heard the military take positions which if wrong had the advantage that no one would be around at the end to know.'[3]

The American blockade was eased on 2 November following Khrushchev's decision to remove all his IL-28 bombers from the island. On that day Kennedy went before the American public on television again. He confirmed that aerial reconnaissance showed the missile bases being dismantled and the missiles and associated equipment being crated, as Khrushchev had promised. Even so the Americans maintained a modified blockade, and kept their forces on DEFCON two alert, until 20 November when the President was satisfied Khrushchev had kept to his side of the bargain. Britain had relaxed its unprecedented alert three status on Guy Fawkes Night, 5 November.

The crisis in the Caribbean arose as a result of adventurism on both sides; a highly dangerous strategy at a time of nuclear confrontation. Kennedy had pursued covert actions against Cuba and had been squarely behind the Bay of Pigs invasion by Cuban exiles. It failed miserably, but it had been devised to overthrow the Castro regime. Khrushchev gambled massively with his secret missile deployment . It was resolved because both men were willing to risk humiliation rather than Armageddon. It was a terrifyingly close run thing, with Britain effectively on the side-lines in the dispute, but in the front-line had the missiles and the nuclear bombers been launched.

The British authorities had been at pains to keep a low-key approach undoubtedly for fear of panicking the UK public. But the Soviet authorities were well aware of the extremely high state of alert of Britain's nuclear forces, and there was a clear belief among senior RAF officers that Bomber Command's actions had contributed to preventing war, and had helped tilt the balance towards a peaceful outcome. Information gained by the British secret intelligence services through the efforts of Col Oleg Penkovsky, made it clear a high priority for Soviet military intelligence was, not unnaturally, warning of a nuclear attack. In the early 1960s the USSR had few warning radars and reconnaissance satellites. They relied on phone intercepts and a network of 'base watchers' in the UK to observe unusual activity which might point to an increased alert status. Undoubtedly, despite

Macmillan's insistence on no overt measures, the Soviet authorities knew of the very high state of readiness within the V-Force and on Thor launch bases as the crisis reached its peak.

Air Marshal Sir Kenneth Cross, was adamant that for the deterrent to be effective it was 'systems at readiness that counted.' That was proved true. The risks were high, and the stakes even higher. But in the end it was sanity that prevailed, and the Cold War never dropped to such a level of dangerous 'deep freeze' again.

Khrushchev's last two years in power were a time of relative desperation. After the collapse of his Cuban adventure much of his energy and flair seemed to have gone. His colleagues were wary of his bluff and bluster and increasingly moved against him. The humiliation of Cuba gave momentum to the anti Khrushchev cabal in the Kremlin. His authority oozed away and he was ousted in October 1964 and sent into retirement. He died in 1971. There was no Red Square funeral for him and he was buried quietly at Novodevichy Cemetry. It took the family four years to get permission to erect a monument.

After the crisis, the pace of Soviet missile production and deployment picked up. Before the Cuban adventure the USSR armoury contained just a handful of inter-continental missiles. When Khrushchev was removed from office, two years later, the Soviet Union's intercontinental reach had grown to some 200 ICBMs. By September 1968 the Soviets commanded a larger force of missiles capable of intercontinental range even than the United States.

Shortly after the Cuban crisis *The Times* in Britain published a letter signed by forty-two leading Labour politicians. It said: If Russian missiles in Cuba were a threat to American cities (as we believe they were) then United States missiles ringing the USSR are equally a threat to Soviet cities. This is the lesson that millions have learned from the terrifying events of the Cuban crisis. Now that Mr Khrushchev has withdrawn his missiles, Mr Kennedy should respond similarly. Unless the west makes some counter-concession, Mr Khrushchev's present policies may be replaced by tougher ones. We in Britain should press the United Kingdom Government to ask Mr Kennedy to remove his Polaris and Thor missiles bases from our country immediately. These bases heighten world tension. They also make it certain that the British people would be incinerated in the first hours of a world war.'

It was a forceful plea, but the opposition politicians were unaware of two facts. America had agreed to take its missiles out of Turkey and there had been a joint American and British decision to dismantle the Thor bases in England. It was recognised the Thor rockets were fast becoming an obsolete technology. They were vulnerable. They took time to be fuelled and brought to a launch stage. And the new inter-continental missiles being developed by the Americans were more efficient and coming on stream in increasing numbers. Thor had been a stop-gap weapon. It had been a sabre that was rattled effectively during the crisis, but was now destined to be phased out. By August 1963 all the missile launch pads in England had been dismantled. Some believed that they had been withdrawn as part of the same covert deal that Kennedy struck with Khrushchev over the Jupiters in Turkey. They were not. The ironic fact is that when the Cuban missile crisis broke, the imminent disbandment of the RAF's Thor squadrons had already been decided. America had no need any longer of a defensive missile fence this side of the Atlantic. Nevertheless, the American Strategic Air Command bomber bases remained on British soil.

There were some very positive outcomes of the dangerous days of tension in October 1962. Most importantly for the safety of the world was the creation of the hot line, a direct communications link between Moscow and Washington to allow the leaders of west and east to talk directly to each other in any future crisis. It eliminated the problems of time difference which had frustrated some of the most crucial negotiations during the Cuban stand-off. The events of those terrifying days had illustrated starkly the appalling consequences of one false decision, or one fatal misunderstanding.

Within twelve months the world's two super-powers made three significant arms-control agreements. The hot line was established in June 1963. In August the same year a nuclear test ban treaty was signed by the United States, the Soviet Union, and Great Britain. Finally, the crisis led to talks that eventually resulted in 1969 in a treaty on the non-proliferation of nuclear weapons. The Cold War dragged on, dominating lives across the world. There were periodic incidents when tensions mounted. On each side, technology generated weapons that were more sophisticated, more frightening and more accurate. But, thank goodness, in the three decades of the Cold War that remained, the world never again approached so close to that ultimate threshold which could have destroyed mankind.

Notes

1. McGeorge Bundy: *Danger and Survival: Choices About the Bomb in the First Fifty Years*, New York, Random House, 1988.
2. Nikita S Khrushchev: *Khrushchev Remembers*, translated by Jerrold Schecter and Vyacheslav Luchkov, Little, Brown: Boston, 1990.

Chapter 20

And Still The Facts Were Witheld

One of the really striking things of that time was the quite exceptional and unnecessary secrecy in Britain.

Denis Healey (now Lord Healey),
Defence Secretary 1964–70

Perhaps the comment that best sums up the British dimension of the Cuban crisis was made by the Commander in Chief Bomber Command, Sir Keith 'Bing' Cross, the man who as far as Britain's deterrent forces were concerned was at the sharp end of it. His comment, referred to in an earlier chapter, emphasised that during the crisis, control of Britain's nuclear deterrent worked perfectly from him downwards; but from him upwards, he perceived, nothing worked at all. It is a striking indictment of what the commander of Britain's V-Force and Thor missile squadrons thought of the relationship he had with his political masters, as the international situation moved threateningly towards a Third World War.

The record suggests senior politicians in London – including the foreign secretary and the defence secretary – were not entirely up to speed with the dramatically increased alert stance of British nuclear forces during the crisis. The late Sir Solly Zuckerman, chief scientific adviser to the Ministry of Defence in 1962, has been quoted by the American author Scott Sagan in his book *The Limits of Safety* as saying that, although he was at the centre of things during those fateful days, he did not recall the Prime Minister, the secretary of state, or the chief of the defence staff being directly involved with the order to raise the state of readiness of Bomber Command beyond Macmillan's request for 'appropriate steps', to a full alert three. 'To the best of my knowledge,' he recalled, 'the Ministry of Defence did not order him (Air Marshal Cross) to increase the state of readiness of his force.'[1]

Lord Healey (Denis Healey) who became Secretary of State for Defence in the Labour Government two years after the crisis, told me in 2007 that politicians were absolutely not aware that Bomber Command had ordered such a high state of readiness. 'One of the really striking things of that time was the quite exceptional and unnecessary secrecy in Britain. Bomber Command was able to prepare for a massive raid on the Soviet Union without even letting the Ministry of Defence know, let alone parliament.'[2] Nobody in the general public had the slightest idea of what was going on in the UK. They saw the TV reports; they heard what was being said on the radio; they read the newspapers, but the media was reporting what was happening on the other side of the Atlantic, not the nuclear strike being prepared on RAF and USAF bases here in the UK.

Lord Healey commented that in the wake of the Cuban crisis it was clear a government that wanted to retain public support for its defence policy had to be honest about what it was doing.

During the crisis the Ministry of Defence explicitly told the British press that increased alert measures were not being taken by British deterrent forces. So the British public was ignorant that its nuclear forces had gone to the brink. Macmillan made no mention of the military stance when he told the Commons on 30 October: 'The world has had a shock. We have been very near the edge.'

The Macmillan Government had previous 'form' in keeping disturbing news out of the public eye. In 1957 the Prime Minister had taken steps to heavily censor the report into the fire at the atomic energy authority's Windscale plant in Cumbria, caused almost certainly by ministerial pressure on scientists to meet the demands of producing Britain's first megaton bomb. Macmillan, desperate to prove to the Americans that the UK was a reliable partner with which to share nuclear secrets, ensured his government remained tight-lipped about the alarming extent of radioactive fallout from the accident at Britain's first reactor. The first really major accident of the nuclear age was the subject of a political cover-up not dissimilar to that which followed the ordering of the UK's deterrent forces on close to a wartime footing during the Cuban crisis.

The first inkling the public had that covert events had moved the UK closer to nuclear conflict than at any other time in the Cold War, far closer than most people ever knew, came in a front page report in the *Daily Mail* on 18 February 1963, three and a half months after the crisis had been resolved. Under a prominent front-page headline, 'When Britain went to the Brink', the article by the *Daily Mail*'s defence correspondent Stevenson Pugh, said 'The sixty Thor rockets and the V-bombers in this country were "all systems go" for attack during the Cuban crisis.[3] Categorical denials were given at the time that any preparations were being made. Now I learn that for the first time, the Thors were poised in anger with H-bomb warheads in place; the bombers also had bombs ready.'

The report said the alert had been surrounded by official secrecy and that Macmillan had been within hours of informing the nation of his decision to back Kennedy all the way, when Moscow radio announced Khrushchev's decision to back down. At that point, the report continued, Bomber Command had been on its hair-trigger alert for eight days.

The *Daily Mail* reported that Air Marshal Sir Kenneth Cross, issued his first alert on 20 October. On that day, it said, he found that fifty-nine out of the sixty Thor rockets were serviceable. It was a Saturday, but a proportion of bomber crews and V-bombers were also on stand-by in a state of readiness at the end of the runway at each V-bomber base. On the Monday, the sixtieth Thor, which was 'out' of operational use for training, was ordered to war readiness. All the bomber crews were stood by. Sir Kenneth then received a request from US Strategic Air Command for a statement on his readiness. The request came on his own H-war network from SAC HQ in Omaha. The report commented that there seemed to have been no similar communication on the political network in Whitehall, despite the fact that the Thors and V-bombers were supposed to be responsible for a vital proportion of SAC's first-wave targets.

Records now released, and the recollections of those who were involved at the time, bear out the basic facts in the *Daily Mail*'s report, although the dates in the newspaper report were clearly wrong and conflict with RAF and government records. However, when a few days later, opposition MPs questioned Macmillan on the newspaper report in the House of Commons and pressed for a statement, the Prime Minister denied that anything other than what would be con-sidered 'normal' had taken place. He persisted in concealing the full truth from parliament and the nation about the highest level of alert the UK's nuclear forces went to during the whole Cold War era, despite strong questioning from Labour members.

Labour MPs reacted furiously. Mr Stephen Swingler asked Macmillan why he had not informed the nation that he had given authority for alerting all V-bomber crews and Thor rocket bases in preparation for nuclear war. Mr K Zilliacus asked the reason why the Prime Minister had authorised the nuclear deterrent forces in the UK to be put in a state of instant readiness for attack during the United State's arms blockade of Cuba. Mr Tom Driberg questioned why official denials that any such alert action had been taken were issued at the time in response to press inquiries. The Liberal leader, Mr Jo Grimond, asked what steps the government was taking together with its allies to develop more effective joint planning and control of nuclear weapons used by the alliance, so that there would be greater co-ordination with NATO in major foreign policy and defence decisions.

To all these questions Macmillan answered very defensively. He told MPs that 'the V-bomber force and the Thor rockets in this country are always at a very high state of readiness. During the period of tension, thought not, in fact on the date mentioned in the newspaper report, certain precautionary steps were taken, but more than this was not necessary.' On the matter of NATO, he said the government was discussing with Britain's allies a whole range of problems arising from the development of NATO's nuclear forces.[4]

This in no way satisfied opposition MPs. Mr Swingler challenged the Prime Minister again. Was he calling the *Daily Mail*'s defence correspondent a liar, he asked. Or does the Prime Minister's answer about precautionary measures contain a formula for concealing the fact that the government was 'preparing a national suicide threat' at the time of the Cuban crisis?

Macmillan's reply gave nothing further away. 'Naturally, if the deterrent is to play its role, it is always kept at a high state of readiness. During a period of tension certain additional steps were taken, but they are of a kind which is merely intended and normal and were no more than normal.'

That did not satisfy some of the more critical and outspoken MPs. Mr Zilliacus asked: 'Is the Prime Minister telling the House that he was prepared to enter into a nuclear war which would have destroyed the people of this country, in support of an act of aggression by the United States which had resorted to force in violation of the United Nations charter?' Why did the Prime Minister deny that any such action had been taken?

Mr Macmillan replied that the honourable member was making a quite false deduction from what he had said or from what was done. Mr Warbey then asked 'exactly what was the purpose of the precautionary measures' that the Prime Minister had mentioned. 'Were they directed towards ensuring that the missiles and V-bombers could be more instantly used for attack or were they directed towards ensuring that they could be immobilised, so that in the event of nuclear war ensuing from the Kennedy-Khrushchev dispute over Cuba, this country would have been able to stay out and the lives of its people protected?'

Macmillan replied that he was not prepared to add to what he had already said. Mr Driberg persisted with his question asking for an explanation why, since he had said that certain precautionary steps had been taken, categorical denials had been given to reputable defence correspondents by the Ministry of Defence and Bomber Command.

The Prime Minister responded that what had been denied was that some 'abnormal' action was taken. But, protested Mr Grimond, cannot the Prime Minister be more explicit about what is meant by the word 'normal'? 'This seems to have been a very abnormal situation. Surely people are entitled to know what abnormal steps were taken. Is it not usual that any crisis in the west affects all the nations of the west if they are of any power whatever? If that is so, is it not vital that the nations of the west should consult not only about the final crisis but about the diplomatic and defence decisions which lead to it?' Again the Prime Minister said he had nothing to add. 'It is clear that with weapons of this kind, if one has them they must, if they are to be credible, be kept at a very high state of readiness. At certain periods of tension certain additional steps are taken. That is not unreasonable.'

Macmillan's final word was that the lesson of Cuba was that the strength of the alliance as a whole 'was of very great value in reaching a settlement. It is also a fact that these terrible forces on both sides did deter war, because all governments must shrink from any action which could bring them into play.'

The Prime Minister had managed to play a 'straight bat' to a House of Commons that was beginning to realise the UK had come much closer to nuclear confrontation than Macmillan was prepared to admit. In the intense media glare that exists now, fifty years later, with twenty-four-hour news the norm, no government today would succeed in keeping such a tight lid on potential life and death issues. But the period of highest tension had passed and people wanted to get on with their lives. Nevertheless the crisis had exposed the fragility and the intense risks of the nuclear stand-off the Cold War represented.

On 10 November 1962 a remarkable memorandum arrived on the desk of Sir Alec Douglas-Home at the Foreign Office, It was from 'our man in Havana', the British Ambassador to Cuba, Mr Herbert Stanley Marchant, and it gave a long and full account of the Cuban crisis as he viewed it from the island. 'I doubt whether a month ago any reputable publisher would have given a moment's consideration to a story in which Soviet Russia was to be credited with shipping some four dozen assorted giant missiles, each one longer than a cricket pitch, across the Atlantic to Cuba, where Russian military technicians disguised as agricultural advisers would set them up in secret on launching sites – some of them just off the main road less than fifty miles from Havana. Certainly no publisher could have accepted a chapter two in which less than a week later the same missiles were being feverishly dismantled, packed up and re-shipped back across the Atlantic.'

The ambassador went on to say that as observers he and his staff in Havana had been curiously isolated in the tense, unnatural calm of the eye of the cyclone which had so shaken the world. Mr Marchant told the foreign secretary that it was generally accepted in Cuba that the Russians were just building ground to air rocket sites. 'What we did not see anything of until too late, was the vital equipment and the larger missiles which were almost certainly moved only by night. In fact we saw no rockets of any kind until 25 October when a convoy of several ground to air missiles appeared in the city itself in daylight and larger ones, presumably ground to ground missiles after dark.'

The ambassador went on to note that there was no lack of evidence of a hurried evacuation of troops and technology to the ports. On 5 November a Russian passenger ship had left Cuba crowded with technicians.

Assessing the motive for Khrushchev to install offensive weapons on Cuba, the ambassador admitted that no one realised the high stakes the Russian leader was prepared to play for. 'We have with us now in Havana, Mr Mikoyan, who has brought with him a large pocketful of prizes and presents for good behaviour!'

'Castro had called the country to arms to defend itself against threatened invasion and against an embargo the Cuban leader described as an "inhuman blockade instituted by war-mongering imperialist Yankees and designed to starve and bring to their knees the peace-loving people." It was not until Castro's broadcast speech on 1 November that the majority of Cubans learnt for the first time of the existence of offensive rockets in their country, and even then they were referred to as "strategic weapons". They also learnt at this juncture that the weapons in question were operated and manned by Russian military technicians, that the Soviet Union had decided to withdraw them, and that there had been differences of opinion between the Cuban and Soviet Governments. By now however the relief generally felt, if not publicly expressed, at moving a step back from the brink of a nuclear war, was in itself sufficient to take the sharp edge off any immediate urge to complain, much less to resist or revolt.'

'To discover in the early stages of an eighteen round contest that you are not even one of the contestants but only the prize money, is not an easily forgotten experience for a sensitive young nation.

But better to be humiliated than wiped out, and I do not think it impossible, with the help of an extensive propaganda campaign showing how Khrushchev has saved the peace of the world, both Castro and the Cuban nation will very soon regain confidence in their international sponsor the USSR and be able to convince themselves that it has all been for the best.'

By far the most striking comment the ambassador made in his report back to his government was the observation that 'an early interest in the possibility of evacuation subsided, as it became evident that if it was a nuclear war we were heading for, Cuba was perhaps a better place to be than Britain.'[5]

As an assessment from an experienced ambassador of the chances of survival if the Cuban crisis had triggered nuclear war, that comment is eye-opening!

Macmillan in his memoirs refers to another striking sentiment. On 27 November, a month after that terrifying weekend when the world stood at the brink of nuclear war, the Prime Minister received a letter from Khrushchev. It said: 'I fully share your view, as well as that of President Kennedy, that the Cuban crisis has led to a better understanding of the need for prompt settlement of acute international problems.'

'An admirable sentiment,' Macmillan comments. 'But leaving a lot unsaid!'[6]

Notes

1. Scott D Sagan: *The Limits of Safety: Organisations, Accidents and Nuclear Weapons*, Princeton University Press, 1993.
2. Lord Healey interviewed 2007.
3. *Daily Mail*, 18 February 1963.
4. Hansard House of Commons Debate, 28 February 1963 Vol. 672, ccl 439–44.
5. Document AK1261/667 From British Embassy Havana to Foreign Office London, 10 November 1962.
6. Macmillan, *At the End of the Day*, p. 220.

Appendix

Crisis Timeline

1956

February   Nikita Khrushchev gives 'secret speech' to the twentieth party congress in Moscow denouncing Stalin's 'cult of personality.' His position as first secretary of the Soviet Communist Party takes him to the top of the post-Stalin leadership.

1957

January   Harold Macmillan becomes British Prime Minister.

March   Macmillan and President Eisenhower announce agreement to deploy Thor intermediate range nuclear missiles in UK.

October   USSR launches Sputnik one, the first artificial satellite to be fired into space. It was a major shock to the Pentagon and the American public who had to admit to the Soviets being ahead in the 'space race'. Sputnik appeared to give the Soviets a lead in development of inter-continental ballistic missiles.

1958

September   First Thor missile base in UK operational.

1959

January   Fidel Castro assumes power in Cuba.

October   Turkey and the United States sign agreement to base US nuclear-tipped Jupiter missiles in Turkey.

1960

February   Soviet First Deputy Prime Minister, Anastas Mikoyan attends Soviet trade exhibition in Havana and negotiates economic agreements with Cuba.

May	Soviet Union and Cuba establish diplomatic relations.
September	First large arms shipments from Soviet Bloc to Cuba.
October	Cuba nationalises US private investments worth some one billion dollars.

1961

January	Khrushchev states that Soviet rockets, based in the USSR 'protect' Cuba and there are 'no Soviet bases in Cuba.'
January	At his inauguration as President, John F Kennedy vows the United States will 'pay any price' to preserve western interests.
January	CIA deliver to would-be assassins a box of poisoned cigars in an effort to get Castro killed.
April	Fourteen hundred Cuban exiles attempt an invasion of Cuba at the Bay of Pigs. One hundred and fourteen are killed and 1,189 captured. Castro orders the arrest of thousands of suspected dissidents. The CIA authorises a last-minute bombing effort with six US airmen. Four are shot-down.
April	Khrushchev warns the United States against arming Cuban émigrés for further attacks on the island.
June	Kennedy and Khrushchev meet in Vienna. Khrushchev delivers an ultimatum on Berlin: settle the issue or the USSR will hand over control of the East Berlin zone to East Germany. Kennedy says the prospects for war are 'very real.'
July	Kennedy doubles US military reserves, increases the military services draft, and pushes forward civil defence measures.
August	The Berlin Wall is erected sealing off the eastern sector of Berlin.
August	Soviet Union explodes a massive fifty-eight-megaton H-bomb.
September	Dangerous tank-to-tank stand-off at check-point on the Berlin wall.
September	A US national intelligence report suggests the Soviet inter-continental ballistic missile programme is far behind previous US estimates.

November	Kennedy authorises 'Operation Mongoose' to covertly destabilise Castro.

1962

January	New Year's Day parade in Cuba demonstrates the extent of Soviet Bloc arms deliveries to Cuba.
February	American joint chiefs of staff give 'first priority' to the completion of all contingency plans for military action against Cuba.
April	US Jupiter missiles in Turkey, manned by American personnel, become fully operational.
April	Khrushchev decides to deploy Soviet missiles to Cuba.
July	Castro visits Moscow and agrees missile and arms deployment.
Mid July	First Soviet cargo ships head from the Black Sea for Cuba with false cargo declarations and shipping weights: Altogether forty intermediate and medium range ballistic missiles; twenty-four surface to air missile batteries; eighty-four MIG-21 jet fighters; IL-28 nuclear bombers; missile boats; submarines; mobile tactical nuclear weapons; and 40,000 elite troops.
Late August	Kennedy is informed that a U-2 reconnaisance mission confirms the presence of surface to air missiles in Cuba.
4 October	Kennedy advises 'massive activity' should be undertaken including the mining of Cuban harbours.
6 October	US Atlantic command reports increased readiness so that it can mount a full-scale invasion of Cuba.
14 October	Major Richard Heyser, flying a U-2 reconnaissance plane, obtains the first photographic evidence of Soviet medium range ground to ground ballistic missiles sites in Cuba.
16 October	Kennedy convenes his executive committee of advisers. The committee is informed the Soviet missiles will be operational in two weeks.
18 October	Kennedy meets with Soviet Foreign Minister, Andrei Gromyko. Gromyko denies categorically that the Soviet Union has placed offensive nuclear

	weapons on Cuba. Kennedy does not reveal he already has photographic evidence.
19 October	Kennedy meets with his joint chiefs of staff. Air Force chief, General Curtis Le May, argues that if the US fails to use force it would be 'as bad as the appeasement at Munich.' Kennedy orders a blockade or 'quarantine' of Cuba.
21 October	Kennedy discusses the clandestine deployment of missiles on Cuba with British ambassador, Sir David Ormesby-Gore.
23 October	Kennedy tells the American people on national television that a 'world crisis' was at hand as a result of the secret Soviet nuclear deployments in Cuba. US military ordered to DEFCON three. High proportion of US nuclear bombers in the US and UK armed with nuclear weapons for the only time in Strategic Air Command history. fifty-four nuclear armed aircraft on continuous patrol. One hundred and thirty six Atlas and Titan intercontinental ballistic missiles prepared for launching. Defense Secretary, Robert McNamara, in confidential report lists requirements for an invasion of Cuba: 250,000 men, 2,000 air sorties against Cuban targets. Castro mobilises military on Cuba.
	In London, Macmillan, Sir Alec Douglas-Home (foreign secretary) and Lord Mountbatten (chief of the defence staff) shown reconnaissance photos by American Ambassador, David Bruce. North Atlantic council briefed. Macmillan persuades General Lauris Norstad, supreme allied commander in Europe not to call a full NATO alert for fear of exacerbating the situation.
	In Moscow Colonel Oleg Penkovsky of Soviet intelligence arrested by the KGB for spying on behalf of the west.
23 October	Poll indicates one in five Americans believe a blockade will result in the Third World War.
24 October	Soviet ships reach the quarantine line and stop dead in the water. Kennedy receives letter from Khrushchev calling the quarantine an 'act of aggression.' Kennedy issues order for the

countdown to Operation Scabbard, the invasion of Cuba on 30 October.

25 October   US military in US and UK ordered to DEFCON two, one stage below all-out war.

26 October   Letter from Khrushchev states the Soviet Union will remove their missiles provided Kennedy will publicly guarantee the US will not invade Cuba. Robert Kennedy, American attorney general, meets Soviet ambassador Anatoly Dobrynin, and secretly agrees a trade-off with the nuclear missiles in Turkey is possible.

27 October   A US U-2 spy-place accidentally flies into Russian air-space via Alaska. Another U-2 is shot down over Cuba and its pilot killed. Kennedy receives a letter from Khrushchev saying the US must promise publicly not to invade Cuba and must remove the Jupiter missiles from Turkey. Robert Kennedy in a meeting with Ambassador Dobrynin, gets agreement that the quid pro quo element of removal of the Jupiter missiles is to be kept confidential.

In London a hastily convened meeting of the British army, navy and Air Force chiefs is told by the Prime Minister that the V-Force should be dispersed to remote airfields in the event of positive indications that the US propose to launch an invasion of Cuba. Chief of air staff, Sir Thomas Pike, told by Macmillan that Bomber Command should covertly take all 'appropriate steps.' Air Marshal, Sir Kenneth Cross, officially orders the V-Force and Thor ballistic missiles to alert condition three, the highest stage of readiness in the whole of the Cold War.

Tense situation aboard nuclear armed Soviet submarine B-59 while under attack from American depth-charges. Captain orders nuclear tipped torpedo readied for firing. Argument breaks out between the submarine's senior officers finally leading to the submarine surfacing to seek orders from Moscow.

28 October   Khrushchev announces on radio Moscow the dismantling of the Soviet missiles on Cuba and

does not refer to the US missiles in Turkey. Castro is furious that the decision has been made 'over his head.'

In UK V-Force ordered to 'enhanced alert three' increasing the numbers of nuclear armed aircraft on QRA.

5 November	V-Force's unprecedented alert three state stood-down.
20 November	American blockade of Cuba withdrawn and defence condition two relaxed when it became clear Khrushchev had kept his side of the bargain.
21 November	Kennedy terminates the quarantine measures against Cuba.

1963

April	Kennedy is informed that the last Jupiter missile has been removed from Turkey.
5 August	United States signs the limited test ban treaty with Russia.
18 October	Prime Minister Macmillan resigns due to illness, Sir Alec Douglas-Home becomes British Prime Minister.
22 November	President Kennedy is assassinated.
December	Dismantling of Thor missile bases in UK starts.

1964

October	Khrushchev is replaced in a bloodless coup and is sent into retirement.

1969

June	Submarines equipped with Polaris nuclear missiles take over British nuclear deterrent from RAF V-Force.

1991

September	Soviet President Mikhail Gorbachev announces he will withdraw all Soviet troops from Cuba.

2008

February	Fidel Castro retires as President of Cuba and commander in chief, handing over to his brother Raul Castro.

Bibliography

Andrew, Christopher, *The Defence of the Realm: Authorised History of MI5* (Allen Lane, London, 2009).

Blight, James, Allyn, Bruce and Welch, David, *Cuba on the Brink: Castro, the Missile Crisis and the Soviet Collapse* (Pantheon, New York, 1993).

Blight, James and Welch, David, *On the Brink: Americans and Soviets Re-Examine the Cuban Missile Crisis*, (Hill & Wang, New York, 1989).

Boyes, John, *Project Emily: Thor IRBM and the RAF* (Tempus Publishing, 2008).

Bundy, McGeorge, *Danger and Survival: Choices about the Bomb in the First Fifty Years* (Random House, New York, 1988).

Campbell, Duncan, *The Unsinkable Aircraft Carrier: American Military Power in Britain* (Michael Joseph, London, 1984).

Catterall, Peter, *The Macmillan Diaries, Volume 2 1957–1966* (Macmillan, London, 2011).

Evans, Harold, *Downing Street Diary: The Macmillan Years 1957–1963* (Hodder & Stoughton, London, 1981).

Fursenko, Aleksandr and Naftali, Timothy, *One Hell of a Gamble: Khrushchev, Castro & Kennedy 1958–1964* (Norton, New York, 1997).

Gaddis, John Lewis, *The Cold War* (Allen Lane, London, 2006).

Gordievsky, Oleg and Andrews, Christopher, *KGB: The Inside Story* (Hodder & Stourton, 1990).

Hennessy, Peter, *The Prime Minister: The Office and its Holders since 1945* (Allen Lane, London, 2000).

Hennessy, Peter, *The Secret State: Preparing for the Worst 1945–2010* (Penguin Books, 2010).

Kennedy, Robert F, *Thirteen Days: A Memoir of the Cuban Missile Crisis* (Norton, New York, 1969).

Khrushchev, Nikita S, *Khrushchev Remembers*, translated and edited by Strobe Talbott (Bantam, New York, 1971/Little, Brown, Boston, 1970).

Khrushchev, Sergei N, *Nikita S Khrushchev: Krizisy i Rakety* (Novosti, Moscow, 1991).

Khrushchev, Sergei, *Khrushchev on Khrushchev: An Inside Account of the Man and his Era* (Translated/edited by William Taubman, Little, Brown, Boston, 1990).

Lovell, Sir Bernard, *Astronomer by Chance* (Macmillan, London 1990).

Macmillan, Harold, *At the End of the Day 1961–63* (Macmillan, London, 1973).

Macmillan, Harold, *Pointing the Way 1959–61* (Macmillan, London, 1965).

Menaul, Stewart, *Countdown: Britain's Strategic Nuclear Forces* (Robert Hale, London, 1980).

O'Brien, Michael, *John F Kennedy: A Biography* (Thomas Dunne Books, New York, 2005).

Penkovsky, Oleg, *The Penkovsky Papers* (Collins, 1965).

Pincher, Chapman, *Too Secret Too Long* (Sidgwick & Jackson, London, 1984)

Reeves, Richard, *President Kennedy: Profile of Power* (Simon & Schuster, New York, 1993).

Rusk, Richard, *As I Saw It* (Norton & Co, New York, 1990).

Sagan, Scott, *Limits of Safety: Organisations, Accidents & Nuclear War* (Princeton University Press, 1993).

Sagan, Scott, *Moving Targets: Nuclear Strategy and National Security* (Princeton University Press, 1989)

Schecter, Jerrold and Luchkov Vyacheslav, *Khrushchev Remembers* (Little, Brown, Boston, 1990).

Schlesinger, Arthur M Jr, *A Thousand Days: John F Kennedy in the White House* (Fawcett Crest, New York, 1967).

Schlesinger, Arthur M Jr, *Robert Kennedy and his Times* (Random House, New York, 1978).

Scott, L V, *Britain and the Cuban Missile Crisis, 1962: Political, Military and Intelligence Dimensions.*

Scott, Len, *Kennedy, Macmillan, and the Cuban Missile Crisis.*

Suvrov, Victor, *Soviet Military Intelligence* (Grafton Books, 1986).

Taubman, William, *Khrushchev: The Man and his Era* (Norton, New York, 2003).

Troyanovsky, Oleg, *The Making of Soviet Foreign Policy.*

Wilson, Jim, *Launch Pad UK: Britain and the Cuban Missile Crisis* (Pen & Sword, 2008).

Woolven, Robin, *UK Nuclear History Working Paper No 3* (Mountbatten Centre for International Studies).

Wright, Peter, *Spy Catcher* (William Heinemann, 1987).

Zuckerman, Sir Solly, *Monkeys, Men and Missiles* (Collins, London, 1988).

Index

195

197

200